Law in Sport

TITLES IN THE SPORT MANAGEMENT LIBRARY

Case Studies in Sport Marketing

Developing Successful Sport Marketing Plans, 3rd Edition

Developing Successful Sport Sponsorship Plans, 3rd Edition

Economics of Sport, 2nd Edition

Ethics & Morality in Sport Management, 3rd Edition

Financing Sport, 2nd Edition

Foundations of Sport Management, 2nd Edition

Fundamentals of Sport Marketing, 3rd Edition

Media Relations in Sport, 3rd Edition

Sport Facility Management:
Organizing Events and Mitigating Risks, 2nd Edition

Sport Governance in the Global Community

Sport Management Field Experiences

Law in Sport

—FOURTH EDITION—

Annie Clement, PhD, JD
University of New Mexico

John Grady, JD, PhD
University of South Carolina

Fitness Information Technology
A DIVISION OF THE INTERNATIONAL CENTER FOR PERFORMANCE EXCELLENCE

262 Coliseum, WVU-CPASS
PO Box 6116
Morgantown, WV 26506-6116

The content of this text is not intended to be legal advice. It is provided solely for educational purposes. Legal counsel should be consulted for advice on all legal matters.

Library of Congress Control Number: 2012941259

ISBN: 978-1-935412-41-0

Cover Design: 40 West Studios

Cover Photo: Book and gavel photo: © Ken Cole | Dreamstime.com; 50-yard line photo: © David Leindecker | Dreamstime.com; Volleyball photo: © Diloreto | Dreamstime.com; MarineBicyclist © Mark Turney; Female golfer photo: © BigStockPhoto.com

Typesetter: 40 West Studios

Production Editors: Matt Brann, Rachel Tibbs

Copyeditor: Rachel Tibbs

Printed by: Data Reproductions Corp.

10 9 8 7 6 5 4 3 2 1

Fitness Information Technology
A Division of the International Center for Performance Excellence
West Virginia University
262 Coliseum, WVU-CPASS
PO Box 6116
Morgantown, WV 26506-6116

800.477.4348 (toll free)
304.293.6888 (phone)
304.293.6658 (fax)
Email: fitcustomerservice@mail.wvu.edu
Website: www.fitinfotech.com

Contents

Acknowledgments

I wish to thank my family, friends, and University of New Mexico students and colleagues. To the many students and colleagues at Cleveland State University, Florida State University, and Barry University, thank you for your support and inspiration for the earlier editions. A special thank you to John Grady, Rachel Tibbs, and Matt Brann for making the text a reality.

—Annie Clement

Special thanks for the continued support from my family and my colleagues in the Department of Sport and Entertainment Management at the University of South Carolina. Also, thank you to my current and former students who serve as the inspiration for the examples in this book. Finally, thanks to Annie Clement, Rachel Tibbs, and Matt Brann for their efforts in creating this textbook.

—John Grady

Preface

This fourth edition of *Law in Sport* is designed to make the basic legal concepts that are significant to sport management easy to understand. Once these concepts are understood, the study and analysis of court decisions will acquaint the student with the application of law in sport. The fourth edition of this textbook is recommended for use in courses that cover legal aspects of sport, and is crafted for both undergraduate and graduate sport management programs. *Law in Sport* serves as a resource for students in sport management and related fields who wish to learn relevant legal theories and understand their application to the management of sport. By viewing current legal issues through the lens of a sport practitioner, students will obtain a deeper appreciation of the context in which these legal issues may arise and will be able to avoid exposing the agencies for which they work to liability.

This textbook explains the law to students who already understand the fundamentals of sport and how sport agencies function. One of the most important attributes of this book is that it provides just enough legal information so that the sport business professional appreciates the importance of law in making decisions and the need to seek legal advice in relation to each of these decisions.

Introduction

The Study of Law in Sport

"LAW IN SPORT" OR "SPORT LAW"?

An ongoing debate exists over the use of the terms "law in sport" and "sport law" (Davis, 2001). "Law in sport" is the wide range of legal concepts faced in the day-to-day decisions in the sport industry. These concepts have been taken from the laws of negligence, intentional torts, product liability, contracts, constitution, labor, agency, intellectual property, and others. They are applied to sport and physical activity just as they are applied to non-sport situations.

Sport law, on the other hand, refers only to the basic law and court decisions that are unique to sport. A body of law, including case law and law reviews, unique to sport continues to develop. Specialized courses dedicated only to the law unique to sport now exist in several law schools as well as some graduate and undergraduate programs in sport management. *Already developed into a field of Law*

An example of one of the many unique aspects of law in sport is the draft system found in professional team sports. The draft involves the rating of athletes and the opportunity of teams to select and employ individual athletes according to an inverse relationship, which is based on the win/loss record of the league's teams the previous year. If this were a general business practice, we would find each year's MBA graduates rated by grades or some other formula, waiting to be picked by industries according to the previous year's profits of the industries. Those industries with the lowest profits would select first. No MBA student would have a choice of location or company.

In addition to the example listed above, the following items are just a few of the myriad unique aspects of law that exist because sport differs from traditional business practices:

- antitrust issues as a result of lockouts by major professional sport leagues in the United States
- the dual union/representation combination found in professional team sport contracts
- free agency
- drug testing of professional and amateur athletes
- high levels of assumption of risk far beyond what is expected in business in general

- intellectual property cases involving fantasy sports
- sex of the team rather than sex of the coach used as a factor in discrimination
- stadium accessibility requirements under the Americans with Disabilities Act
- restructuring naming rights deals during an economic downturn
- legal issues resulting from revenue sharing among professional teams and leagues

STATUS OF LAW IN SPORT

The study of law in sport, physical activity, and related areas began in the 1980s. In response to negligence suits occurring in physical activity and the dedicated interest in risk management practices, sport specialists began to look to the legal profession for help. Communication was difficult, as lawyers saw "sport" as mainly professional sport and viewed the legal needs of professional teams and leagues as focusing on contract, labor, and agency law. Sport professionals, however, viewed law as personal injury and civil rights issues. While there were very few sport specialists who served the legal industry as expert witnesses at the time, these individuals are credited for forming the connection between law and sport that exists today. As sport management grew as an academic field of study, the need for the business components of law that had originally been championed by the legal profession became increasingly important to sport professionals at all levels (professional, collegiate, Olympic).

Law in sport and physical activity continues to grow and evolve. Current legal trends that developed and were shaped in the context of sport have become part of the mainstream in the popular press and are now discussed on sport law blogs, demonstrating interest by a far wider audience than ever before. Moreover, the separate area of risk management and compliance in sport exemplifies the return to the originally identified need for negligence and civil rights law. The chapter on risk management (Chapter 11) included in this text reflects best practices in stadium management that have evolved since September 11, 2001, and provides students with an introduction to the risk management process since many students may not have access to an entire course in this area.

COMPONENTS OF A LAWSUIT

Anyone can be sued. A lawsuit can be brought against any person or agency. A suit is brought when a person believes that he/she has been wronged and decides to place liability for that wrong on another person or agency. Court records verify that persons in nearly every profession have been forced by a court of law to defend their employment practices, programs, supervision, and management. All professionals should assume they can be sued; think through what a suit would mean emotionally, physically, and financially; and plan strategies that will provide a good chance of succeeding in a court of law.

Monetary damages are nearly always the goal in tort situations; in recent years, civil rights decisions have also resulted in monetary damages. In a court of law, the object of a damage award is to return the injured party to his/her condition prior to the incident. This is often called making the person "whole." A quadriplegic can never be returned to a walking and running person. Therefore, a specific sum of money is agreed upon by the court as a replacement for that person's capacity to walk and run. Personal injury litigation usually results when a victim has sustained a substantial financial loss. The loss may be a result of medical bills, lost wages, or rehabilitation fees. In addition, the loss may include future losses for persons who will require continuous assistance and rehabilitation. The expense of a catastrophic injury can be high.

Selection of an Attorney

When an individual determines that he/she has been harmed, the next step is usually to select an attorney for guidance. The attorney must understand the circumstances of the incident, become conversant with accepted professional standards of care both in sport and physical activity, and in civil rights concerns. Once the attorney understands the incident and the appropriate standard of care, the attorney is ready to advise the client. Among the client's choices is to bring a cause of action (lawsuit) against the party (or parties) that caused the harm. Every effort is made by the attorney and client to settle the differences among the parties; a lawsuit is considered a last resort. If one of the parties refuses to negotiate or there is a significant difference of opinion about the facts of the case, a formal complaint is filed.

Stages of a Lawsuit

A suit is divided into four stages: complaint, discovery, trial, and appeal.

Complaint

The complaint is a written statement alleging the cause of action, rights of the injured parties, legal theories, and award sought. The court issues a summons that is served on the defendant—the person or agency alleged to have caused the harm. An answer to the court is filed by the defendant in a specified period of time (usually 30 or 45 days). Once an individual receives a summons, legal counsel should be obtained. The ideal approach is for the defendant to have retained legal counsel that has been involved in risk and business decisions, and thus understand the environment in which the alleged injury occurred.

Discovery

Once a formal complaint is filed, both parties are in a favorable position to obtain information about the incident. This period of time is referred to as the discovery period. During the discovery period, parties learn as much as possible about the incident in which the alleged injury occurred, and value the injury in the context of similar incidents. Information is obtained by subpoena of records and by interviewing persons involved in the incident. The results of these discussions are made permanent as affidavits and depositions (statements of persons, under oath) of parties directly involved. Furthermore, the depositions of experts can assist the lawyers, the court, and ultimately the jury, in establishing standards of care and best business practices.

A case can be settled at any time during the discovery period. Members of the court stay in touch with the lawyers and their clients throughout the discovery period. The majority of court claims are settled during this period. The discovery period has a starting and finishing date. If the dispute is not resolved on the final date of discovery, the parties move into the motion phase and prepare for trial. Motions are requests to the court, controlled by the rules of the court and assist the parties in resolving disputes. Motions for settlement may be made prior to and during trial.

Trial

The trial is bench or jury. In a bench trial, a group of judges makes the decision. In a jury trial, people selected by the lawyers and judge make the decision. The decision is based on the testimony at trial and the documents produced. Once the jury is selected, the attorneys for the plaintiff and defendant make opening statements to the court summarizing their case. After the opening statements, the plaintiff presents his/ her case. The defendants are permitted to cross-examine each witness provided by the plaintiff. When the plaintiff has completed the presentation, the defendant presents his/her case. Again, the opposing counsel is permitted to cross-examine all witnesses.

At any time, but usually at the completion of either the plaintiff's presentation or the defendant's presentation, a motion can be made to the court to settle the case. If no motion is made or if the motions made are not granted, the attorneys move (or request) that the court go to closing arguments. Following closing arguments, the judge instructs the jury. The jury deliberates and returns a verdict to the judge. The verdict determines who wins and who loses. The judge usually accepts the jury's verdict and announces the decision.

Appeal

If the party that loses believes that there has been error, or that new information about the facts of the case are available, he/she will usually appeal the trial court's decision to a higher court (the court of appeals for the state or the state supreme court). The appellate court (consisting of a panel of judges) reviews the record of the trial. Attorneys for both sides file briefs and/or summaries. The appellate court may affirm, reverse, or remand the case for further study.

THE LEGAL SYSTEM

To work effectively with legal concepts, it is helpful to possess knowledge of both how law is created and the role of the courts in the interpretation of law. Understanding sources of law and the structure and role of federal and state courts will provide such foundational information.

Sources of Law

Law in the United States is derived from federal and state constitutions, legislative enactments, and the results of decisions rendered by federal and state courts. The United States Constitution and the constitutions of each state create the federal and state judicial systems, respectively. Federal government powers are limited to those identified in the U.S. Constitution. The Tenth Amendment to the U.S. Constitution provides that all powers not specifically granted to the federal government in the U.S. Constitution be made available to the states.

Federal and state statutes, executive orders, and city ordinances form the basis for statutory law. Congress, state legislatures, city councils, and county boards of commissions have authority to enact laws dealing with a wide range of topics. Their powers are limited only by federal and state constitutions. For example, states, communities, and local municipalities have the power to regulate, within their jurisdiction, resources and human activity for the promotion of health, safety, and welfare. Compliance with an occupancy limit at a stadium, for instance, would be used by a city to promote public safety, particularly during emergencies.

Administrative law covers the rules, regulations, and directives issued by the executive branch of government within the scope of the acts of Congress. Specific administrative agencies such as the Office of Civil Rights are charged with the responsibility of overseeing the execution of the rules, regulations, and directives of the executive branch.

Case law forms the basis for common law in the United States. Under common law or judge-made law, the results of court decisions in state and federal courts establish legal precedent, which is then used by courts as a guide in deciding future cases under stare decisis. Stare decisis is the legal principle by which courts must honor past precedent. As noted by Moorman and Grady (2011), determining the precedential value of a court decision involves first identifying the level of court deciding the case, then analyzing legal sources to put the court decision in the context of case law that existed before the current decision was made. As a result of the use of precedent, laws may differ from one state to another, from one court to another, or from one federal jurisdiction to another. This means that a particular legal decision may be used in Minnesota, while a slightly different precedent or decision may be used in Florida.

Determining whether the precedent is binding or persuasive is also important. "A decision rendered by the U.S. Supreme Court is binding on all lower federal courts and carries the highest precedential value, whereas a state court decision has limited impact only to the one state and represents the opinion of just one court" (Moorman & Grady, 2011, p. 179). In cases involving sport and physical activity, these differences are not extreme. Laws discussed throughout the text will relate to the general principles of law and will avoid unique regional decisions.

This textbook facilitates future sport professionals' acquisition of knowledge related to the legal decisions appropriate to their professional needs. The student will acquire knowledge of the United States Constitution and skill in locating the constitution and case law in the student's respective state. Furthermore, the student will become acquainted with federal, state, and local statutes, executive orders, and city ordinances. All of these sources of legal knowledge are pertinent to the student's future role in managing sport and physical activity.

Courts

The United States has two judicial systems: one at the federal level and one in each state. Though certain aspects of their responsibilities interrelate, these systems are largely independent. Each state is governed by its own state constitution and the U.S. Constitution. Jurisdiction of the federal court system extends to all cases and controversies arising under the U.S. Constitution and all statutes and treaties pursuant to the U.S. Constitution. State and local courts are responsible for controversies arising under the constitutions for each state and the laws of cities and counties.

Local courts also hear the cases of citizens, unless the issue relates to a citizen's right that has been proscribed or limited by the Constitution. When such rights have been affected, the cases are under the jurisdiction of the federal courts. Should the laws of a county, city, or state be in conflict with the Constitution, the controversy will be brought to the federal courts. In some situations, the state court will be the court of last resort. In other circumstances, the federal court will be the final court. Sometimes, the state and federal court systems will have concurrent jurisdiction or joint responsibility for law enforcement.

Federal Courts

The federal courts are structured in three tiers: the District Court at the lowest level, the Courts of Appeals at the intermediate level, and the Supreme Court at the highest level (see Figure A). Other courts established by the U.S. Constitution include the Court of Claims, Court of Military Appeals, and Customs Court. The national judiciary also includes legislative and administrative agencies created by Congress. These agencies perform judicial functions subject to review by the courts. It should be noted that the word "review" refers to the power of a court to examine decisions made by administrative units. Such examinations ascertain the validity of the rulings in light of applicable statutes, regulations, previous opinions, and findings of fact.

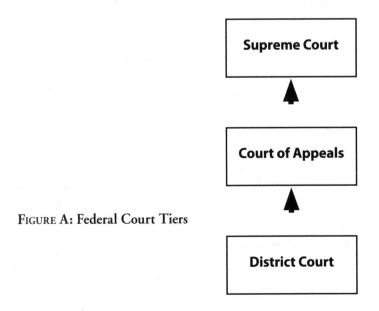

FIGURE A: Federal Court Tiers

Federal courts deal with certain kinds of cases (often referred to as federal questions) and with certain parties to a dispute from different states. The phrase "federal question" means the case involved an interpretation and application of the U.S. Constitution, Acts of Congress, or Treaties. Diversity of citizenship refers to a case between parties who reside or do business in different states; a citizen of the United States and an alien; or a United States citizen and a foreign government.

Article III of the U.S. Constitution extends federal jurisdiction to all cases involving the Constitution, as well as all statutes and treaties that may be made in pursuance of it. Admiralty and maritime law, statutory and international in character, fall under the exclusive jurisdiction of the federal courts. Controversies involving persons such as ambassadors, public ministers, and consuls also fall under the jurisdiction of the national judiciary, as do controversies involving two or more states.

District Courts

The district courts are the basic civil and criminal trial courts in the federal system. Most cases in federal law originate here, and no case is appealed to a district court. There are 92 district courts in the 50 states, the District of Columbia, Puerto Rico, the Virgin Islands, the Canal Zone, and Guam. Each court is presided over by a single judge who has been appointed by the President of the United States. District courts usually establish the record used to determine the guilt or innocence of the defendant in criminal matters and the determination of legal responsibility in civil issues. The report containing the facts of the controversy is usually established in the district court.

Courts of Appeals

The courts of appeals are the intermediate courts. They take cases only on appeal from a federal district court or from a regulatory commission, such as the Securities and Exchange Commission. The United States is presently divided into 11 courts of appeals districts, each having a group of three to nine judges. Cases are heard and decisions rendered by as few as two judges; however, three is a more standard number. Appeals courts review the proceedings of the original trial court to ascertain whether the substantive and procedural rights of the parties involved have been honored. The court also decides whether the statute or regulation under which the indictment was brought is constitutional.

Supreme Court

The Supreme Court, the highest court of the United States, is presided over by one chief justice and eight associate justices (28 USC, Section 1). The justices are appointed by the President of the United States subject to the approval of the Senate. "The judges serve during 'good Behaviour' which has generally meant a life term" (Supreme Court, n.d.). The U.S. Constitution gives the Supreme Court original jurisdiction, or the capacity to create the record only for cases involving ambassadors, public ministers, and consuls, and for proceedings in which a state is a party. Its appellate jurisdiction is more flexible, as it can be altered by an act of Congress. It should be noted that the phrase "appellate jurisdiction" means the record is reviewed to ascertain that the substantive and procedural rights of the parties involved have been honored and that the statute or regulation under consideration is constitutional.

At present, the Supreme Court may review cases which originate in the state courts, in the lower federal courts, or in the federal regulatory boards and commissions. The Supreme Court is required to take an appeal from the highest state court, from a United States court of appeals in a case in which a federal statute or treaty has been declared invalid, or when a state constitutional provision or statute appears to violate the U.S. Constitution or an act of Congress. It should be noted that the route of appeal from the highest state court is directly to the Supreme Court and not through the lower federal structures.

Many of the cases that go to the Supreme Court are by a writ of certiorari and not by the appeals route. A writ is an order issued by the court calling up an important case for review because the case is constitutionally significant. The Supreme Court makes its decision to take cases on certiorari and on appeal. The refusal of the Supreme Court to hear an appeal or to accept a petition for certiorari generally means that the members have decided to accept as valid the decision of the highest state court or the lower federal court.

State Courts

Court systems differ from state to state. It should be noted that effort has been made to make generalizations with reference to the state courts. Therefore, the discussion within this textbook may not mirror the exact judicial form in every state. For example, state judges are either appointed by the governor or elected by popular ballot.

Courts are classified by the types of cases presented: juvenile courts meeting the needs of youth, criminal courts hearing offenses against society, and civil courts adjudicating issues involving the rights of the private sector. Although courts may differ from state to state, all states have trial and supreme courts. A minority of states have courts of appeals (see Figure B). All states have administrative agencies that perform judicial functions and are subject to judicial review.

State Trial Courts

When parties decide to resort to the judicial system to settle a dispute, their initial contact will be with a trial court. Civil and criminal cases are usually tried in different courts at this level. Trial courts decide disputes of fact. Detailed findings of fact based upon the evidence provided are then subjected to rules of law. Therefore, the judge and jury (or the judge standing alone) render a decision.

State Courts of Appeals

A party wishing to appeal a judgment made by the trial court can take the case to a court of appeals. With the exception of a few states, both civil and criminal cases generally go to the same court of appeals. Courts of appeals make decisions both by using the record of facts obtained in the trial court and by reviewing the questions of law. If one of the parties is not satisfied with the decision of the state court of appeals, the issue may be taken to the state supreme court.

State Supreme Court

The state supreme court is the highest appellate court and the court of last resort on matters of state law. As a court of appeals, the state supreme court will examine the record to be sure the substantive and procedural rights of the parties have been properly adjudicated and that the constitution, statutes, and regulations of the state have been adequately interpreted. When appropriate, a state supreme court decision can be appealed directly to the U.S. Supreme Court.

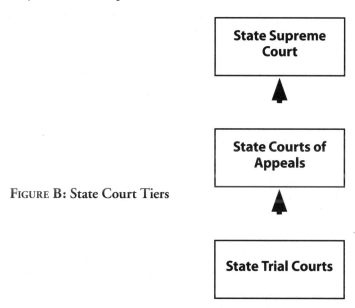

FIGURE B: State Court Tiers

THE LEGAL RESEARCH PROCESS

The legal research process is fundamentally different from other research paradigms with which the reader may be familiar. A goal of conducting qualitative research may be to seek an in-depth understanding of a phenomenon affecting sport management practice, such as interviews with executives from companies sponsoring the Olympics about perceptions of ambush marketing. A goal of quantitative research, on the other hand, may be to observe variables in the sport environment to come to a conclusion about a hypothesis, such as predicting factors impacting spectator motivations to attend wheelchair basketball events. While sharing some of these same goals, the goal in conducting legal research is distinct: to develop a comprehensive understanding of a legal topic, including analyzing all sides of a legal issue. Through legal research, "the researcher must employ a combination of sources to ensure that the research is comprehensive" (Moorman & Grady, 2011, p. 176).

In searching for and analyzing applicable sources of authority, the legal researcher uses a non-linear process to begin the research process with a broad legal topic in mind and continues to refine it by going back and forth between sources as relevant sources continue to be located (Moorman & Grady, 2011). The researcher continually narrows his/her focus on a specific legal issue. For example, a researcher may want to investigate the constitutionality of pat-down searches at NFL stadiums. The researcher could begin to understand the "big picture" by locating published cases involving pat downs at similar public places where large numbers of people gather similar to stadiums, such as at airports. He/she could then begin to narrow the search for cases specifically involving pat-down searches at sporting events. This would likely lead to cases of drug testing of athletes, factually dissimilar from the topic of searches of spectators but possibly analogous and of value to the researcher. This "road block" may require searching for additional sources more directly on point, such as for cases involving pat downs of spectators at high school athletic contests. The sources often identify and provide guidance about subtle changes in the legal landscape over time that may impact the narrow legal topic that a beginning researcher may not be able to identify from reading a handful of cases.

Similar to the research process used by qualitative researchers, the legal researcher "moves back and forth between primary and secondary sources, integrating the information rather than providing a linear summary of each source" (Moorman & Grady, 2011, p. 189). This process of continually narrowing the focus of the research has been described as an inverted pyramid analytical approach (Dernbach, Singleton, Wharton, & Ruhtenberg, 2007). This approach has been adapted for use in legal research in sport management (Moorman & Grady, 2011, pp. 189–190).

Once a legal concept is clearly understood through use of the research process described above, the researcher can then research additional legal materials as well as find additional support in articles relating to sport management in order to better grasp the application of the legal concept to the management and practice of sport and physical activity. For example, once the concept of negligence in sport is generally understood through analyzing primary sources like court cases, a researcher may want to analyze how negligence has been applied by the courts specifically in crowd management situations at sport facilities. Another person may be interested in the impact of negligence on lifeguards, while yet another may be interested in how negligence will impact his/her personal training business. Each of these issues can be further studied using secondary sources of legal materials, such as law review articles and legal or trade journals.

This remainder of this introduction guides student researchers through the legal research process described above using cases, law review articles, journals, and books related to the application of law to sport and physical activity. It also enables individuals to locate statutes and case law cited in this text and in legal periodicals and to utilize various sources of legal materials in preparing presentations and publications.

Legal publications can be found in courthouses, public libraries, public and private institutions that offer law-based courses, and university and college law schools. Numerous private law firm libraries—while at times more difficult to access—also exist and contain numerous research collections. With advances in technology and growth of the Internet and digital content, there is now more widespread access to legal research materials than ever before, and everyone from legal scholars to undergraduate sport management students can learn to conduct legal research.

LexisNexis Academic

A commonly available legal research retrieval system created for general university use is called LexisNexis Academic. It allows students enrolled in subscribing institutions an opportunity to electronically search for many sources of legal information, including court decisions, statutes, and constitutions.

LexisNexis Academic can commonly be found under the electronic library databases of subscribing university websites. The search process is similar to conducting an Internet search with the option to narrowly search for specific legal topics. For example, a student may decide to search for "negligence" involving "soccer" in the student's home state or in all of the United States. Cases identified through the search (e.g., negligence) and soccer will appear in the search results using case titles. The student can scan each case to ascertain its value to his/her research interest and then read in detail only those valuable cases. To gain familiarity with LexisNexis Academic, a recommended strategy is to find a case of interest in any chapter of this textbook and perform a search using LexisNexis Academic to identify subsequent cases in which the original case has been cited or discussed (also referred to as Shepardizing).

LexisNexis Academic also allows students to search for law review articles. Many of the law review articles specifically devoted to the study of law and sport are written to educate lawyers about the context and nuances of sport as well as how to apply legal theory uniquely to situations involving sport. These articles are often very valuable to sport management students in courses in law but also in finance, governance, and management. LexisNexis Academic has a tutorial to assist the user in acquiring a range of search strategies.

SOURCES OF LEGAL INFORMATION

Legal materials can be separated into two categories: primary and secondary sources. Primary sources are actual statements of the law and include legislative statutes, court decisions, executive decrees and orders, and administrative regulations and rulings. Federal and state statutes and appellate court decisions are the primary documents most often used in legal research. Primary sources can be relied upon to determine what the law is and what the law requires (Moorman & Grady, 2011). Secondary sources explain, interpret, and comment on the law or its application (Moorman & Grady, 2011) and include textbooks, law review articles, treatises, practice manuals, commentaries, restatements, and periodicals.

Case Law

Case law plays an important role in sport and physical activity, as many legal theories have evolved as a result of case decisions. Cases can be located through researching topical areas in case digests and citations from textbooks and periodicals. Results of case law are published according to the organization of the courts with reporters for the U.S. Supreme Court, the federal appellate courts, and all state appellate and supreme courts. All of these materials can be found on an electronic retrieval system.

Statutes and Codes

A systematic compilation of statutes and regulations is usually identified as a Code. The regulations of federal agencies are first published in the Federal Register and later codified into the Code of Federal Regulations. The United States Code Annotated (USCA) contains federal, legislative, and congressional statutes. Each state has a similar code. Putnam (2003) notes that "the body of law represented by statutory law has expanded greatly. Many matters once governed by common law are now governed by statutory law" (p. 49). Through statutory analysis, a lawyer, researcher, or student can determine whether a statute, such as an "open records" statute, applies to communications generated by a state university's athletic compliance department, how it applies, and the effect of that application (Putnam, 2003).

Annotated Reports

Annotated reports are legal references reported according to subject matter. For example, American Law Institute Reports include past developments and current laws in most states and future trends.

Legislative History Reports

Researchers often will trace the history of a law to locate documents which will reveal the intent of Congress or a state legislature. Statutory research will include pre-enactment history of earlier statutes and the current status of law under consideration. Legislative historical documents include presidential messages, congressional bills, reports of hearings, committee reports, debates, House and Senate hearings, and Senate executive reports.

Administrative Documents

Administrative materials are located under the title of the agency. Therefore, knowledge of the agency is important to the researcher. Such information also can be located in the United States Government Manual, Federal Register, Code of Federal Regulations, and Administrative Rules and Decisions.

Periodicals

Many periodicals address issues of law in sport and physical activity on a single-article basis, while others dedicate an entire volume or publish only in the area of sport. The indexes of legal periodicals and their electronic databases will identify these articles.

SYSTEM FOR CASE ANALYSIS

After a judge renders a decision in a case, an explanation of the reasoning behind the decision is written. The explanation and a summary of the presentation to the court are published as an opinion. When several judges have participated in the decision and agreement does not exist among the judges, one judge writes the opinion of the majority of the judges. Disagreeing judges are free to write their dissenting opinions either as a group or as individuals. A case opinion will usually contain the following general categories: title, facts, issues, decision or holding, and the reasoning of the court.

SUMMARY

A difference exists between the phrases "law in sport" and "sport law." "Law in sport" is the selection of a wide range of legal concepts that are relevant to the day-to-day decisions made in the sport industry. These concepts have been taken from the laws of negligence, intentional torts, product liability, contract, constitution, labor, agency, intellectual property, and others. By contrast, "sport law" refers only to the basic law and court decisions unique to sport.

The constitutions, statutes, administrative decisions, and the results of court cases constitute the law used in the United States. Congress, through the Senate and House of Representatives, has the power to create new law. Court systems are organized for the federal government and within each state. Each system consists of a lower court, in which the facts are ascertained for the record prior to judicial decision; and a series of higher order courts of appeals, in which the record is examined for procedural or substantive errors.

Case analysis is used to learn details of litigation and the topics that could become the subject of litigation. That knowledge can be used to create and implement risk management programs or to prepare research reports. It is significant to ascertain whether the results of the case establish new law or utilize existing law from other jurisdictions (i.e., other states or regions). Case analysis can identify patterns of litigation, where the litigation is occurring, and what activities appear to have been called into court.

REFERENCES

Davis, T. (2001, Spring). What is sports law? 11 *Marq. Sports L. Rev.* 211.

Dernbach, J. C., Singleton, R. V., Wharton, C. S., & Ruhtenberg, J. M. (2007). *A practical guide to legal writing and legal method* (3rd ed.). New York, NY: Aspen.

Moorman, A. M. M., & Grady, J. (2011). Legal research. In D. P. S. Andrew, P. M. Pedersen, & C. D. McEvoy. *Research methods and design in sport management.* (pp. 173–195), Champaign, IL: Human Kinetics.

Putnam, W. H. (2010). *Legal research, analysis, and writing* (3rd ed.). Clifton Park, NY: Delmar Cengage Learning.

Supreme Court of the United States. (n.d.). The Court as an institution. Retrieved from http://www.supremecourt.gov/about/institution.aspx

RECOMMENDED READING

Andrew, D. P. S., Pedersen, P. M., & McEvoy, C. D. (2011). *Research methods and design in sport management.* Champaign, IL: Human Kinetics.

Carter, W. B. (1999). What makes a "field" a "field"? 1 *Virginia J. of Sports* L. 235.

Garon, J. M. (2002, Feb.). Entertainment law. 76 *Tul. L. Rev.* 559.

Part I

— TORT LAW —

A tort is an injury or a civil wrong that has caused harm to a person or a person's property for which the courts will provide a remedy. Broad categories of tort found in sport and physical activity are negligence, intentional tort, and product liability. The American Law Institute tracks changes in the law of tort and periodically publishes these changes in a Restatement. The following Restatements have been used in this section of the book:

- *Restatement Third, Torts: Liability for Physical and Emotional Harm* (2010);
- *Restatement of the Law of Torts, Product Liability* (1988); and
- *Restatement Second, Torts* (1965, 1977, and 1979).

In educational terms, each of the *Restatements* presents a contemporary structure of the discipline of tort. Numerous writers, judges, and practicing lawyers were involved in the creation of each of the *Restatements*. The 2010 volume is the result of 29 American Law Institute meetings involving over 300 leaders in the area of tort.

Negligence is covered in Chapter 1. A person acts negligently if the person does not exercise reasonable care under all circumstances. Risky conduct is the term popular in the sport and physical activity industry. Historically, negligence has been the legal theory most often encountered in sport and physical activity. Intentional torts, explained in Chapter 2, are torts caused by a deliberate act. Today, fault is often not found in professional and collegiate team sports until intent is determined. This new approach to fault in sport has evolved since the earlier court decisions. Product liability, discussed in Chapter 3, is the accountability of the manufacturer, retailer, and seller of a dangerous or defective product to those injured by the product.

1

Negligence

OBJECTIVES

Upon completing this chapter, you will:

1) understand the elements of negligence and be able to apply them to a real-life situation;

2) recognize the relationship between duty and foreseeability;

3) be able to articulate the defenses to negligence and give examples of each defense;

4) be confident in identifying and defining the particular kind of assumption of risk necessary in a range of situations;

5) know how to explain comparative negligence to a colleague;

6) recognize the types of premise liability and be able to locate local and state law in the area; and

7) understand the various kinds of immunity.

INTRODUCTION

A person acts negligently if the person does not exercise reasonable care under all circumstances. "Primary factors to consider in ascertaining whether the person's conduct lacks reasonable care are the foreseeable likelihood that the person's conduct will result in harm, the foreseeable severity of any harm that may ensue, and the burden of precautions to eliminate or reduce the risk of harm" (Restatement Third, Torts: Liability for Physical and Emotional Harm, Section 3). It is the person's acts and the person's omissions, or failure to act. Negligence also includes a balancing of risks and benefits or a cost benefit test. The "risk is the overall level of the foreseeable risk created by the actor's conduct and the benefit is the advantages that the actor or others gain if the actor refrains from taking precautions" (*Restatement Third, Torts: Liability for Physical and Emotional Harm*, Section 3 [e]).

ELEMENTS OF NEGLIGENCE

The following five elements must exist for a court to find a person or agency negligent:

- duty;
- breach of duty;
- factual cause;
- scope of liability including foreseeability; and
- damage.

Duty

"An actor ordinarily has a duty to exercise reasonable care when the actor's conduct creates a risk of physical harm. In exceptional cases, when an articulated countervailing principle or policy warrants denying or limiting liability in a particular class of cases, a court may decide that the defendant has no duty or that the ordinary duty or reasonable care requires modification" (*Restatement, Third, Torts: Liability for Physical and Emotional Harm,* Section 7). A relationship sufficient to create a legal duty may arise by statute, ordinance, administrative rule, contract, voluntary assumption, or judicial decision. Three different legal duties or standards of care (explained later) are reasonable person, special relationship, and professional standard. A reasonable person duty is the standard applicable to society in general. Parents are among those with special relationships. Coach-athlete, teacher-student, trainer-client, therapist-client, employer-employee, and principal-agent are relationships that establish a professional legal duty of care. The legal duty of care and the standards of the profession or industry dictate the duty elements of negligence.

Breach of Duty

Once the legal duty or standard of care is established, proof must be provided to the court by the plaintiff (injured person) that the duty was breached. Professional sport and physical activity specialists have specific duties. These legal duties (standards of care) are in writing for some professionals; for others they are unwritten standards commonly accepted by members of the profession. Among a number of sport and physical activity professionals, one legal duty is emergency care. Although professionals do not have to provide emergency care, they must make provisions for such care. Failure to make provisions for emergency care is an example of a breach of legal duty. Instructors, teachers, therapists, and exercise specialists are obligated to provide learning experiences that are challenging but not so difficult or so far beyond the capacity of the learner that injury is likely to occur. When clients or students are injured as a result of being allowed to participate in risk activities far beyond their physical capacity, professionals are in breach of their duty of care. If facilities are not maintained according to the expectations of the industry, professionals will also breach the duty of care.

Factual Cause

When it has been determined that the defendant breached the duty of care, the court identifies the relationship between the breach and the injury. A breach can be an act or omission. Was the breach the cause of the injury? For liability to be found, the breach must be the cause of the injury. The plaintiff must show a direct relationship between the breach of the duty and the injury or damage. For example, was the defendant's negligent act the cause of the injury? Would the same harm have resulted had the negligent act never occurred? Reasonable care is

> the balance between the magnitude of the foreseeable risk and the burden of precaution that can eliminate the risk. The "magnitude" of risk includes the likelihood of a harm-causing incident and the severity of the harm that may occur. If the burden is greater than the magnitude of the risk, the actor who declines to adopt the precaution is generally not negligent. But if the risk is somewhat greater than the burden, the actor is negligent for failing to adopt the precaution. (*Restatement, Third, Torts: Liability for Physical and Emotional Harm*, Section 2 [d])

Scope of Liability Including Foreseeability

After establishing factual cause, scope of liability- foreseeability is ascertained. Foreseeability is the capacity of the defendant to anticipate an accident or incident. Was the harm to the plaintiff a reasonable, foreseeable, consequence of the defendant's actions? Was the defendant responsible? At trial, the court will ask if the accident or incident in which the plaintiff sustained injuries was an event that could or should have been predicted as one that might cause injury. To what extent could it have been predicted that participation in the activity would result in injury? Was the occurrence of the injury foreseeable? The harm must have been foreseeable before the event; decisions about foreseeability are not to be made after the injury has been sustained. Sufficient foresight must exist to enable professionals to prevent or alter actions in an effort to avoid injury. A remote possibility is not sufficient; substantial damage must be probable, not just possible. In sport and physical activity, risk management processes can be used to establish foreseeability.

Damage

For the court to find negligence, substantial damage must exist. Cuts and bruises are not sufficient; the person must be seriously damaged physically or psychologically. If the question exists as to whether the damages are substantial, the question of damages will go to the jury.

STANDARDS OF CARE

There are three basic standards of care: reasonable person, special relationship, and professional.

Reasonable Person

Reasonable person is a hypothetical scenario that asks what an average adult would have done in a similar situation. For example, the court will ask what care an ordinary person would have provided under the circumstances of the incident to avoid injuries to others. Did the defendant behave as a reasonable, prudent adult? Would a reasonable person have recognized the risk and taken steps to avoid it?

There is no duty to act affirmatively on behalf of all other people or "no duty to rescue." A person walking past a playground and observing an injured child has no obligation or responsibility to provide immediate and temporary care for the injured child. Duty exists only when a special relationship has been formed. If the person, walking past a playground decides to provide help to the child, the person is obligated to continue the help until professional emergency medical assistance is on the scene. Once a rescuer begins to give assistance, a special relationship is created. Thereafter, assistance must continue until emergency help arrives. Children are held to the standard of care expected of a child of similar age, education, intelligence, and experience. Children under five or those engaging in a dangerous activity that is characteristically undertaken by adults do not possess the capacity to be negligent.

Special Relationship

Parents and schools are examples of people and agencies with special relationships that dictate a distinct standard of care. An exception to the "no duty to rescue" rule exists for parents. Parents do have an obligation to rescue their child when the child is in danger. The special relationship that exists between spouses and between parents and children is a duty to rescue within the context of skill, knowledge, and ability. Therefore, a parent who did not know how to swim would not have a duty to jump into the water to rescue his/her drowning child, but would have a duty to call for help.

Among a school's responsibilities to children is a duty to be prepared to render emergency medical assistance when it is needed. In *Kleinknecht v. Gettysburg* (1991), the court held that the college had a duty to be prepared for a medical emergency resulting from collegiate athletics. In this case, an athlete suffered a cardiac arrest and died during practice. Also, schools are expected to provide protection for children through age-appropriate supervision.

Professional

A professional standard is established when a body of professional knowledge exists and a recognized level of performance is adhered to by members of that profession. This is the level most relevant to sport and physical activity professionals. The level of duty owed is higher than the level expected of a reasonable person. A person is found negligent under a professional standard for failing to perform at the level expected of a person with the training, knowledge, and skill of a member of the profession. In turn, the public can rely on receiving a predictable level of performance from a professional because of the person's training, knowledge, and skill. The professional's legal duty of care to another is satisfied when unreasonable risks of harm are eliminated. To successfully eliminate unreasonable risks of harm, the professional must recognize and know the dangers of harm inherent in the activities in use.

Among the many professional standards in sport and physical activity are facility inspection, proper use of equipment, supervision, instructional protocols, rescue procedures, and emergency care. The legal duty or standard of care is the written statement or standard accepted by the profession. It may require specific courses or learning experiences, attainment of proficiency in competency tests, and periodic renewal of designated certificates. When a standard does not exist, the legal duty of care is that of a reasonable professional or a reasonable person under similar circumstances.

A legal duty of care may exist even though the professional is not on the payroll. Technical expertise, not job status or wage, is the basis upon which one's duty of care is judged. It is anticipated that certain expertise will accompany specific jobs. As mentioned earlier, a professional will be held to the level of expertise recognized in a job even if the professional does not hold the appropriate credentials for the job. Professionals are often surprised to learn that the same duty of care may exist when they serve as a volunteer as when they are a paid employee working in a professional capacity.

DEFENSES

The defenses against claims of negligence are:

- contributory negligence;
- assumption of risk; and
- comparative fault or comparative negligence.

Contributory negligence uses the objective standard of a "reasonable person," the standard used in negligence cases. The defense of assumption of risk uses a subjective standard based on the victim's knowledge of the risk and willingness to assume the risk. In most states, contributory negligence and assumption of risk are merged into comparative fault.

Contributory Negligence

Contributory negligence means that the plaintiff, or injured person, is responsible in part for his/her injuries. One has a duty to protect one's self from injury. The plaintiff's conduct has somehow contributed, as a legal cause, to the harm the plaintiff has suffered (*Restatement, Third, Torts: Liability for Physical and Emotional Harm,* Section 3 [k]).

The standard of conduct used in negligence, that of a reasonable person under ordinary circumstances, is also the standard applied in contributory negligence. In contributory negligence, the defendant is not relieved of a duty toward the plaintiff. Contributory negligence does, however, become a part of the formula in allocating damages between the plaintiff and defendant. It is also a defense to negligence. It is not, however, a defense to an intentional tort.

Assumption of Risk

Assumption of risk occurs when the victim becomes responsible for some portion of the risk of an activity and, as a result of assuming the risk, assumes liability for that portion of damages. In complete assumption of risk, the victim has contracted away his/her right to a cause of action through a signed written agreement, which is considered a contract. Only adults, not minors, can create contracts. Therefore, minors cannot waive their right to sue. Also, in many states, a minor may sue over an injury sustained while a minor, after he/she becomes an adult.

Warnings, risk education, and signed forms may not bar recovery for all adults but will serve to inform participants of the dangers inherent in the activity. Even though a court may not accept an assumption of risk statement as a contract or a complete bar to recovery, the document will demonstrate that the victim had knowledge of the risk involved in the activity.

Knowledge and Appreciation

When a participant encounters a dangerous situation, the participant must have adequate knowledge to appreciate the danger. Knowledge and appreciation of danger is not based on a reasonable person standard but on a standard tailored for the individual involved. Persons using equipment or taking instructions for the first time are not expected to possess the same level of knowledge and appreciation of danger as persons with considerable experience in the activity. Once the person understands the danger, he/she is able to make informed decisions about taking the risk of participating in the activity.

In many court decisions, knowledge and appreciation of a danger is a question for the jury. A professional's method of demonstrating that students and clients had knowledge and appreciation of the risks in the activity in which they were participating involves the use of instructional protocols, records of progress, and other documents. Assumption of risk involves either express or implied consent. There are two types of assumption of risk, primary and secondary, which will be discussed after the types of consent.

Express Consent

Express consent is usually a signed agreement between the participant and the service provider that meets the standard of a contract and can relieve the provider of a lawsuit for negligence. The plaintiff expressly assumes the risk and agrees, prior to the time of the injury-causing event, to hold the defendant blameless. Some states and courts may refuse to honor these contractual agreements, stating that public policy prohibits injured parties from signing away their rights.

When a person who fully understands the risk of an activity voluntarily agrees to take part and to relieve the defendant of any duty, they are said to have given express consent. Under this agreement the plaintiff must:

- know that the risk exists;

- understand the nature of the risk; and

- freely choose to incur the risk.

The decision to assume the risk must be free and voluntary; some sign or manifestation of consent must be present to relieve the defendant of his/her obligation. Should the plaintiff be placed in a position where the consent was forced, the plaintiff cannot be said to have assumed the risk. Age, experience, and knowledge of information pertinent to the activity are critical factors in determining a plaintiff's ability to comprehend and appreciate a risk.

Implied Consent

In sport and physical activity, persons who understand the risk of an activity can, as a result of participating in the activity, agree to the inherent risks without signing a contract. In implied consent, the defendant is not relieved of a responsibility. Implied consent becomes a part of the comparative fault percentage. The following explanation of the two types of assumption of risk, primary and secondary, is somewhat unique to sport and physical activity.

Primary Assumption of Risk

Primary assumption of risk occurs when a party or potential plaintiff voluntarily participates in a sporting event or activity involving inherent risk and the defendant is under no duty to protect the plaintiff from the inherent risks of the activity. It should be noted that the defendant is liable for injury when his/her behavior becomes reckless. This heightened reckless standard was found in decisions in California, Kentucky, Louisiana, Michigan, Nebraska, Ohio, and Texas and is becoming more frequent across the United States. To recover in a court of law, an injured athlete must show that the injuries sustained in sport and physical activity did not flow from the normal course of participation or competition.

Secondary Assumption of Risk

Secondary assumption of risk occurs when a party voluntarily participates in a risky activity, has not consented to relieve the defendant of his/her duty of care, and the defendant breaches a duty of care owed the plaintiff. Secondary assumption of risk is not a bar to recovery; it becomes part of the comparative fault formula. In summary, primary and secondary assumption of risk are similar to express and implied consent. Primary assumption of risk is essentially consent and relieves the defendant of fault. Secondary assumption of risk does not involve consent and thus may only reduce, not remove, the plaintiff's liability for the harm.

COMPARATIVE NEGLIGENCE/COMPARATIVE FAULT

Comparative negligence is a system in which the percentage of responsibility of the injured party and the percentage of responsibility of the persons or agency that contributed to or caused the harm are balanced in a formula. The contributory negligence of the injured party is used to reduce the recovery for the injured party. Recovery is allocated in proportion to the relative fault of each party. For example, the injured party may be found to be 30 percent at fault (contributory negligence and assumption of risk) and the person causing the injury at 70 percent fault. Table 1.1 shows the allocation of a $100,000 judgment.

TABLE 1.1: Comparative Negligence

Party	Fault	Judgment Sum
Plaintiff	30%	Assumes $30,000 of expenses
Defendant	70%	Pays $70,000 to plaintiff

Comparative fault, in contrast, is the apportionment of damages among the joint defendants according to the percentage attributed to each. Table 1.2 explains the above situation involving three—rather than one—defendants. The three defendants are responsible for 70% of the damage award with Defendant 1 responsible for 30%, Defendant 2 for 25%, and Defendant 3 for 15%.

TABLE 1.2: Comparative Fault

Party	Fault	Judgment Sum
Injured party	30%	Assumes $30,000 of expenses
Defendant 1	30%	Pays $30,000 to injured party
Defendant 2	25%	Pays $25,000 to injured party
Defendant 3	15%	Pays $15,000 to injured party

A modified system of fault allocation used in some states denies the injured party recovery if the injured party's negligence was as great as 50% or 51% of the fault. Other states have a system called "joint and several liability" for the damage award. That means that if only Responsible Party 1 was able to pay, he/she would be responsible for the total or $70,000. If only Responsible Parties 2 and 3 could pay, each would be responsible for 50% of $70,000, or $35,000.

WAIVER OF LIABILITY

A range of educational tools and agreements are used in sport and physical activity to educate and inform participants about risks. These risk and/or informed consent documents will be used by the court to demonstrate that the parties were informed of the risks, understood the risks (provided the forms withstand the scrutiny of the court), agreed to encounter the risks, and signed a statement acknowledging their understanding of the risks. Statements are to be so specific that the participant has an estimate of the probability of sustaining a loss and what the loss might be. Courts have found defendants not guilty of negligence when the plaintiff had signed a waiver of liability that fully conformed with the legal requirements of a contract. The release must be clear, unambiguous, explicit, and concise. On occasion, waivers of liability may be considered by the courts to be so offensive to society that parties are not permitted to sign away those rights. Signed statements of release are often misinterpreted to mean that the participant has agreed not to sue.

In addition to the contract requirements, it should be noted that only adults can enter into a contract; parents cannot sign away the rights of their children, but parents can sign away their own rights to a cause of action for their children. This means that they can agree to the knowledge of a full disclosure of the risks including probability, extent, and magnitude of the harm that could occur to their child while he/she participates in the activity. In the event of a lawsuit, such an agreement will be examined by the court to determine its validity as a defense. Injured children reaching the age of majority have the benefit of their state's statute of limitations, often two years, to bring a cause of action for a harm that occurred while they were a minor. All documents used as educational tools and waivers of liability are to be drafted by legal counsel and are to conform to relevant local and state statutes.

OWNERS AND OCCUPIERS OF LAND

Premises liability is a theory of property liability currently being incorporated into negligence in many states. An understanding of this area is essential for reviewing cases where it remains the law and for the examination of older cases. In early days in the United States, persons owning large tracts of land were encouraged to allow others to use their land for hunting, fishing, and recreation. To protect the owners of these lands from liability, property laws were created in various states. Premises liability defined the duty of care of the owner or person in possession of land to individuals injured on their property. Persons entering the land are classified as either:

- invitees;
- licensees; or
- trespassers.

Invitees have the greatest protection, while licensees are given less care. Trespassers are owed the lowest duty, sometimes referred to as zero duty. Tennessee, Maine, Connecticut, Florida, and Illinois were the first to abolish premises liability. Other states have followed their direction. As states reject the categories of invitee, licensee, and trespasser, they are moving toward a reasonable person standard for the liability of the landowner or person in possession of the land.

Invitee

An invitee is a person who has either expressly or impliedly been invited onto the land of another for an economic benefit to the person in possession of the land (known as a business invitee), or one who enters land open to the public (known as a public invitee). Patrons of stadiums are business invitees; the owner or operator of the stadium is thus responsible for providing a reasonably safe environment. In state and federal recreation areas and parks, the public has been impliedly invited onto the land. Even though no economic motive may influence the invitation to the public, the person or agency in possession of the land is responsible at an invitee level.

Duties owed to the invitee include keeping the premises in a reasonably safe condition and warning of known dangerous conditions. The possessor of land also has a duty to inspect for unknown dangers. The possessor of land is not only responsible for reasonable care and adequate warnings to invitees about known dangers, but also for care and warnings about those conditions of which the possessor/owner should have been aware.

Licensee

A licensee is a person who is on the land with the owner's consent but does not have a business purpose for being on the land. While the licensee is typically a social guest, an individual who goes onto someone's land and is not asked by the owner to leave is also considered a licensee. For example, a person who takes a shortcut through someone's land or a neighbor who is joined in a backyard activity are licensees. Duties owed to the licensee are the same as those owed to the invitee (reasonable care), with one important exception: the licensee is to be warned of or protected from only those harms of which the possessor of the land is aware. The owner must keep the property in a reasonably safe condition and warn or protect persons entering the land from harms of which the owner is aware. There is no duty to inspect or discover dangerous conditions. There is also no duty to make the land safe. Essentially, a licensee accepts the land in the same condition as the landowner.

Trespasser

A trespasser is a person who goes onto another person's land without permission and without the knowledge of the land owner. The owner of the land owes no duty of care to the trespasser. Land owners do not have a duty to inspect the premises, to make the land safe, to warn of dangers, or to use reasonable care in anticipating trespassers. However, when an owner or person in possession of land becomes aware that trespassers may be on their property or that trespassers frequent the property, their duties change. They must either remove the trespasser from the land or secure the land from the trespasser. Failure to do so entitles the trespasser to a licensee status or reasonable standard of care. Under a reasonable care standard, the owner is to exercise care and warn of known dangers.

Attractive Nuisance

When the trespasser is a minor, the reason that the trespasser is on the land becomes important. If the condition of the land or an object on the land is such that it entices someone to enter the land, an attractive nuisance may exist. In this situation, the possessor must foresee the potential attractiveness of the property and the fact that a child could be seriously harmed. Precautions must be taken when the owner or possessor knows or has reason to know that children will be attracted to the land. No defense is available in attractive nuisance, as children are considered too young to appreciate the danger.

Open and Obvious

Section 343A of the *Restatement of the Law of Torts (Second)* was the basis for the open and obvious application in tort. "A possessor of land is not liable to his invitee for physical harm caused to them by any activity or condition on the land whose danger is known or obvious to them, unless the possessor should anticipate the harm despite such knowledge of obviousness" (218). One area in sport and physical activity nearly always considered "open and obvious" is water. Thus, a person taking part in aquatic activities is to know and understand the potential harm water possesses. It is part of assumption of risk. In most states, open and obvious is a complete bar to liability, while in others it is a factor to be considered in determining liability in tort.

VIOLATION OF A STATUTE, ORDINANCE, OR REGULATION

On occasion, the defendant accused of negligence may be in violation of a statute, ordinance, or regulation. State statutes, for example, may define reasonable and prudent care, industry standards, or the application of negligence. Health codes for food preparation, swimming pool depths, and lifeguard-to-swimmer ratios are examples of state and local statutes. Federal statutes tend to influence watercraft and parks.

When negligence is based on the violation of a statute, the following questions are to be answered:

1) Was the statute designed to protect the type of conduct the actor violated?

2) Is the accident victim within the class of persons the statute was designed to protect? (*Restatement of the Law Third, Torts, Liability for Physical and Emotional Harm*, Section 14)

Sport professionals should become acquainted with local, state, and federal statutes, as well as ordinances and regulations that affect their position and profession. Also, professionals need to be aware of how violation of the laws will be enforced by public authorities. An example is exceeding the occupancy code of an arena, which is typically enforced by a city fire marshal.

IMMUNITY

Immunity is freedom from liability or freedom from suit. This special status is found most often in government entities. The Federal Tort Claims Act of 1946 played a major role in the evolution of immunity as we know it today. The act states that when the government engages in activities in which private persons are also engaging, the government cannot be sued; the act gave the public consent to sue the federal government in tort. The act provides "monetary recovery from the federal government where damages, loss of property, personal injury, or death are caused by the negligence or wrongful acts of federal employees acting within the scope of their employment, and where the United States, if a private person, would be liable in accordance with the law of the place where the tort occurred" (28 USCS 2675). Immunity statutes include federal, state, and local government, Good Samaritan, hazardous recreation activity, and volunteer laws.

Governmental Immunity

Sovereign or governmental immunity in the English common law was a system modified and adopted by the United States. An English subject could not sue the king, and America decided that the United States government could not be sued without its consent. Sovereign immunity protects the government against liability but doesn't protect all of the government employees against liability. Immunities and levels of immunity have been crafted for certain responsibilities. Those charged with making the most serious governmental decisions appear to have the greatest amount of immunity. Judges, legislators, and high executive officers usually have absolute immunity.

Immunity among public officials goes back to the statement of our founding leaders: that we cannot be sued without the consent of the federal government. As mentioned earlier, the Federal Torts Claims Act of 1946 provides, with exceptions, that when the government engages in activities in which private persons are also engaging, the government cannot be sued. Among the exceptions to the Federal Tort Claims Act are intentional torts, military personnel, contract interference, and torts committed in the conduct of government business. Thus, federal employees have immunity for discretionary decisions, but they do not have immunity for ministerial decisions. Discretionary functions are usually planning functions; the carrying out of the plan is ministerial and not covered by immunity (*Restatement, Second, Torts,* Section 895D [f, h]).

Immunity is governed by state and local laws, with state governments differing in the reach of immunity legislation. Schools and recreation agencies are among those provided a level of immunity by state and local governments. The law encourages risk management and appropriate insurance to cover potential risks.

Good Samaritan

Good Samaritan laws are state statutes that provide immunity from suit for negligence for persons who administer emergency care to others. In 1959, California was the first state to pass Good Samaritan legislation; the legislation was directed at medical doctors. Many states have enacted similar legislation to enable medical doctors to rescue and aid victims without fear of lawsuits. Some of these state statutes include nurses, paramedics, persons performing CPR, dentists, and others.

The majority of the state statutes grant immunity to anyone who renders emergency care. The rescuer is to work only at the scene of the accident, act in good faith, be a reasonable and prudent rescuer, follow the methods advocated by his/her license or certificate, and provide service gratuitously. California's Business and Professional Code No. 2398 (2010), Aid to Participants in Athletic Events and Contests, states that

> No licensee, who in good faith and without compensation renders voluntary emergency medical assistance to a participant in a community college or high school athletic event or contest, at the site of the event or contest, or during transportation to a health care facility, for an injury suffered in the course of such event or contest, shall be liable for any civil damages as a result of any acts or omissions by such person in rendering such voluntary medical assistance. The immunity granted by this section shall not apply to acts or omissions constituting gross negligence.

Some states have sport-specific Good Samaritan or emergency care statutes. Under these statutes, physicians and other emergency care personnel are exempt from negligence for assistance provided in practice and games. The Wisconsin Statute (895.48, 2011) states that

> Any physician or athletic trainer, … chiropractor, dentist, … emergency medical technician, first responder, … physician assistant, … registered nurse, … or a massage therapist or bodyworker … who renders voluntary health care to a participant in an athletic event or contest sponsored by a nonprofit or a school, … is immune from civil liability for his or her acts or omissions in rendering that care if all of the following conditions exist:
>
> a) The health care is rendered at the site of the event or contest, during transportation to a health care facility from the event or contest, or in a locker room or similar facility immediately before, during or immediately after the event or contest.
>
> b) The physician, athletic trainer, chiropractor, dentist, emergency medical technician, first responder, physical assistant or registered nurse, massage therapist or bodyworker does not receive compensation for the health care, other than reimbursement for expenses.

The California Education Code No. 49409 (2011), immunity statutes for school districts, grants civil immunity to physicians and surgeons who render voluntary emergency medical assistance to participants in school athletic events or contests. The code reads as follows:

> Notwithstanding any provision of any law, no physician and surgeon who in good faith and without compensation renders voluntary emergency medical assistance to a participant in a school athletic event or contest at the site thereof, or during transportation to a health care facility, for an injury suffered in the course of the event or contest, shall be

liable for any civil damages as a result of any acts or omissions by the physician and surgeon in rendering the emergency medical care. The immunity granted by this paragraph shall not apply in the event of an act or omission constituting gross negligence.

Recreational Use Statutes

Recreational use statutes and hazardous recreation sport statutes began to appear in the 1960s. Ski incidents may have prompted some of the early statutes; rights of skiers and rights of ski resort owners and operators are among the most detailed statutes. In most cases, the primary recreational activities of a state are reflected in its statutes. Colorado, for example, defines recreational purpose as including, but "not limited to, any sport or recreational activity of whatever nature undertaken by a person while using the land, including ponds, lakes, reservoirs, streams, paths, and trails ... and includes, but is not limited to, any hobby, diversion, or other sport or other recreational activity" (CRS 33-41-102, 2011).

The California Government Code Section 831.7 (2011) states that:

> Neither a public entity nor a public employee is liable to any person who participates in a hazardous recreational activity, including any person who assists the participant, or to any spectator who knew or reasonably should have known that the hazardous recreational activity created a substantial risk of injury to himself or herself and was voluntarily in the place of risk, or having the ability to do so failed to leave, for any damage or injury to property or person arising out of that hazardous recreational activity.
>
> (b) As used in this section, "hazardous recreational activity" means a recreational activity conducted on property of a public entity which creates a substantial as distinguished from a minor, trivial, or insignificant risk of injury to a participant or a spectator.

The act goes on to say that this does not limit liability in situations where the facility should guard or warn of known dangerous conditions or where injury was caused by negligent failure to maintain a facility.

Volunteer Immunity

Immunity for volunteers has become a popular topic of interest in sport contexts. Volunteer immunity is applicable only in negligence; it does not exist in recklessness. It merely transfers the responsibility for the incident from the non-paid staff to the facility itself; it does not absolve the facility, agency, or organization from liability. The Volunteer Protection Act of 1997, the first federal statute, provides the following limitations on liability for volunteers. Section 14503 (2011) provides:

a) Liability protection for volunteers … no volunteer of a nonprofit organization or government entity shall be liable for harm caused by an act or omission of the volunteer on behalf of the organization or entity if

1) the volunteer was acting within the scope of the volunteer's responsibilities in the nonprofit organization or government entity at the time of the act or omission;

2) if appropriate or required, the volunteer was properly licensed, certified, or authorized by the appropriate authorities for the activities or practice in the State in which the harm occurred, where the activities were or practice was undertaken within the scope of the volunteer's responsibilities in the nonprofit organization or governmental entity;

3) the harm was not caused by willful or criminal misconduct, gross negligence, reckless misconduct, or a conscious, flagrant indifference to the rights or safety of the individual harmed by the volunteer; and

4) the harm was not caused by the volunteer operating a motor vehicle, vessel, aircraft, or other vehicle for which the State requires the operator or the owner of the vehicle, craft, or vessel to (A) possess an operator's license; or (B) maintain insurance.

REMEDIES

In tort, damages are compensatory, occasionally punitive, and seldom injunctive. Compensatory damages are those fees paid for medical expenses, property repair, lost wages, pain or emotional suffering, loss of property, loss of bodily function, and any bills directly related to the incident. Compensatory damage is assessed to make the injured person whole, or to pay for the damage done.

Punitive damages, seldom found in negligent actions, occur in intentional torts and product liability claims. They are assessed in an effort to punish a party for the damage done to society in general, and to the plaintiff in particular. The purpose of a punitive damage award is to deter the person or agency from acting again in a similar manner. These damages are not in response to the bills the plaintiff has obtained as a result of the incident. Financial status and assets of the person or organization that caused the harm are used to arrive at a punitive damage award. The award is the amount of money essential to cause the wrongdoer sufficient financial loss such that they will avoid such harm in the future.

Injunctive relief, a request to the court to require the defendant to stop doing an offensive act, is discussed in Chapters 4 and 5, the civil rights chapters, and in civil rights cases where it is often used. While it is often listed with damages, it is seldom found in tort law decisions.

LITIGATION

The court decisions can be studied under a number of different categories. In this case, legal theories and sport and physical activity specifics will lead the discussion. Among the legal theories discussed are assumption of risk, open and obvious, spectators, statutes, waiver of liability, and risk management.

Decisions in Assumption of Risk

California took the lead in primary assumption of risk and in the theory of co-participant responsibilities in the classic decision of *Knight v. Jewett* (1992). Kendra Knight and Michael Jewett attended a Super Bowl party at the home of friends. During halftime, they were among a group who played touch football. No rules were agreed to prior to play and, at times during play, participants asked that roughness be eliminated. Michael Jewett jumped to catch a ball and collided with Kendra Knight, knocking her down and injuring her hand and finger as he returned to the ground. After three unsuccessful surgeries, one of Knight's fingers was amputated.

Knight filed suit against Jewett on theories of negligence, assault, and battery. Defendant Jewett moved for summary judgment on the theory that assumption of risk was a complete defense for his actions. "Defendant asserted that by participating in the touch football game that resulted in her injury plaintiff impliedly agreed to reduce the duty of care owed to her by defendant … to only a duty to avoid reckless or intentionally harmful conduct and that the undisputed facts established both that he did not intend to injure plaintiff and that the acts of defendant which resulted in plaintiffs injuries were not reckless" (*Knight v. Jewett*, 1992, 698). Also, defendant claimed that plaintiff watched professional football on television and was familiar with the risks associated with playing football. Plaintiff, however, stated that she assumed that the game they were playing was "mock football" and not a serious, competitive sport.

The California Court concluded "that a participant in an active sport breaches a legal duty of care to other participants (i.e., engages in conduct that properly may subject him/her to financial liability) only if the participant INTENTIONALLY injures another player or engages in conduct that is so reckless as to be totally outside the range of the ordinary activity involved in the sport" (711). Jewett's conduct was found to be negligent or careless but not intentional. The touch football game did not breach a legal duty of care owed by defendant to the plaintiff. The case fell within primary assumption of risk, so comparative fault was not used.

The *Knight v. Jewett* case gave the sport industry a pass on liability in contact sports. The 2007 California golf case, *Shin v. Ahn,* took the primary assumption of risk from contact sports to noncontact sports, and what can be observed in the following cases is that assumption of risk has been further defined as part of physical activity. Shin and Ahn were part of a threesome playing golf. As they moved to the next tee, "plaintiff took a shortcut which placed him in front of the defendant and to his left. He stopped … even though he knew (1) that he was in front of the tee box, (2) that defendant was preparing to tee off, and (3) that he should stand behind a player who was teeing off" (583). "Plaintiff's expert stated that golf etiquette requires that a player ensure that no one is in a position to be struck when he or she hits the ball" (583). Shin was hit in the temple by a ball driven by Ahn. Shin sued for negligence as a result of his injury.

The trial court found for the defendant and then reversed itself, saying that issues remained which could be examined by the court at a later date. The California court of appeals affirmed the trial court's decision. The Supreme Court of California affirmed the lower courts' decisions and remanded the case with directions that litigation should continue under primary assumption of risk. An interesting point that sport professionals should consider is the Supreme Court of California's statement that the appeals court "relied too heavily on one of the golf's rules of etiquette involving safety.... Golf's first rule of etiquette provides that players should ensure that no one is standing close by or in a position to be hit by the club, the ball or any stones, pebbles, twigs or the like when they make a stroke or practice swing" (590). The court went on to say that "rules of etiquette govern socially acceptable behavior. The sanction for a violation of a rule of etiquette is social disapproval, not legal liability" (590).

Anand, et al. v. Kapoor (2010) was a New York case that emphasized the results of the *Shin* case. Anand was playing on a nine-hole golf course when he suffered a retinal detachment and permanent loss of vision after being hit in the eye by his partner's golf ball. Kapoor's ball went into the rough and he went to search for it. In the meantime, without waiting for Kapoor, Anand walked along the fairway to his lie. Kapoor found his ball and, without giving a warning, he hit the ball that struck Anand causing the injury. The court ruled for the defendant, finding that being hit by a ball without warning while searching for one's own ball was a risk of playing golf. No mention was made of the rules of etiquette of golf.

Examples of contemporary assumption of risk decision in skiing (*Fontaine v. Boyd,* 2011), trampoline play(*Kelly, et al. v. Roscoe, et al.,* 2009), use of playground monkey bars (*Smith v. City of New York,* 2010), and use of golf clubs (*Rudzinski, et al. v. BB,* 2010) follow.

Deborah Boyd, an intermediate skier, ran over the back of the skies of Andrea Fontaine, an expert skier, causing her to fall. Fontaine required several surgeries and considerable medical treatment, and has permanent injuries to both knees. Fontaine sued Boyd. The first question was the appropriate venue for the case. Fontaine was a Massachusetts resident; Boyd was a Rhode Island resident. The incident occurred in New Hampshire. The case was brought to a Rhode Island court but it was decided under New Hampshire law, the location of the incident. (Remember, tort law is state law.) The court had to determine "whether a claim of negligence by one skier against another skier for injuries sustained when the two friends collided while skiing recreationally is barred as a matter of law by the doctrine of primary assumption of risk under New Hampshire law" (*Fontaine v. Boyd,* 2011). The court found for the defendant, Boyd. The collision, as described, was an inherent risk of skiing.

A seven-year-old child broke her leg while jumping on a home trampoline with two other children (*Kelly, et al. v. Roscoe, et al.,* 2009). Kelly's mother filed suit on behalf of her daughter against the trampoline owners, the Roscoes, for "negligent supervision of the trampoline" (1008). The trial court found for the defendant. The injury was part of the ordinary risk associated with using a trampoline with other children. Kelly appealed. The court of appeals examined the issue of multiple persons on a trampoline and whether the potential risks were among the ordinary risks associated with trampoline activity. The court also noted that the parents of the injured child had forbidden their daughter to jump with others on the trampoline because she could be injured, which confirmed that the risk was foreseeable. A combination of the foreseeability by the parents and primary assumption of risk enabled the court to affirm the trial court's decision.

Nine-year-old Isaiah Smith was injured when he fell from the monkey bars at a playground owned and operated by the City of New York (*Smith, et al. v. City of New York, et al.,* 2010). He was instructed by his parents not to play on the monkey bars; however, he chose to ignore his parents' instruction. He used the bars, fell, and sustained injuries. His parents sued under negligent supervision. An interesting statement in the case was the following: "It is well settled that one is deemed to have assumed, as a voluntary participant … those commonly appreciated risks which are inherent in and arise out of the nature of the sport [physical activity] generally" (3). Defendant's motion for summary judgment was granted; the City of New York won.

Assumption of risk has consistently been upheld in golf for those persons whose golf balls hit others on the course; however, it was also found to be a valid defense when one golfer hit another with his club (*Rudzinski, et al. v. BB,* 2010). Two children, ages 9 (BB) and 11 (DB), were playing golf. The nine-year-old had never played before, so the eleven-year-old provided some instruction. "As BB was preparing to swing, DB saw an extra ball near the ball BB intended to strike, told BB not to swing, and went to move it" (2). DB was hit in the face, requiring hospitalization, but sustained no permanent injuries. Rudzinski filed suit on behalf of DB against BB for negligence, carelessness, gross negligence, and recklessness. The question for the court was whether the risk of being hit by a golf club was an inherent risk of golf. The court ruled for the defendant. Because the plaintiff's conduct was "consistent with the inherent risks presented by golf, and because there is no evidence of intentionally injurious or reckless conduct, the court finds that DB has failed to establish that BB's duty of care encompassed the risk involved" (11).

Decisions Finding Open and Obvious

"Open and obvious" tends to appear most often in water incidents. *Sholer v. ERC Management Group, et al.* (2011), and *Davis, et al. v. Accor North America, Inc., et al.* (2010) are examples of this pattern. Cassidy Jane Sholer became a quadriplegic after diving into an apartment swimming pool. The pool was open, lights were on, and there was no signage regarding pool depth, prohibiting diving or unsupervised swimming. She made a shallow dive and hit her head. She sued under negligence. The apartment complex countered with open and obvious. They also stated that the victim had been at least mildly intoxicated. The person who rescued her claimed that the shadows in the pool were such that the depth was difficult to recognize. The trial court and the court of appeals ruled for the defendants on the basis of open and obvious danger. The Supreme Court of Oklahoma reversed the trial court's decision, and returned the case to the lower court for an analysis of whether the pool may have had a hazard.

Davis presented a claim for wrongful death for the death of her husband in a hotel pool. The Davis family and their goddaughter were swimming and playing in the shallow, three-foot end of the hotel pool when a foam noodle floated toward the nine-foot deep end of the pool. None of the family members were competent swimmers. Shylettia, the goddaughter, went after the noodle, got into trouble, and Mrs. Davis rescued her. In the confusion, Mr. Davis also jumped into the pool, pushed Mrs. Davis to safety, and drowned. The water in the pool was so cloudy that rescuers had to use walking search techniques to find him. Confusion occurred among the people sent to the front desk to call 911. Although the hotel had violated numerous provisions of the Ohio Administrative Code for the maintenance of swimming pools, the United States District Court for the Southern District of Ohio, Western Division, found for the hotel on the theory of open and obvious.

A case involving failure to pad a softball field fence post was considered open and obvious (*Kaitbenski v. Tantasqua Regional School District*, 2009). Taryn T. Kaitbenski, playing catcher in a varsity softball game, ran into an uncovered and unpadded fence post as she tried to catch a pop fly, and sustained injuries as a result. She sued the construction companies that built the stadium. They argued that she needed expert testimony to prove her claim and that her injury was open and obvious. This case points out the need for risk management in the areas of construction and for knowledge of safety standards by those engaging in the building of facilities.

Decisions Involving Spectators

Spectators have been injured from a flying ball or puck during the game (*Sciarrotta v. Global Spectrum, et al.*, 2008) and by a player who entered the spectator seating area (*Pickel v. Springfield Stallions, Inc., et al.*, 2010). The *Sciarrotta* decision contains a detailed discussion of the limited duty rule influencing safety planning for facilities housing sports where objects may fly into the seating areas, notably baseball and hockey facilities. Mrs. Sciarrotta attended an ice hockey game at the Sovereign Bank Arena in Trenton, New Jersey, to see her daughter sing the national anthem. She was injured when hit by a hockey puck driven from the rink during the team warm-up. Her seat was six or seven rows from the ice and above the Plexiglas protective barrier. She sued, alleging negligence by Global Spectrum, the facility, and by Comcast Spectator Co., owners and operators, and others responsible for the facility.

The limited duty rule originated in *Schneider v. Am. Hockey & Ice Skating Center, Inc.* (2001) and was further developed in *Maisonave v. Newark Bears Professional Baseball Club, Inc.* (2005) and in the New Jersey Baseball Spectator Safety Act of 2006. The limited duty rule

> applies to sports venues in respect of a specific peril, that of objects leaving the field of play that may injure spectators in the stands. Under the rule, a sports venue owner or operator that provides screened seating (1) sufficient for those spectators who may be reasonably anticipated to desire protected seats on an ordinary occasion, and (2) in the most dangerous section of the stands, has satisfied its duty of care. The rule applies not only while the game itself is in progress, but whenever spectators are located in the stands. (*Sciarrotta v. Global Spectrum, et al.*, 2008, 701)

In *Sciarrotta,* the court debated as to whether the application of the limited duty rule was adequate for the hockey warm-up session when many pucks were in play, or only for game play involving one puck. The trial court found for the facility; they had fulfilled the limited duty rule. The intermediate appellate court found a question as to whether the protection was adequate for the practice play when so many pucks were in the air, and reversed the decision, holding for Sciarrotta. The New Jersey Superior Court, Appellate Division, reversed and found for the facility; the limited duty rule was satisfied.

Wendy Pickel, a spectator at an indoor football game, was injured when one of the players fell over the wall separating the players from the playing court and ran into her. She sued the owners of the facility and the team for negligence. The defendants argued "that because football was a contact sport in which violent collisions were inherent in the game…. [This] required plaintiff to plead a greater culpability on behalf of the team than mere negligence" (879, 880). The trial court agreed and held for the defendants. Pickel appealed, arguing that the contact sport exception did not apply to spectators, only to participants. The court of appeals reversed and found for Pickel.

Decisions Under Statutes

Three examples of cases settled under statutes will be discussed. One was settled under a New Jersey Equine Activities Liability Act (*Hubner, et al. v. Spring Valley Equestrian Center,* 2010), and two others were settled under state recreational use statutes (*University of Texas Health Science Center at Houston v. Garcia,* 2011; *Coan v. New Hampshire Department of Environmental Services,* 2010).

Gloria Hubner was injured when she fell from her frightened horse as the horse backed into training poles. She sued claiming negligence. The trial court found for the defendant as the claim was barred by the New Jersey Equine Act. Hubner appealed. The Appellate Court reversed and remanded the decision for further proceedings. After several rounds of appeals, the Supreme Court of New Jersey found her claim was barred by the Equine statute. The Equine Act can operate as a complete bar to plaintiff if her injuries were caused by one of the inherent risks of the activity. The court analyzed the statute in the following manner:

1) Does the situation mirror the words of the statute?

2) Purpose of the statute is to protect equine activities due to their economy and open space preservation. Participant assumes defined risks.

3) Those assuming the defined risks are barred from recovery. It is one of a number of statutes "using assumption of risk principles to allocate responsibility for injuries sustained in inherently dangerous recreational activities."

4) In a previous case, the court discussed the allocation of losses for inherently dangerous recreational injuries. The "primary" assumption of the risk refers to an obvious inherent risk, as to which the facility operator owes participants no duty and a claim based on the risk is barred. The "secondary" sense of assumption of risks arises where the operator has a duty and breaches it, but asserts as

an affirmative defense that the participant "voluntarily exposed himself to a risk negligently created" by the operator.

5) Risks are to the listed.

6) The difference between the inherent risks and conditions within a facility's control are identified.

7) An exception to the statute is made where the operator acted with "negligent disregard for the participant's safety." (*Huber, et al. v. Spring Valley Equestrian Center,* 2010, 618, 619).

The Texas Recreational Use Statute and premises liability law became the focus of the *University of Texas Health Sciences Center at Houston v. Garcia* case (2011). Garcia sued the university for injuries to his big toe sustained while playing on the outdoor sand volleyball court. He stated that the institution knew or should have known that the court needed to be inspected, maintained, and repaired: the failure to do so was the cause of his injuries. The university said the claim was barred by sovereign immunity under the Recreational Use Statute. Before sovereign immunity could be waived, duty had to be determined. Under premises liability law, the plaintiff was owed the duty of care that a private person owes to a licensee on private property unless he/she paid to be on the premises. The Texas Recreational Use Statute states that:

> If an owner ... gives permission to another to enter the premises for recreation, the owner, ... by giving permission does not:
>
> 1) assure the premises are safe for that purpose;
>
> 2) owe to the person to whom permission is granted a greater degree of care than is owed to a trespasser on the premises; or
>
> 3) assume responsibility or incur liability for any injury to any individual or property caused by any act of the person to whom permission is granted. (Tex. Civ. Prac. & Rem. Code Ann. Section 75.002[c])

The court of appeals held that the Recreational Use Statute applied. They reversed the trial court's order denying the defendant's motion to dismiss, and remanded or returned the case to the trial court for further proceedings.

Coan brought a wrongful death and negligence suit against the New Hampshire Department of Environmental Services for the drowning deaths of three young people—ages 16, 20, and 9—which resulted from the release of an additional 375 cubic feet per second to the flow coming out of the Dam into the lake in which they often swam. No warning or information about the flow was posted. The trial court found for the defendant under recreational use immunity; there was no duty to warn or place safety devices on the shore. The Supreme Court of New Hampshire affirmed the judgment.

Decisions Involving Waiver of Liability

Stelluti v. Casapenn Enterprises, LLC, et al. (2010) featured a situation where the waiver of liability won the case for the defendant despite the fact that the fitness equipment fell apart. Gina Stelluti, a member of spinning class, fell forward while her feet remained strapped to the peddles of the bike when the handlebars were dislodged. She sued under negligence, alleging failure to maintain the equipment, set up the equipment, and properly instruct her on the use of the equipment in such situations. The fitness center countered with the liability waiver she had signed. Trial, Appeals, and Supreme Courts of New Jersey all found for the defendant on the basis of the liability waiver.

Jakubovsky was skiing down a slope at Blackjack Mountain in Michigan when a snowboarder, coming at a high rate of speed, hit her, causing significant injuries as she was pushed into a fence (*Jakubovsky v. Blackjack Ski Corporation, et al.,* 2009). The snowboarder was never identified. She sued the resort. The resort claimed immunity under Michigan's Ski Area Safety Act which "provides that skiers are deemed to accept the dangers inherent in the sport of skiing, including injury from skier-to-skier collisions" (3). Jakubovsky claimed that the resort was not immune under the statute because it had violated the act "by failing to warn skiers of the unmarked trail which the snowboarder took prior to the accident" (3). The Michigan Ski Area Safety Act states the following:

> Each person who participates in the sport of skiing accepts the dangers that inhere in that sport insofar as the dangers are obvious and necessary. Those dangers include, but are not limited to, injuries which can result from variations in terrain; surface or subsurface snow or ice conditions, bare spots, rocks, trees, and other forms of natural growth or debris, collisions with ski lift towers and their components, with other skiers, or with properly marked or plainly visible snow-making or snow-grooming equipment. (*Jakubovsky v. Blackjack Ski Corporation, et al.,* 2009, 4)

The defendant succeeded based on the Michigan Ski Area Safety Act. Similar acts exist in many states where ski resorts are located and, in most cases, the act enables the resort to succeed in a court of law.

SUMMARY

Negligence occurs when a person does not exercise reasonable care under all circumstances. It must be foreseeable that a person's conduct will result in harm. The five elements of negligence are duty, breach of the duty, factual cause, scope of liability including foreseeability, and damage. Violation of statutes, ordinances, or regulations are, on occasion, the basis for a negligence action.

The standards of care in sport and physical activity are reasonable person, special relationship, and professional. The reasonable person is a hypothetical person that represents what an ordinary person would do in the situation. Parents and schools have special relationships with children that make them responsible for certain standards of care. A professional standard is established when a body of knowledge exists and a clearly recognized level of performance is adhered to by members of the profession. Defenses to negligence are contributory negligence, assumption of risk, and comparative negligence. Contributory negligence means that the victim contributed to his/her own injuries. Assumption of risk is that the participant knew and agreed to the risk when he/she chose to participate in the activity. Comparative negligence is a system of fault used to identify the extent of fault of the victim and the extent of fault of the person(s) responsible for the victim's injuries.

Premises liability is classified as invitee, licensee, and trespasser. An invitee has been invited onto the land, typically for a business purpose. The owner must keep the premises in a reasonably safe condition, inspect for problems, repair as needed, and warn of known dangers. A licensee is on the land with the owner's consent but does not have a business interest; he/she is a guest. The owner must keep the land in reasonable condition and warn of any known problems; he/she is not required to inspect the land. The trespasser is on the land without the owner's permission and is owed "zero duty."

Immunity is freedom from liability. The types of immunity include governmental immunity, Good Samaritan laws, and volunteer immunity. Damages in tort are compensatory and punitive.

DISCUSSION QUESTIONS

1. Identify the elements of negligence and describe the elements in the context of a sport environment.

2. Explain the Good Samaritan Laws and identify when they are used.

3. What is contributory negligence and when does it occur?

4. Do recreational use statutes cover scholastic and collegiate athletics?

ACTIVITIES

1. Read two assumption of risk cases in a sport in which you are familiar. Given your knowledge of rules and safety within the activity, including age appropriate understandings, assess the court with reference to sport.

2. Read the dissent and the statements on the etiquette of golf in the *Shin vs. Ahn* case. Did the California court choose to overrule the laws of golf in their decision?

3. Select a sport. Identify five issues of foreseeability in the sport. Outline an assumption of risk statement for the sport.

REFERENCES

Anand, et al. v. Kapoor, 942 N. E. 295 (2010).

Coan, et al. v. New Hampshire Department of Environmental Services, et al., 161 N. H. 1; 8 A. 3d 109 (2010).

Davis, et al. v. Accor North America, Inc., et al., Case No. 1:08-CV-425, 2010 U.S. Dist. LEXIS 40057.

Federal Tort Claims Act (1946). 28 USC 1346(b), 2671–2680.

Fontaine v. Boyd, C.A. No. WC-2007-0794, 2011 R. I. Super. LEXIS 27.

Hubner, et al. v. Spring Valley Equestrian Center, 1 A. 3d 618 (2010).

Jakubovsky v. Blackjack Ski Corporation, et al., Case No. 08-C0206, 2009 LEXIS 120889.

Kaitbenski v. Tantasqua Regional School District & others, 26 Mass. L. Rep. 128 (2009).

Kelly, et al. v. Roscoe, et al., 925 N. E. 2d 1006 (2009).

Kleinknecht v. Gettysburg College, 989 F. 2d 1360 (1991).

Knight v. Jewett, 3 Cal. 4th 296; 834 P. 2d 696 (1992).

Maisonave, et al. v. The Newark Bears Professional Baseball Club, Inc., et al., 881 A. 2d 700 (2005).

Pickel v. Springfield Stallions, Inc., et al., 398 Ill. App. 3d 1063; 926 N. E. 2d 877 (2010).

Restatement of the Law of Torts (Second). (1976). St. Paul, MN: American Law Institute.

Restatement Third, Torts: Liability for Physical and Emotional Harm. (2011). St. Paul, MN: American Law Institute.

Rudzinski, et al. v. BB, C/A No. 0:09-1819-JFA, 2010 U.S. Dist. LEXIS 68471.

Schneider, et al. v. American Hockey and Ice Skating Center, Inc., 342 N. J. Super 529 (2001).

Sciarrotta, et al. v. Global Spectrum, et al., 194 N.J. 345; 944 A. 2d 630 (2008).

Shin v. Ahn, 165 P. 3d 581 (2007).

Sholer v. ERC Management Group, et al., Case Number: 108024, 2011 OK 24.

Smith, et al. v. The City of New York, et al., 117109/07, 2010 NY Slip Op 30680U (2010).

Stelluti v. Casapenn Enterprises, LLC, et al., 203 N. J. 286; 1 A. 3d 678 (2010).

The Volunteer Protection Act of 1997, 42 USCS Sec. 14503.

University of Texas Health Science Center at Houston v. Garcia, No. 14-10-01021-CV. 2011 Texas App. LEXIS 5686.

RECOMMENDED READING

Cole, M. G. (2007). No blood no foul: The standard of care in Texas owed by participants to one another in athletic contests. 59 *Baylor Law Rev.* 435.

Davis, T. (2008). Emerging legal issues affecting amateur & professional sports: Tort liability of coaches for injuries to professional athletes: Overcoming policy and doctrinal barriers. 76 *UMKC L. Rev.* 571.

Harlan, B. P. (2008). The California Supreme Court should take a Mulligan: How the Court shanked by applying the Primary Assumption of Risk doctrine to golf. 29 *Loy. L. A. Ent. L. Rev.* 91.

2

Intentional Torts and Criminal Law

OBJECTIVES

Upon completing this chapter you will:

1) know the difference between civil and criminal law: courts, decisions, and punishments;

2) be able to differentiate between negligence and intentional torts in sport and physical activity;

3) understand and be able to describe the role of immunity as a defense to torts;

4) recognize the differences between battery and assault; and

5) be able to explain the role of a release to your supervisor.

INTRODUCTION

Intentional torts are injuries caused by a deliberate act. Under the law, intent means that "the person acts with the purpose of producing a consequence (act) or the person acts knowing that the consequence is substantially certain to result" (*Restatement Third, Torts: Liability for Physical and Emotional Harm*, Section 1). The actor may not intend to injure someone. The intentional torts most often encountered in sport and physical activity are torts to persons and property. Sport managers will also encounter intentional torts in economic relations. The accepted contact between players in many sports and the violent nature of some competitions have caused the courts to find most incidents of play or practice involving injury among sport teammates or opposing players to be intentional torts. They are not considered to be negligence, something one did not know would happen. The intentional tort categories in which violent actions are intended are the vehicle for many sport decisions. The court will ask if the athlete intended to injure the fellow athlete or if the actions were so violent that recklessness bordered on intent.

An example of an intentional tort is a person hitting another in the heat of competition. The actor expects the act to be carried out; however, the actor does not intend that an injury will be sustained because of the act. In an intentional tort in sport, the court will attempt to ascertain if there was intent merely to do the act or there was intent to do the act and to harm the plaintiff. An act executed with intent to harm another is not only an intentional tort but could become a criminal offense. If a substantial injury or death should occur, the person who carried out the act could be accountable for a criminal act.

INTENTIONAL TORT LAW VERSUS CRIMINAL LAW

There are major differences between intentional tort law and criminal law. The purpose of intentional tort law is to vindicate and honor the victim while enforcing appropriate standards of care. The role of criminal law, in contrast, is to support the state's interest in deterring crime. Litigation in tort law is between individuals or individuals and agencies. In criminal law, the state or federal government brings a cause of action against an individual or agency. For example, the State of New York brings an action against a person. On occasion, the same act can result in both tort and criminal law. An example of this is a state bringing a cause of action to prosecute a person for a crime, while the person harmed brings an action to recover compensation.

INTENTIONAL TORTS TO PERSONS

Intentional torts to persons include battery, assault, false imprisonment, and recklessness. They occur between persons engaging in an activity, or between a coach, teacher, or supervisor and a player or client. The civil rights statute 42 USC 1983, as it relates to intentional torts, is also reviewed in this section.

Battery

Battery is intentional, harmful, or offensive contact with another person, without that person's consent. The physical contact must be intentional; however, there does not have to be intent to injure, and injury or damage does not have to occur. Continuous intentional tagging and pushing in game play or engaging in locker room pranks could, given the right circumstances, become batteries. Horseplay is often found to include battery.

Numerous batteries, seldom recognized as such, exist in the traditional rituals of recreational and competitive sports. Today, hazing is considered to be among these batteries. In addition to batteries within the competitive arena, there are also batteries that occur as a result of athletes injuring spectators. For years, aquatic competitions ended with winners, losers, coaches, officials, and spectators being thrown into the water. When aquatic officials complained of these unsafe practices, administrators responded by stating that restricting such behavior would take the fun out of the event. Finally, serious life-threatening and debilitating injuries resulting from horseplay caused administrators to view this behavior in a different light. Today, most national swimming meets no longer finish with everyone in the water.

Pushing, shoving, chasing, and tagging are to be avoided in physical activity environments unless such activity is an element of regular game play, and officials are present to control the level of physical contact and safety. The majority of serious injuries attributed to horseplay occur in the home or in unsupervised recreational areas.

Battery does not take place if the other party consented to the act. Consent, however, is difficult to assess. For example, does a person's competing in and winning a swimming event give consent to a fellow team member to toss that person into the water in celebration of the victory? No matter the context, sexual contact among adults without consent is battery. Sexual contact between an adult and a minor with or without consent may be a criminal act.

Assault

Assault is the apprehension or belief that one will experience imminent contact; assault does not require physical contact. Again, the person has not consented or agreed to the act. When a person is threatened by an action such that he/she believes another is preparing to hit him/her, an assault has occurred. It is not necessary that the assaulting person intends to harm the individual. The person threatened need not be in fear of the other person's actions; only apprehension or threat is required. An example of an assault is a 6'4" basketball coach lunging toward a 5'2" seventh-grade athlete, telling him to move toward the basket now! If the two are in fairly close range, the young person may be in fear of being hit although he is not touched. This is an assault. The threat must be physical—words alone will not constitute an assault. If contact is made, it is a battery.

False Imprisonment

False imprisonment is the unjustified, unlawful, and intentional confinement, restraint, or detention of a person within specific boundaries against that person's will. Wrongful intent need not exist, nor is there a need for substantial damage. For example, store managers who restrain shoppers suspected of shoplifting could be charged with false imprisonment. While no false imprisonment court decisions currently exist in sport and physical activity, professionals who routinely restrain persons in locker rooms or gymnasiums as punishment could be liable for false imprisonment.

Recklessness

Recklessness describes a significantly high level of risk of which the actor is aware. A person acts recklessly in engaging in conduct if:

a) the person knows of the risk of harm created by the conduct or knows facts that make the risk obvious to another in the person's situation; and

b) the precaution that would eliminate or reduce the risk involves burdens that are so slight relative to the magnitude of the risk as to render the person's failure to adopt the precaution a demonstration of the person's indifference to the risk (*Restatement Third, Torts: Liability for Physical Harm*, Section 2, 2010).

In the past, recklessness was a tort of professional sport; today, intentional torts occur in many forms and at all levels of competition. For years, the courts found it difficult to assess sport injuries as intentional torts. As players have increasingly sustained severe injuries from the violation of game rules, these acts have been called intentional torts. Just how far beyond the rules of the game can a player—even a professional player—be expected to assume a risk of injury? The courts appear to sense a need to declare that a player assumes all risks of injury up to the limits of the rules; however, when the injury is a clear violation of the rules, it becomes an intentional tort.

42 USC 1983

42 USC 1983 is a statute often used in civil rights cases that permits tort claims for deprivation of federal rights under the color of state law. Defendants are state or local government officials: victims may also sue under this law as private individuals.

> Section 1983 provides a private right of action for damages to individuals who are deprived of "any rights, privileges, or immunities" protected by the U.S. Constitution or federal law by any person acting under the color of state law.... As such state officials may be held liable under Section 1983 if there is, at minimum, an underlying constitutional tort.... However, the defense of qualified immunity generally shields officials in the performance of their discretionary duties from liability of civil damages "insofar as their conduct does not violate clearly established statutory or constitutional rights of which reasonable person would have known." (U.S. Code, 2011, 111, 112)

Victims of intentional torts may use 42 USC 1983 in place of or in addition to intentional torts to gain personal rights. *J. K. v. Arizona Board of Regents, et al.* (2008) and *Fitzgerald v. Barnstable School Committee* (2009) are cases involving 42 USC 1983. *J. K.* is discussed under battery while *Fitzgerald* follows here because the case established the connection between sexual assault and 42 USC 1983.

In 2001, a kindergarten student, Jacqueline Fitzgerald, told her parents that when she wore a dress to school, "an older student on her school bus would bully her to lift her skirt" (*Fitzgerald v. Barnstable School Committee*, 2007, 169). Later, the third grader also asked her to do more. Her mother reported the incidents to the school. The school studied the situation and the local police department held an investigation. All decided that insufficient information existed to find the young man criminally involved. Their solution was to provide a different bus schedule for Jacqueline or separate the kindergarteners from the third graders on the bus by three rows of seats. Mrs. Fitzgerald felt the solution was a punishment for her daughter and recommended that the young man be moved to a different bus. The school refused. There was a second encounter between the students in a gym class and Jacqueline began to miss a great deal of school and all of her gym classes.

In April of 2002, the Fitzgeralds sued the Barnstable School Committee and the superintendent. The claim against the school committee was for violation of Title IX; the claim against both the School Committee and the superintendent was under 42 USC 1983. A number of miscellaneous claims were also filed against both parties. The two major statutes addressed in this case were Title IX and 42 USC 1983. For a Title IX complaint to succeed, the following elements had to exist: the school was be under Title

IX; the harassment was severe, pervasive, and offensive; the student had to be deprived of educational opportunities as a result of the incidents; and educators had to have had actual knowledge of the situation and had done nothing about it. The case met all elements except the last one; the school had addressed the situation and provided a solution, which the parents deemed unreasonable. Thus, the Title IX statute failed to protect the plaintiff. The statute 42 USC 1983 was also a part of the pleadings to the court. The United States Court of Appeals for the First Circuit ruled that the plaintiff had to comply with Title IX, not with 42 USC 1983. *Fitzgerald* lost in the court of appeals; however, the case was appealed to the United States Supreme Court. The U.S. Supreme Court reversed the decision of the court of appeals, stating that 42 USC 1983 and the equal protection clause of the Fourteenth Amendment to the Constitution, in addition to Title IX, needed to be considered by the courts. The case was remanded to the lower court for further proceedings. No further information was available. Often, cases that are remanded are then settled and do not return to the courts.

42 USC 1983 "provides a right of action for any person who, at the hands of a state actor, has experienced the derivation of any rights, privileges, or immunities secured by the Constitution and laws of the United States" (*Fitzgerald, et al. v. Barnstable School Community,* 2007, 176). The court ruled that "the comprehensiveness of Title IX's remedial scheme—especially as embodied in its implied private right of action—indicates that Congress saw Title IX as the sole means of vindicating the constitutional right to be free from gender discrimination" (2007, 179). The Fitzgeralds appealed, and the appeal was accepted by the United States Supreme Court (2009). The Supreme Court reversed the lower court's decision, concluding "that Title IX was not meant to be an exclusive mechanism for addressing gender discrimination in schools or a substitute for 1983 suits as a means of enforcing constitutional rights….[and that a] 1983 suit on the Equal Protection Clause remained available to the plaintiff" (*Fitzgerald,* 2009, Case Overview).

INTENTIONAL INTERFERENCE WITH PROPERTY

Intentional interference with property includes trespass to land, trespass to chattel, and conversion. Substantial damage is not required in intentional interference with property. Trespass to land (real estate) is an intentional entry—walking onto land or the projection of an object (e.g., shooting an arrow or hitting a golf ball) onto the land in possession of another. The action must have been executed without permission (either implied or expressed) from the owner of the property. The intent need only be to enter; no intent to harm is required. For example, a coach or teacher who advises his/her students to pass through a property owner's yard on their way to a playing field or campgrounds could be found liable for encouraging minors to trespass on land.

Trespass to chattel is interference with a person's personal possessions. The action must be intentional. Stealing a motorboat is trespass to chattel; intentionally hitting a sailboat in open waters may be trespass to chattel. Actual damage must exist. Trespass to chattel exists when a person who rightly has access to the property of another refuses to return the property. Conversion is trespass to land or chattel that so substantially interferes with the owner's possession of the property that it is only fair to require the defendant to pay for the property (*Restatement of the Law of Torts, Second*, 1965, 222A). Many courts hold that a purchaser of stolen property is a converter whether or not he/she is aware that it is stolen. Other states have ruled that a person who becomes aware that property was stolen and returns the property will not be held for conversion.

BUSINESS TORTS: FRAUD, DECEIT, AND MISREPRESENTATION

Fraud and deceit are torts often appearing in athletics. Recruiting is an area in which fraud, deceit, and misrepresentation have been alleged. Fraud and deceit may also appear in the purchase of equipment and the construction of buildings. According to the *Restatement of the Law of Torts, Second* (1965), the elements of fraud and deceit are:

1)   a false representation of a material fact;

2)   knowledge that the fact is false;

3)   intention to induce the other party to rely on the representation;

4)   the other party's reliance on the representation; and

5)   substantial damage as a proximate result of the other party's reliance. (525)

A school's description of a league rule and a health spa's explanation of anticipated health improvements are examples of situations that could make agencies vulnerable to litigation under misrepresentation. The opinions of coaches, teachers, trainers, therapists, doctors, and lawyers—on issues about which they are expected to possess knowledge—may be considered facts.

A misrepresentation of a law will not be actionable unless it is made by a person in a position of confidence, or by one expected to have knowledge of the law. A college coach, administrator, or recruiter may be actionable for misrepresenting the National Collegiate Athletic Association (NCAA) rules. An athletic recruiter may be liable for misrepresenting a university's requirements to a potential student-athlete.

The difference between fraud and misrepresentation is that fraud involves the intent to deceive. The deception was planned. Misrepresentation is:

•   falsely denying knowledge of the facts;

•   actively concealing the facts;

•   disclosing only parts of the facts; or

•   providing a false picture.

Persons who claim misrepresentation have to differentiate between non-disclosure and misrepresentation. If the question was never asked, the person making the representation may not have been obligated to disclose the facts. Non-disclosure or failure to disclose is usually not actionable unless there is a relationship between the plaintiff and the defendant that required that there be disclosure, or the plaintiff relied on the defendant's special skill and knowledge in making the decision.

Unlike other intentional torts, there must be substantial damage before one can make a claim under fraud, deceit, or misrepresentation. Damages usually include losses resulting from the injury. They may include lost work time, customers, time in school, or money. Some courts' awards are only for out-of-pocket expenses or expenses that can be verified by receipts; others may permit more abstract losses to be covered. Only when recklessness is involved are punitive damages awarded.

DEFENSES TO INTENTIONAL TORTS

Defenses to intentional torts are reasons to justify the actions of the actor. They include consent, self-defense, defense of other people or one's own property, necessity, and discipline.

Consent

Consent occurs when a reasonable person does not object to or attempt to stop the action of another. It may be verbal consent, or implied consent as a result of silence. A minor is not able to consent. As the minor moves closer to the age of majority or gains the ability to understand and weigh risks, he/she becomes capable of consenting. If the consent occurs under duress, it will not be considered valid in the eyes of the court. Participation in a game involves a manifestation of consent to those bodily contacts which are permitted by the rules of the game. It should be noted that a person must know the risks involved in an activity and the extent of the damage that could occur before giving informed consent.

Self-defense

Self-defense and defense of others permits a person who is under attack to take reasonable steps to prevent harm to him/her or to others, when there is not time to obtain professional assistance. Reasonable force may be used to prevent threatened harm, offensive touching, or bodily contact. An individual must sense imminent extreme danger; revenge is not a defense. A person can use deadly force in self-defense or defense of others only when that degree of force is essential to prevent imminent harm. A person who is attacked should retreat if he/she can do so safely. A person defending him/herself and others in that person's own home may use deadly force and need not retreat. In addition, a person may use reasonable force to defend the rights of family members and others against attack. The property owner may use force that is necessary to protect property. Verbal commands are to be used first. If the verbal commands are not successful, the owner may use force.

Necessity

Necessity is a privilege, due to unusual circumstances, to harm a person or property even though the person or property has done nothing wrong. A sailing group that is subject to threatening weather can tie its craft to a private dock and make camp on a private shore. In this case the necessity is seeking shelter in a life-threatening situation. Those who use necessity are financially responsible for the extent of any damage to property; however, they are not liable for having entered the property of another without permission.

CRIMINAL LAW

Tort law, previously studied, was civil law; the injured party or plaintiff brought a cause of action against the defendant, the person(s) who had caused the harm. In criminal law, the wrong is considered harm to society, not a wrong to another individual. Therefore, a prosecutor, an official of the federal or state government, brings a cause of action against the person accused of the harm (defendant) in a criminal court. The prosecutor has the burden of proving "beyond a reasonable doubt" the elements of the crime. In both criminal and civil court a judge or jury determines the guilt or innocence of the defendant. Criminal law is a combination of federal and state law. Federal law applies when the incident occurs in a military, international, interstate, or navigational environment. Although state laws differ, they tend to have considerable commonality. In an effort to demonstrate the differences among states, details of criminal law in Florida, New York, and California are described in the following.

In criminal law, a guilty defendant is punished by jail or prison, execution, the death penalty, and fines paid to the state or federal government. There are two broad classes of crimes, felonies and misdemeanors. In general, felonies carry a maximum incarceration sentence of more than a year. Misdemeanors usually carry a sentence of less than a year. In criminal litigation the burden of proof is always on the state. The state must prove guilt. Also, criminal litigation requires that the state or federal government satisfy each element of the statutory definition of the crime and that the defendant has been found culpable "beyond a reasonable doubt". Usually a warrant is issued on "probable cause," a much lower standard.

In Florida, a misdemeanor offense is classified as first degree or second degree. Offenses include driving with a suspended license, battery, petit theft, and possession of marijuana. Second degree misdemeanors require no more than sixty days in jail, six months of probation, and a $500.00 fine. A first degree misdemeanor requires no more than one year in jail, one year probation, and a $1,000 fine. Felony offenses are classified as third degree, second degree, and first degree, capital, or life offense. These include a DUI with injuries, robbery, burglary, and possession of cocaine. Third degree results in up to five years in prison, five years' probation, and a $5,000 fine. Second degree results in up to 15 years in prison, 15 years' probation, and a $10,000 fine. First degree results in up to 30 years in prison, 30 years' probation, and a $10,000 fine. A life felony results in up to life in prison; if released, probation for the rest of one's life, and a $15,000 fine. Capital death results in life in prison without the possibility of parole.

In New York, the offenses are classified as felonies, misdemeanors, and third category violations. Felonies are classified A through E with A the most severe. A I results in 15 years to life in prison, A II has a maximum of life in prison. B has a maximum of 25 years in prison, C has a maximum of 15 years in prison, D has a maximum of 7 years in prison, and E has a maximum of 4 years in prison. Misdemeanors are listed under A and B. A has a maximum of one year in jail while B has a maximum of 90 days in jail. Violations are usually fines and/or community service, and on occasion, up to 15 days in jail.

California is one of twenty-four states that has a three-strikes law requiring that a person convicted of three serious crimes be sent to prison for 25 years. They also have the death penalty for first degree murder. Murder can also result in life in prison, without parole, for 25 years to full life. A conviction of rape results in three to six years in prison while robbery results in three to nine years in prison.

LITIGATION IN INTENTIONAL TORTS

Litigation in sport-specific intentional torts differs from general intentional tort cases. An intentional tort requires only the intent to execute an act; results of court decisions in sport require the intent to act, and the intent to injure.

Battery and Assault

Examples of court decisions of battery in sport include a volunteer coach beaten by opposing team coaches in a Little League baseball tournament (*Hill, et al. v. Bridgeview Little League Association, et al.*, 2000, 2001), a person injured by a drunken spectator at a tailgate party (*Bearman v. Notre Dame*, 1983), a head injury in a high school basketball game (*Brokaw v. Winfield-Mt Union Community School District, et al.*, 2008), and two sexual assaults (*J. K. v. Arizona Board of Regents, et al.*, 2008, and *Kaster v. Smith*, 2008). John Hill was attacked and beaten by the Loy brothers while coaching third base in a Little League tournament. The brothers were coaching the opposing team. Hill sustained several injuries including a gouged eye and a broken nose. He sued the Loys; Bridgeview Little League (Bridgeview), the opponents; and Justice Willow Springs Little League (Justice), the sponsor of the tournament. Negligence claims were filed against Bridgeview and Justice for failing to protect Hill. The trial court "entered an order of default against the Loys for failure to answer or otherwise plead" (1177).

The jury verdict for Hill was $632,710 and $125,000 for his wife. Fault was apportioned equally between Bridgeview and Justice. Defendants appealed, challenging the finding of negligence and the exclusion of the Loys from the fault apportionment. The Supreme Court of Illinois reversed the trial court's decision finding that Bridgeview could not foresee the actions of the Loys, and that Justice did not owe a duty to Hill. Hill, however, could sue the Loys for intentional tort.

One of the most publicized cases of spectator violence was *Bearman v. Notre Dame* (1983). Christenna Bearman suffered a leg fracture when she was knocked down by a drunken spectator as she returned to her car following a football game at the South Bend campus. The Circuit Court, St. Joseph County, granted the university a motion for judgment on the evidence. Bearman appealed, arguing that

> she was a business invitee of the University of Notre Dame; therefore, Notre Dame owed to her a duty to protect her from injury caused by the acts of other person on the premises. On the other hand, Notre Dame argues that absent notice or knowledge of any particular danger to a patron, the University cannot be held liable for the acts of third persons (1197).

The Court of Appeals of Indiana reversed the judgment of the trial court, and re-manded for further proceedings based on the following statement:

> The University is aware that alcoholic beverages are consumed on the premises before and during football games. The University is also aware that "tailgate" parties are held in the parking areas around the stadium. Thus, even though there was no showing that the University had reason to know of the particular danger posed by the drunk who injured Mrs. Bearman, it had reason to know that some people will become intoxicated and pose a general threat to the safety of other patrons. Therefore, Notre Dame is under a duty to take reasonable precautions to protect those who attend its football games from injury caused by the act of third persons. (1198)

Although this case involved a battery and is often thought of as a battery case, the final legal analysis was under the liability of property ownership.

In *Brokaw, et al. v. Winfield-Mt Union Community School District and McSorley,* 2008, Jeremy Brokaw, a high school junior and starting guard for the basketball team, was struck in the head by the elbow or fist of an opposing team guard, Andrew Mc-Sorley. Jeremy fell to the floor sustaining head injuries including headaches, hallucina-tions, post-concussion syndrome, and epilepsy spectrum. McSorley was ejected from the game on a technical foul. He received a one game suspension from the league and a five game suspension from his high school. Brokaw's parents sued McSorley for as-sault and battery including punitive damages, and sued McSorley's school district for negligence supervision. The district knew that McSorley behaved aggressively and they did nothing about it. The trial court ruled that McSorley committed a battery and awarded Brokaw's parents $13,000 for their son's medical expenses and $10,000 in damages to Jeremy. Punitive damages were denied as the incident did not rise to the level of recklessness. The claim for negligent supervision was also denied.

Two examples of the many sexual assaults deemed batteries by the courts include an assault of a woman by a football player (*J. K. v. Arizona Board of Regents, et al.,* 2008), and assaults by a high school swimming coach of a number of female students (*Kaster v. Smith,* 2007, 2008). J. K. was allegedly raped by a football player in a University of Arizona dorm where they both resided. J. K. had never met Darnel Henderson, the football player, before the attack. The football player had a history of misconduct and sexual harassment. A university investigation concluded "that the 'football player' had more likely than not sexually assaulted J. K. in violation of the Student Code of Con-duct" (9). In addition, the Arizona University Department of Public Safety's "formal investigation concluded that Henderson had non-consensual sexual intercourse with J. K. and that there was probable cause for criminal prosecution" (9). The Maricopa County Attorney refused to prosecute the athlete for the rape. No reason was provided in the case for this decision.

J. K. filed a complaint against the football player and the Arizona Board of Regents, et al. in the Maricopa County Superior Court; defendants removed the case to the

United States District Court for the District of Arizona. The complaint included a violation of Title IX of the Education Amendments of 1972 in the conduct of the proceedings and follow-up on campus; and a violation of her due process rights under 42 USC 1983 against Koetter, the football coach. The plaintiff contends that

> but for: a) Koetter's knowledge of Henderson's predatory sexual harassment and threatening behavior, b) his affirmative actions in facilitating and permitting Henderson to return to ASU in August 2003 after already being expelled from the Summer Bridge for sexual harassment, c) his affirmative action in concealing relevant information from Clubb and Sullivan at Student Affairs ... In addition to alleging that Koetter failed to act, Plaintiff alleged that Koetter affirmatively ensured that Henderson returned to school, where he was assigned to the very dormitory where his acts of sexual harassment against females had occurred just one month earlier. (22)

As a result of these findings coach Koetter's motion for summary judgment was denied.

Many of the individual defendants for the Arizona Board of Regents were dismissed and the issue of ASU's willful destruction of documentation regarding the football player's earlier misconduct was settled. In reference to the Title IX claim the court also denied the motion for summary judgment, claiming that "the court cannot hold as a matter of law that ASU's response to Henderson's known misconduct during the Summer Bridge program, as well as J.K.'s allegation that Henderson raped her, were not 'clearly unreasonable'" (53, 54).

Kaster v. Smith was a case of sexual relationships between minor girls and the coach of their swimming team. The facts involve "two counts of sexual assault by a school staff member, one count of fourth-degree sexual assault, and one count of disorderly conduct with respect to a sexual relationship with a student" (Case Overview). Mr. Kaster, a swimming coach for both men and women at a Green Bay, Wisconsin, high school from 1983 to 1999 was convicted of the offenses mentioned above under Wisconsin Statute 948.095 that makes sexual contact between a student and a member of the school staff illegal. "The statute defines 'school staff as 'any person who provides services to a school or a school board, including an employee of a school or a school board and a person who provides services to a school or a school board under a contract" (951). While the case was an attempt by the defendant to claim that the fact he was not a teacher, but a contract coach, meant that he was not under the above statute. The court found that his position was under the definition of the statute.

Recklessness

Recklessness is a concept that often relates to sport cases in that an athlete assumes certain risks when engaging in sport, risks beyond those assumed in regular life activities, and that the rules of each game or activity and the duties of the referees and persons in charge, when appropriate, are to control the situation. Unfortunately, games and activities get out of control and those injured in these out of control situations need a legal cause of action. Recklessness is one of those necessary legal causes of action. We begin with the early cases that paved the way for the standard recklessness and move to contemporary decisions made in a range of sports and activities.

Hackbart v. Cincinnati Bengals, Inc. (1979) played an important role in establishing the concept of recklessness. On September 16, 1973, Dale Hackbart, a veteran free safety for the Denver Broncos, was involved in a play that resulted in a pass interception by the Broncos. Acting as an offensive player, Hackbart attempted to block Charles Clark, an offensive back for Cincinnati, by throwing his body in front of him. Clark struck Hackbart, who was still on his knees, with a blow to the back of his head. No penalty was called and Hackbart continued to play. Later, Hackbart had pain, and when he sought medical attention, it was discovered that he had a neck fracture. The trial court judge resolved the liability issue in favor of the Cincinnati Bengals and Clark reasoning that

> professional football is a species of warfare and that so much physical force is tolerated and the magnitude of the force exerted is so great that it renders injuries not actionable in court, that even intentional batteries are beyond the scope of the judicial process…. Despite the fact that the defendant Charles Clark, admitted that the blow which had been struck was not accidental, that it was intentionally administered, the trial court ruled as a matter of law that the game of professional football is basically a business which is violent in nature, and that the available sanctions are imposition of penalties and expulsion from the game. (518–519)

This case weighs the notions of violence, consent, and assumption of risk. The court of appeals reversed and remanded the case for a new trial, holding, among other reasons, that the tort law was applicable to an athletic event and that recklessness, not assault and battery, was a standard for measuring liability in this situation.

Reckless misconduct, later referred to as recklessness, was applied in an amateur sport league for high school age boys in *Nabozny v. Barnhill* (1975). Nabozny was the goalkeeper for the Hansa team; Barnhill was a forward for the Winnetka team. The goalkeeper was kicked in the head by a midfielder while the goalkeeper was on his left knee in the penalty zone. Experts agreed that the contact in question should not have occurred. The court stated:

> That when athletes are engaged in an athletic competition; all teams involved are trained and coached by knowledgeable personnel; a recognized set of rules governs the conduct of the competition; and a safety rule is contained therein which is primarily designed to protect players from serious injury, a player is then charged with a legal duty to every other player on the field to refrain from conduct proscribed by a safety rule. A reckless disregard for the safety of other players cannot be excused. To engage in such conduct is to create an intolerable and unreasonable risk of serious injury to other participants. We have carefully

drawn the rule announced herein in order to control a new field of personal injury litigation. Under the facts presented in the case at bar, we find such a duty clearly arose. Plaintiff was entitled to legal protection at the hands of the defendants.... It is our opinion that a player is liable for injury in a tort action if his conduct is such that it is either deliberate, willful or wanton or with a reckless disregard for the safety of the other players so as to cause injury to that player, the same being a question of fact to be decided by a jury. (260–261)

The case was reversed and remanded to the circuit court for a new trial.

Examples of contemporary cases are taken from a recreation league, colleges, including spectators, theme park, golf, and ski/snowboard. *Feld, et al. v. Borkowski, et al.* (2010) involved teammates on an intramural slow-pitch softball team composed of high school students. Feld was playing first base while Borkowski was practicing batting, when he hit a high flying ball and let go of the aluminum bat, hitting Feld. Borkowski yelled a warning but it was too late. Feld's left eye was severely injured. Feld, through his parents, filed suit in negligence. Borkowski responded that softball was a contact sport and was an exception to the rule of negligence. Feld than changed the charge to reckless conduct. To support the reckless conduct action an expert witness stated that the "only way a right-handed batter could hit a first baseman with a bat in such a manner is if the batter followed though and rotated around after striking the foul ball and deliberately threw the bat or let go of the bat in such a way that it was flung with considerable force through the air toward the first base position" (74). The district court granted Borkowski's motion for summary judgment noting that softball was a contact sport. The Felds appealed. The court of appeals affirmed the lower court's decision.

Plaintiff Mary Kalan and defendant Adrienne Fox were members of opposing teams competing in a recreational softball league (*Kalan v. Fox,* 2010). As Kalan was catching the ball to make a tag she collided with Fox. Plaintiff's injuries required hospitalization. Kalan sued Fox alleging negligence and reckless conduct; the conduct was beyond the rules of the game. Defendant argued that the state's recreational use statute precluded recovery for a person's injuries (Recreational Use Statutes were explained in Chapter 1). A point of debate was whether Fox, the homebound runner, had slide into base. She claimed she was in a slide. If it was a slide, she was within the rules of the game. The trial court found for the defendant runner. Plaintiff appealed. Again, the issue was the position of the runner at the time of impact. Evidence was produced to show that the runner was on her feet, not sliding, at the time of impact. Thus, the court reversed the judgment on the issue of recklessness.

Another adult case, this time in ice hockey, was *Archibald v. Kemble* (2009). Both men were playing in an adult "no check" league. No check means no body contact. Kemble, an eighteen-year-old, jammed his right skate into Archibald's left skate, sending Archibald into the boards and shattering his femur. Archibald was transported to the hospital by ambulance. He received multiple surgeries and has been advised that the injury is permanent. The trial court called it recklessness. A debate existed as to whether recklessness in sport should be analyzed under negligence or intentional tort. The court permitted the case to go to trial. No further information was available.

The United States Coast Guard Academy was playing a varsity soccer match with Trinity College when Cadet Trujillo was struck in the head by Yeager, a Trinity player. Trujillo sued Yeager for careless neglect and reckless use of force in creating the injury (*Trujillo v. Yeager, et al.,* 2009). He also sued Yeager's coach, Pilger, for negligence in failing to properly educate his athlete. Yeager, the defendant, moved to dismiss the complaint stating that one cannot be held liable for negligence for injuries occurring in the course of a competitive contact sport. Trujillo's negligence count was dismissed. Most states have adopted an intentional or reckless standard of care for injuries occurring in competitive sport. Trujillo's complaint against the opponents' coach also failed, with the Court "holding that coaches liable in negligence, particularly to players on a different college's team, would unreasonably threaten to chill competitive play" (91).

In *Nalwa v. Cedar Fair,* plaintiff broke her wrist when her bumper car in a fair was hit from behind and then in front. The lower court found for the fair on primary assumption of risk of the plaintiff. She appealed, "The court of appeals reversed the judgment holding that the primary assumption of risk doctrine was inapplicable to regulated amusement parks, where the activities involved an illusion of risk rather than actual risk" (*Nalwa v. Cedar Fair,* 2011, Case Overview). The Court concluded that issues of liability and cause of action for willful misconduct existed for the fair.

Recklessness incidents seem to occur more often in golf and skiing than in other sports. In golf, two courts, one in Ohio (*Alexander v. Tullis,* 2006) and one in Hawaii (*Yoneda v. Tom, et al.,* 2006) involved golfers struck by fellow golfers' balls, one in the eye. The courts found for the defendants, in *Yoneda,* stating that "there was an inherent risk that golf participants would be hit by errant shots and because plaintiff adduced no evidence that defendant golfer intentionally injured him or acted recklessly beyond the ordinary activities of golf, the doctrine of primary assumption of risk applied, barred plaintiff's actions against defendant golfer" (*Yoneda v. Tom, et al.,* 2006, Case Overview). The same reasoning occurred in the *Alexander* decision.

In skiing the incidents involved equipment problems (*Jozewicz v. GGT Enterprises, LLC; K2 Corporation, et al.,* 2010) and insufficiently marked resort boundaries (*Ciocian v. Vail Corporation,* 2010, and *Anderson v. Vail Corporation,* 2010). Laura Jozewicz's binding released for no reason on her rental ski causing her to fall and injure her neck. It was discovered that the company had failed to remove a binding from her rental ski that was on recall by the Consumer Product Safety Commission. The defendants countered with the fact that she had signed an equipment rental and release agreement which included the following:

> I understand that the binding system cannot guarantee the user's safety. In downhill skiing, the binding systems will not release at all times or under all circumstances where release may prevent injury or death, nor is it possible to predict every situation in which it will release.... I understand that the sport of skiing, snowboarding, skiboarding, snowshoeing

and other sports (collectively "RECREATIONAL SNOW SPORTS") involve inherent risks of INJURY and DEATH. I voluntarily agree to expressly assume all risks of injury or death that may result from these RECREATIONAL SNOW SPORTS, or which relate in any way to the use of this equipment. . . . (Alta Ski Resort, 3)

The United States District Court for the District of Utah, Central Division, held that the pre-injury release was unenforceable and invalid as a matter of public policy. They noted that the "implication of allowing distributors and retailers to contract away liability for noncompliance with established safety standards would increase the risk of injury and would be contrary to Congress's express public policy concerns.... Public policy should encourage compliance with safety laws, not disregard for such laws" (11).

Two Colorado cases in which the court found that ski area boundaries were not adequately marked were *Ciocian v. Vail Corporation* (2010) and *Anderson v. Vail Corporation* (2010). Both skiers, Ciocian on a snowboard and Anderson on skis, skied off a 19-foot retaining wall onto a paved access road, sustaining serious injuries. The trial courts found for the resort; there was no issue of material fact, and the resort's exculpatory agreement was clear and unambiguous and did not violate public policy. These cases were combined on appeal. The markings of the boundaries of the resort became the issue. Was the area of the injury properly marked according to Colorado Revised State Statute 33-44-107 (2010)? Evidence provided by the skiers and ski patrols present at the scene of each of the respective incidents was that the boundary signs were not readily visible to a skier, or as one mentioned, "there was no way she could have known" (*Ciocian, et al. v. Vail Corporation, et al.*, 2010, 1132). The Court of Appeals of Colorado, Division Three, reversed the lower court's decision and remanded the cases for further proceedings. No further proceedings were available at time of publication.

In Minnesota (*Meyers v. Lutsen Mountains Corporation*, 2009) and in California (*Gregorie, et al. v. Alpine Meadows Ski Corporation*, 2010) the resort releases in question were enforced by the courts at the trial and court of appeals levels. Meyers, a self-described expert skier, "lofted" into an area of rocks and trees on the edge of an intermediate hill, sustaining severe injuries. Again, the release was detailed and upheld by the court because Meyers had signed away his rights. Jessica Gregorie sustained injuries resulting in death while snowboarding when she lost control, slid down an icy slope, and went over the marked ski area boundary into the rocks. Although the markings of the boundary lines were an issue, the court found for the resort because the "fatal injuries resulted from risks inherent in snowboarding" (188).

Hazing

Hazing may be treated as a civil or criminal incident. In a national survey conducted by Allan and Madden (2008) of 11,480 students enrolled in 53 universities, they found that 55% of college students involved in clubs, teams, and other extra-curricular organizations reported having been hazed. An example of one of the many extreme cases follows. "Brian Seamons was tied unclothed to a horizontal towel bar with athletic tape by his Sky View High School football teammates in the boys' locker room" (*Seamons, et al. v. Snow, et al.*, 1996, 1229). He had been grabbed while showering, his genital area taped, and he was hung on the towel bar. A girl he had dated was brought into the locker room to see him. According to the case (*Seamons, et al. v. Snow, et al.*, 1996), members of the football team looked on.

> Brian reported this incident to school administrators and other authorities, including the football coach ... and the school principal.... The coach brought Brian before the football team, accused Brian of betraying the team by bringing the incident to the attention of the administration and others, and told Brian to apologize to the team. When Brian refused to apologize, the coach dismissed Brian from the team. The five individuals who assaulted Brian were permitted to play in the next football game. The school district responded to the whole incident by canceling the final game of the season, a state playoff game.
>
> Brian alleges that he was subjected to a "hostile environment" because he was branded as the cause for the football team's demise, and that he was threatened and harassed. Eventually the principal suggested to Brian and his parents that Brian should leave the high school. Brian did so and enrolled in a distant county. (1230)

Seamons's complaints were under constitutional and tort law. The trial court found for the school and its employees. The plaintiff appealed. The court of appeals affirmed all decisions except the First Amendment claim. The court reversed and remanded the claim for further proceedings. In 1998, the United States District Court for the District of Utah, Northern Division, failed to find for Seamons on the First Amendment complaint. The United State Court of Appeals for the Tenth Circuit (2000), however, reversed the decision of the earlier courts for the school and the student and remanded the case for further proceedings.

A fourteen-year-old ninth grade boys' basketball team member was punched and sexually assaulted while waiting for the team bus (*Golden, et al. v. Milford Exempted Village School Board of Education, et al.*, 2009). His parents filed a complaint against the school board, coach, students, and parents of students who conducted the hazing. The complaint included negligence, sexual harassment, intentional infliction of emotional distress, vicarious liability, civil hazing, and negligent supervision. The trial court found for the defendants on all of the claims but the civil hazing and negligent supervision; immunity for the administrators was also refused. The school board appealed. The court of appeals reversed the trial court's decision and found for the school on hazing as the pleadings were insufficient; the negligent supervision was reversed on the grounds that the defenses set forth did not apply. The case was remanded for further study.

CRIMINAL LITIGATION

In criminal law, the state or federal government charges the person with a crime. *State of Ohio v. Guidugli* (2004) occurred in an intramural basketball game at the University of Cincinnati. Campus police were called to the situation. There were few eyewitnesses, and a great deal of pushing and shoving. The intramural supervisor, Steinman, saw Guidugli punch one of the opposing players with a full swing toward the player's eyes. The defendant, Guidugli, was convicted of misdemeanor assault for his role in the fight with the opposing team. He unsuccessfully pleaded self-defense. Guidugli was formally charged with criminal assault that resulted in a 180-day suspended jail sentence.

A recent Florida decision in an area other than sport, in which a minor threw a stapler with intent to hit a fellow student but it hit an employee instead, was viewed under both civil battery and criminal battery and provides the reader with an understanding of how a sport battery might be viewed by the courts in a future decision (*S. G., A Child v. State of Florida*, 2010).

> Section 784.081(2)(c) of the Florida Statutes (2008) reclassifies the crime of battery from a misdemeanor of the first degree to a felony of the third degree when the battery is committed upon "any elected official or employee of: a school district; a private school; the Florida School for the Deaf and the Blind; a university lab school; a state university or any other entity of the state system of public education, as defined in s.1000.04; a sports official; an employee or protective investigator of the Department of Children and Family Services; an employee of a lead community-based provider and its direct service contract providers; or an employee of the Department of Health or its direct service providers, when the person committing the offense knows or has reason to know the identity or position of employment of the victim.... (*S. G., A Child v. State of Florida*, 2010, 385)

A case that stunned the sport nation was the State of Kentucky's action against Jason Stinson, a football coach at Pleasure Ridge Park High School, in Louisville, Kentucky. A fifteen-year-old player under his direction collapsed and died from a heat stroke, sepsis, and multiple organ failure. The athlete's body temperature was found to be 107 degrees. Prior to the day of the incident the same athlete had collapsed during a practice in 94-degree heat. The local prosecutor charged Stinson with reckless homicide. Although Stinson was found not guilty at trial, the incident has served as a warning to coaches practicing in severe weather and other conditions (Marck, 2011).

SUMMARY

Intentional torts are injuries that are caused by deliberate acts or deliberate failure to act. Intentional torts to persons include battery, assault, false imprisonment, and recklessness. Intentional torts to property include trespass to chattel, trespass to personal property, and conversion. Business torts are fraud, deceit, and misrepresentation.

Defenses to intentional torts include consent, self-defense, defense of others, necessity, and discipline.

Criminal law involves harms to society. A prosecutor brings the cause of action against the person who caused the harm. The burden of proof must be "beyond a reasonable doubt." Crimes are usually listed as felonies or misdemeanors with punishments including jail and prison sentences, fines, community service, and in some states a death sentence. For years, society and the courts held that the person engaged in physical activity assumed all the risks inherent in the sport. In some cases, the triers of fact have even ruled that participants assume the risk of intentional torts that might occur in the heat of battle.

DISCUSSION QUESTIONS

1. Contrast negligence with intentional tort. When does each occur?

2. How does the application of criminal law differ from the application of civil law?

3. What is the difference between battery and assault?

ACTIVITIES

1. Persons aspiring to employment in collegiate athletic departments are to read the case *J. K. v. Arizona Board of Regents, et al.* (2008) in detail and create a risk management outline to be used by management in such a situation. Legal, ethical, and public relations decisions are to be considered.

2. Locate two recent cases involving hazing in either college or scholastic athletics. Did the state in which the case was decided have a hazing statute? If such a statute existed what role did it play in the decision?

3. Read the Feingold and Marck articles and decide how heat and other serious issues in athletics should be handled.

REFERENCES

Alexander v. Tullis, 2006 Ohio 1454.

Allan, E., & Madden, M. (2008). Hazing in view: College students at risk. Initial findings from the national study of student hazing. Retrieved from http://www.hazingstudy.org/publications/hazing_in_view_web.pdf

Anderson v. Vail Corporation, et al., 251 P. 3d 1125 (2010).

Archibald, et al. v. Kemble, 971 A. 2d 513 (2009).

Bearman v. University of Notre Dame, 453 N. E. 2d 1196 (1983).

Brokaw, et al. v. Winfield-Mt Union Community School District and McSorley, 2008 Iowa App. LEXIS 1138.

Ciocian, et al. v. Vail Corporation, et al., 251 P. 3d 1130 (2010).

Feld, et al. v. Borkowski, 790 N. W. 2d 72 (2010).

Fitzgerald, et al. v. Barnstable School Committee, 129 S, Ct. 788 (2009); 504 F. 3d 165 (2007).

Golden, et al. v. Milford Exempted Village School Board of Education, 2009 Ohio 3418.

Gregorie, et al. v. Alpine Meadows Ski Corporation, et al., 2011 U.S. Dist. LEXIS 20275; 405 Fed. Appx. 187 (2010).

Hackbart v. Cincinnati Bengals, Inc., 601 F. 2d 516 (1979); cert denied 100 S. Ct. 275 (1979); 435 F. Supp. 352 (1977).

Hill, et al. v. Bridgeview Little League Association, et al., 745 N. E. 2d 1166 (2000); Petition for rehearing denied 2000 Ill. LEXIS 249.

J. K. v. Arizona Board of Regents, et al., 2008 U.S. Dist. LEXIS 83855.

Jozewicz v. GGT Enterprises, LLC, et al., 2010 U.S. Dist. LEXIS 53937.

Kalan v. Fox, et al., 933 N. E. 2d 337 (2010).

Kaster v. Smith, 290 Fed. Appx. 949 (2008).

Marck, D. (2011). Necessary roughness?: An argument for the assignment of criminal liability in cases of student-athlete sustained heat-related deaths. 21 *Seton Hall J. Sports & Ent. L.* 177.

Meyers v. Lutsen Mountains Corporation, 587 F. 3d 891 (2009).

Nabozny v. Barnhill, 334 N. E. 2d 258 (1975).

Nalwa v. Cedar Fair, L. P., 196 Cal. App. 4th 566 (2010).

Restatement of the Law of Torts, (Second). (1965). St. Paul, MN: American Law Institute.

Restatement Third, Torts: Liability for physical and emotional harm. (2010). St. Paul, MN: American Law Institute.

S. G., A Child v. State of Florida, 29 So. 3d 383 (2010).

Seamons, et al. v. Snow, et al., 206 F. 3d 1021 (2000); 15 F. Supp. 2d 1150 (1998); 84 F. 3d 1126 (1996).

State of Ohio v. Guidugli, 811 N. E. 2d 567 (2004).

Trujillo v. Yeager, et al., 642 F. Supp. 2d 86 (2009).

Yoneda v. Tom, et al., 133 P. 3d 796 (2006).

RECOMMENDED READING

Davis, T., & Smith, K. E. (2009). Eradicating student-athlete sexual assault of women: Section 1983 and personal liability following Fitzgerald v. Barnstable. 2009 *Mich. St. L. Rev.* 629.

Feingold, D. (2011). Who takes the heat? Criminal liability for heat-related deaths in high school athletics. 17 *Cardozo J. L. & Gender* 359.

Lee, J. W., & Lee, J. C. (2009). *Sport and criminal behavior.* Durham, NC: Carolina Academic Press.

Otto, K. A. (2009). Criminal athletes: An analysis of charges, reduced charges, and sentences. 19 *J. Legal Aspects of Sport* 67.

Rapp, G. C. (2008). The wreckage of recklessness. 86 *Wash. U. L. Rev.* 111.

Scales, A. (2009). Student gladiators and sexual assault: A new analysis of liability for injuries inflicted by college athletes. 15 *Mich. J. Gender and Law* 205.

3

Product Liability

OBJECTIVES

Upon completing this chapter, you will:

1) understand the policy rationale for imposing liability on the manufacturers and sellers of defective sports and physical activity equipment;

2) be able to differentiate between manufacturing and design defects;

3) understand the importance of warnings to protect users from harm;

4) be able to distinguish express and implied warranties; and

5) be able to explain the defenses available to manufacturers in product liability cases.

INTRODUCTION

Product liability is of concern to manufacturers, retailers, and sellers of sport and physical activity equipment. Owners and agencies leasing sport and physical activity equipment may also be sued under product liability. Historically, product liability has been considered strict liability, where the manufacturer, wholesaler, and retailer of a faulty product are automatically liable for putting an unreasonably dangerous product in the marketplace. And, with the exception of the very few courts that have decided to include a product liability category of negligence in a decision, it remains strict liability today. While "services" are not covered under product liability, occasionally a service provider may be included as a defendant in a product liability lawsuit.

Participants in sports and physical activity generally assume that the products they purchase or lease are safe and will enable them to perform to their maximum capacity in the sport or activity. Often, however, the product is so technically complex that users are not able to examine the equipment for any faults or flaws. This complexity increases with advances in technology and, in many cases, makes it impossible for even skilled performers to assess the condition of their equipment. Because sport and physical activity equipment is expensive, users expect the equipment to be safe and appropriate to the activity. Furthermore, since the user is typically not in the best position to assess the safety of the equipment he/she is using, the responsibility for discovering product defects and correcting them is appropriately borne by those who design and manufacture the product, rather than the consumers of such products.

Sport professionals, sport personnel, team or sport club managers, and others responsible for the selection and purchase of sport and fitness equipment need to be aware of product liability. They must be able to protect their organizations against the purchase and installation of faulty products, know the organizations' rights when products fail, and effectively relay manufacturers' warnings to appropriate audiences.

Under product liability, the manufacturer, wholesaler, retailer, supplier, and vendor are liable for placing a defective product—one that might cause injury—on the market. Product liability theory presumes that the manufacturer and seller are in the best position to become aware of problems, to eliminate defects, and to absorb losses from product changes and/or litigation. A product is considered defective under product liability when the defect existed at the time the product left the manufacturer or retailer (defendant) and the defect caused the injury. Components of the product liability statute also include non-compliance with safety standards, misrepresentation, and failure to recall. The Consumer Product Safety Commission also allows for an action in federal court against a manufacturer in violation of a consumer product safety rule.

Defenses to product liability include contributory negligence, assumption of risk, misuse, and the Uniform Commercial Code (UCC) disclaimers. Product liability is governed by state and federal laws. States may differ in their laws and in the interpretation of similar laws. *Restatement (Third) of Torts: Product Liability* (1998) is the guide for the discussion that follows. It defines a product as a "tangible personal property distributed commercially for use or consumption. Other items, such as real property and electricity, are products when the context of their distribution and use is sufficiently analogous to the distribution and use of tangible personal property" (267). A person, according to Section 20, who sells or distributes a product is defined in the explanation below:

(a) One sells a product when, in a commercial context, one transfers ownership thereto either for use or consumption or for resale leading to ultimate use or consumption. Commercial product sellers include but are not limited to, manufacturers, wholesalers, and retailers.

(b) One otherwise distributes a product when, in a commercial transaction other than a sale, one provides the product to another either for use or consumption or as a preliminary step leading to ultimate use or consumption. Commercial nonsale product distributors include, but are not limited to, lessors, bailors, and those who provide products to others as a means of promoting either the use or consumption of such products or some other commercial activity.

(c) One also sells or otherwise distributes a product when, in a commercial transaction, one provides a combination of products and services and either the transaction taken as a whole, or the product component thereof, satisfies the criteria in ... (a) or (b). (284)

CATEGORIES OF PRODUCT DEFECT

Product liability exists when a manufacturer, retailer, or seller sells or distributes a defective product. The categories of product defect include a manufacturing defect, a design defect, or defect as a result of providing inadequate instructions or warnings. According to the *Restatement (Third) of Torts: Product Liability* (1998), Section 2, a product

(a) contains a manufacturing defect when the product departs from its intended design even though all possible care was exercised in the preparation and marketing of the product;

(b) is defective in design when the foreseeable risks of harm posed by the product could have been reduced or avoided by the adoption of a reasonable alternative design by the seller or other distributor or a predecessor in the commercial chain of distribution, and the omission of the alternative design renders the product not reasonably safe;

(c) is defective because of inadequate instructions or warnings when the foreseeable risks of harm posed by the product could have been reduced or avoided by the provision of reasonable instructions or warnings by the seller or other distributor, or a predecessor in the commercial chain of distribution, and the omission of the instructions or warnings renders the product not reasonably safe. (14)

Manufacturing Defect

A manufacturing defect is an unreasonably unsafe product created in the construction process; it may include the improper construction of a part (or parts) or the improper assembly of the parts. A manufacturer's defect means that the product does not perform or was not built as the manufacturer planned or according to the design. As a result of the change, an unsafe product has been created. The manufacturer's defect may occur in all of the products or may occur only in a few random products.

For example, in 2009, the U.S. Consumer Product Safety Commission (CPSC) in association with the manufacturer issued a nationwide recall of a specific brand and model of basketball hoops. Approximately 1,700 in-ground basketball hoops were recalled because the bolts at the base could fail, causing the unit to fall. This would be considered a manufacturing defect because the defect occurred during the manufacturing stage rather than during the design process and some, not all, of the hoops manufactured were defective.

To determine liability for manufacturing defects, strict liability is used.

Design Defect

A design defect means that the product, when built according to the manufacturer's plan, contains a design flaw or fault that will subject the user of the product to unreasonable harm; the original plans or specifications are flawed. A design defect makes all of the products unreasonably dangerous, not just a few of them. This unreasonable danger is one that has not been contemplated by the user or consumer. The manufacturer is held to the status of an expert in the design area. An examination of the manufacturer's schematics or design plans must reveal a flaw in the design and analysis of the manufacturing protocol which demonstrates that the product was created according to the faulty design. Those persons who created the design and specifications will ultimately be held responsible. Bessinger and Cade (2010) noted that there has been a dramatic increase in design defect litigation, which has also been seen in sport litigation.

The role of the manufacturer and the seller or distributor for failure to note the design flaw will be based upon whether the defendant had expertise or reason to know (through complaints or otherwise) that the design flaw might exist. However, a recent trend being used by some courts is considering the obviousness of the danger as one factor in determining if the product is unreasonably dangerous, rather than as a complete defense to product liability.

The *Restatement (Third) of Torts: Product Liability* (1998) exclusively adopts a risk/utility analysis in determining whether a design defect exists. Under this approach, a product will be found defective as designed only if the magnitude of the risk created by the design is greater than the utility of the product (*Restatement [Third]*, Sec. 2[b]). Specifically, the *Restatement (Third) Torts* Section 2(b) provides that a product is defective when "the foreseeable risks of harm posed by the product could have been reduced or avoided by the adoption of a reasonable alternative design by the seller or other distributor, or a predecessor in the commercial chain of distribution, and the omission of the alternative design renders the product not reasonably safe" (14).

Instructions

Adequate instructions on how the product is to be used and information about potential hazards in the use of the product are to be provided. These instructions are to include: assembly, cleaning, periodic inspection, routine care, and method of repair. If the equipment is to be installed under supervision, it should be noted.

The nature of some products causes them to be considered dangerous. At times, the purchaser may not understand the obvious danger of a product he/she is using. For example, all boats and personal watercraft present a hazard to any person who is unable to right his/her body and come to the surface after being thrown into the water. For anyone unable to execute this minimal personal rescue skill, the use of all watercraft is hazardous.

Warnings

When manufacturers or sellers become aware of a dangerous product, they have an obligation to warn the user about the specific danger(s) involved. Merely placing a warning label on a product is not enough. The product must be manufactured to be as safe as is reasonable. What cannot be incorporated into the safe manufacture of the product must be explained in the warning. Warnings must be adequate to perform their intended function of risk reduction (*Pell v. Victor J. Andrew High School and AMF*, 1984). Warnings may be inadequate, however, if they

- do not specify the risk presented by the product;

- are inconsistent with how a product should be used;

- do not provide the reason for the warnings; or

- do not reach foreseeable users.

When the danger is not apparent, there is a duty to warn the user of the product. When the danger is obvious, some courts have ruled that there is no duty to warn. Other courts have ruled that even though the danger might be considered obvious to some people, the duty to warn remains with all involved in manufacture, retail, and leasing. When the user has knowledge of the danger of a product as a result of his/her experience and expertise, there is no duty to warn. For example, a competitive surfer has knowledge of the dangers of surfing and understands the precautions taken to use surfing equipment safely. No duty to warn exists when the dangers of a product are known within a profession. The duty to warn cannot be delegated.

In understanding the nuances of product liability law, it is necessary to differentiate between defective and dangerous products. Defective products are to be removed, while dangerous products should contain warnings. Products may be dangerous only when used or misused in certain ways. If manufacturers or sellers can foresee any of these uses or misuses, or alternatively if a court of law could decide that they should have foreseen a use or misuse, the manufacturer or seller must warn users about foreseeable dangers. Manufacturers must simulate how products will be used by consumers and whether the product could be dangerous in its present or future use. They should reasonably anticipate the environment in which it could be used and warn against dangers they can foresee. For example, children using a portable basketball hoop in a driveway or on a neighborhood street may not appreciate that dunking on the hoop may cause the entire structure to tip over, potentially injuring the participants or others nearby, because the hoop is not permanently fixed in the ground.

The objective of a warning in product liability, but also in tort law generally speaking, is to alert the user to a danger of which the user is not aware. Determining whether a danger is obvious to the user must take into account the user's expertise, skill, and knowledge. Therefore, products that may typically be expected to be used by children, where the user may not have the expertise or maturity to appreciate the danger, are particularly prone to requiring warnings.

Manufacturers, sellers, and owners (including sport and physical activity professionals) may have a duty to warn. They need to be aware of when to warn and have a systematic process of informing clients about the warnings. A person held to a duty to warn, according to Wittenberg (1985), is to provide a warning that is:

1) Conspicuous—it will attract the user's eye

2) Specific—it will be understood by the user

3) Forceful—it will convince the user of the range and magnitude of the potential harm that could occur. (pp. 1–33)

Manufacturers, wholesalers, retailers, sellers, and persons supervising the use of a product can be held for failure to adequately warn users of foreseeable dangers or failure to pass on the warnings to others. These dangers include foreseeable use and misuse of the product. A warning of danger must: a) identify the risk, b) provide the reason for the warning, and c) reach the user. The user is to be warned and to understand the importance of the warning. Warnings are to be written in such a manner that users recognize the significance of the warning. When the significance of the warning is obvious, there is a far greater chance the warning will be taken seriously. Manufacturers, retailers, and wholesalers must place the warning on the product in such a way that it cannot be missed.

The manufacturer is to provide the product user with information and directions regarding the qualities, characteristics, and uses of the product. The information is to be written in such a way that if caution were essential, a reasonable person would recognize the need to exercise caution. The objective is to avoid injuries that could occur from ignorant misuse of the product. Instructions are to be provided to enable the purchaser to pass on the instructions and warnings to all potential users of the product.

When a warning is justified, the courts will determine the adequacy of the warning on a case-by-case basis, considering whether it was noticeable, accurate, clear, and strong. It must capture the attention of those who will use the product and inform them of the dangers in the use of the product. Even in situations where the user is sophisticated, a warning to remind the user of the potential danger associated with the product may be in order.

Manufacturers, retailers, and supervisors of activity have a duty to instruct the participant on the safe use of the equipment and to warn against dangers. The warning must be sufficient to enable the average person to understand the probability, frequency, and magnitude of the occurrence of the risk and the extent of the potential injury. It is this duty to warn and to instruct about the dangers of the use of certain equipment that is the responsibility of those who supervise, manage, or teach physical activity.

When a manufacturer provides a warning to a sport professional, such as the manager of a fitness center, the manufacturer also gives responsibility to that person to properly inform or pass on the warning to those who will use the equipment. Warnings are to be placed on the face of the equipment or on the wall above the equipment; they are not to be thrown out in the empty cartons used to ship or deliver the product.

Professionals have an additional duty to inform and to warn participants about the skill and physical capacity essential to safely use certain pieces of equipment. This includes the duty to warn and to provide instruction sufficient to enable the average person to ascertain the need for experience before using various pieces of equipment. Participants need to know and understand when the equipment is beyond their skill level. Warnings need to be tailored to the specific skill level of the performer.

MISREPRESENTATION

Misrepresentation is an inaccurate statement that leads another to believe a "fact" that is not actually true. The statement may be an unintentional error or an intentional falsehood. In *Restatement of Torts (Third): Product Liability* (1998) Section 9, it is stated that "One engaged in the business of selling or otherwise, distributes products, who, in connection with the sale of a product makes a fraudulent, negligent, or innocent misrepresentation concerning the product is subject to liability for harm to persons or property caused by the misrepresentation" (187).

When product facts and use statements are misrepresented by the seller, an injured plaintiff may have a cause of action for misrepresentation. The product does not have to be defective or unreasonably dangerous. However, a claim may only be brought for physical injury. Care should be taken to ensure that advertisements, brochures, and salespersons' comments given face-to-face or over the phone or Internet do not directly or inadvertently cause product misrepresentations. Salespersons are to be monitored by management to ensure that purchasers are informed of the potential hazards and risks in the use of equipment.

BREACH OF WARRANTY

A warranty is a guarantee by a manufacturer, wholesaler, or retailer to a buyer that the product will perform according to identified standards for a specified period of time. Requirements for maintenance, intended use, and other specifications must be given to the buyer. The warranty is a part of the contract between the buyer and seller. If the seller violates the warranty, the seller breaches the contract; if the buyer violates the warranty, the buyer breaches the contract. In warranty, the liability of the industry exists without regard to fault. For example, if the product does not meet the specifications of the fitness industry, the liability of the manufacturer, retailer, or wholesaler is automatic; there is no need to investigate the intent of the parties. Breach of warranty, also covered by the Uniform Commercial Code (UCC), may occur through breach of express or implied warranty.

Many laws relating to business are similar from state to state. "The states, not the federal government, are the primary source of law on commercial transactions in the U.S. In all 50 states and the District of Columbia, at least some of that commercial law is based on the UCC" (Cornell Legal Information Institute, n.d.).

Express Warranties

Express warranties are written statements about the product; implied warranties are warranties the purchaser assumes. An express warranty is a statement or document containing promises or descriptions of the product. Sections 2-313, 2-314, and 2-315 of the Uniform Commercial Code (UCC) cover express or verbal warranty, implied warranty of merchantability, and implied warranty of fitness for a particular purpose. UCC 2-313 explains the express warranties that a manufacturer, wholesaler, retailer, or supplier may make:

UCC 2-313 *Express Warranties by Affirmation, Promise, Description, Sample*

(1) Express warranties by the seller are created as follows:

   (a) Any affirmation of fact or promise made by the seller to the buyer which relates to the goods and becomes part of the basis of the bargain creates an express warranty that the goods shall conform to the affirmation or promise.

   (b) Any description of the goods which is made part of the basis of the bargain creates an express warranty that the goods shall conform to the description.

   (c) Any sample or model which is made part of the basis of the bargain creates an express warranty that the whole of the goods shall conform to the sample or model.

(2) It is not necessary to the creation of an express warranty that the seller use formal words such as "warrant" or "guarantee" or that he have specific intention to make a warranty, but an affirmation merely of the value of the goods or a statement purporting to be merely the seller's opinion or commendation of the goods does not create a warranty. (UCC 2-313)

In breach of an express warranty, the plaintiff must establish that:

• The warranty was made. The seller made the statement.

• The seller's statement was part of the bargain. The purchaser relied upon the seller's statement in making his/her decision to purchase.

• The product did not conform to the warranty. The product's behavior is not in line with the warranty.

• A causal connection exists between the breach of the warranty and the plaintiff's economic or physical injury.

A breach of an express warranty occurs when the plaintiff is injured and the seller or manufacturer made statements of fact about the product that were false. These statements may be express; for example, the plaintiff was told or it was implied that the lifejacket would support a person of ordinary size in deep water. The statement must be made to the plaintiff or made generally to the public. The plaintiff has to have relied on the statement, and the reliance on the statement or "facts" has to be the cause of the injury.

When the goods are described—and that description is made a basis of the bargain or relied upon by the purchaser—there is an express warranty that the goods shall conform to the description (UCC 2-313 [1, b]). The description can be contained in a brochure, blueprint, written specification, or sample model.

Implied Warranties

Implied warranties exist at the time the person contracts for an article of goods. The purchaser assumes that the product will be what it purports to be and that it will be fit for its intended use. These warranties do not have to appear in writing, nor be mentioned. It is assumed that a boat will float and that a bathing suit will not shrink in water. The goods are expected to pass without objection in the trade and are to be fit for the ordinary purposes for which such goods are used.

Implied warranties include merchantability and fitness for a particular purpose. Merchantability means that the product is suitable for the purposes for which it was created. The level of suitability is to be average or reasonable; it need not be perfect. According to UCC 2-314, this section's ultimate objective "is to require the seller to assume responsibility for a substandard product."

> UCC 2-314 *Implied Warranty: Merchantability: Usage of Trade*
>
> 1) Unless excluded or modified … a warranty that the goods shall be merchantable is implied in a contract for their sale if the seller is a merchant with respect to goods of that kind. Under this section the serving for value of food or drink to be consumed either on the premise or elsewhere is a sale.
>
> 2) Goods to be merchantable must be at least such as
>   a) pass without objection in the trade under the contract description; and
>   b) in the case of fungible goods, are of fair average quality within the description; and
>   c) are fit for the ordinary purposes for which goods are used; and
>   d) run, within the variations permitted by the agreement, of even kind, quality, and quantity within each unit and among all units involved; and
>   e) are adequately contained, packaged, and labeled as the agreement may require; and
>   f) conform to the promises or affirmations of fact made on the container or label if any.
>
> 3) Unless excluded or modified … other implied warranties may arise from course of dealing or usage of trade. (UCC 2-314)

Fitness means that the product has been made for a particular purpose. UCC 2-315 describes fitness in the following way:

> Where the seller at the time of contracting has reason to know any particular purpose for which the goods are required and that the buyer is relying on the seller's skill or judgment to select or furnish suitable goods, there is unless excluded or modified under the next section an implied warranty that the goods shall be fit for such purpose. (UCC 2-315)

When the buyer identifies a particular purpose for the product, the seller must address that purpose when making the sale. A clear statement of the product's fitness for that purpose should be presented. Often, sports and physical activity products have written labels or hangtags identifying the fitness of the product for certain purposes. For example, a bicycle used for racing may be differentiated at the point of sale, in terms of labeling or advertising, from a bike primarily intended for leisure purposes. A prospective buyer should be able to ascertain the fitness of a particular piece of equipment to achieve the desired purpose at the point of sale, through product descriptions or talking with a salesperson. For example, if a runner is purchasing a new pair of shoes to be used in a marathon and discloses the particular purpose for which the shoes are being purchased to the seller, the seller must sell the runner a pair of running shoes that are fit or suitable for this particular purpose. When a product is not fit for that purpose, the buyer has a cause of action under implied warranty of fitness for a particular purpose.

FEDERAL CONSUMER PRODUCT SAFETY ACT

The National Commission on Product Safety was created by Congress in 1968. Its purpose was to explore the need for federal regulation of consumer products. Congress found a high level of unacceptable products—ones from which people were not able to protect themselves (15 USCA 2051 [1]). The Commission recommended the establishment of the Consumer Product Safety Act (CPSA). This act was established

> to protect the public against unreasonable risks of injury associated with consumer products; to assist consumers in evaluating the comparative safety of consumer products; to develop uniform safety standards for consumer products and to minimize conflicting state and local regulations; and to promote research and investigation into the causes and prevention of product-related deaths, illnesses and injuries. (15 USCA 2051 [b])

The CPSA requires manufacturers to inform the Commission of substantial product hazards—ones believed to cause serious harm to users. The term

> "consumer product" means by article, or component part thereof, produced or distributed (i) for sale to a consumer for use in and around a permanent or temporary household or residence, a school, in recreation, or otherwise, or (ii) for the personal use, consumption, or enjoyment of a consumer in or around a permanent or temporary household or resident, a school, in recreation, or otherwise. (15 USCA 2051 [1])

Under safety information and research mandates, the CPSA maintains a National Electronic Injury Surveillance System (NEISS) that gathers information from representative hospital emergency rooms in the United States and its territories. Statistically valid estimates of frequency and severity of injuries associated with specific consumer products are the reported results.

An individual injured by a product whose manufacturer is in violation of the consumer product safety law may bring an action in federal court. The plaintiff must prove that the manufacturer has distributed a product which presents a hazard, and that the manufacturer failed to give notice to the CPSA despite knowledge of the hazard. The failure to give notice must be the proximate cause of the plaintiff's injury. In addition to being made whole or receiving compensatory damages, a successful victim may recover the costs of the lawsuit and attorney fees.

Professionals may not "manufacture for sale, offer for sale, distribute in commerce, or import into the United States any consumer product which is not in conformity with an applicable consumer product safety standard" (15 USCA 2068). Any person who knowingly violates Section 2068 is subject to a civil penalty of $5,000 or less for each violation. The maximum penalty is not to exceed $1,250,000 (15 USCA 2069). These figures are to be adjusted yearly for increases. The Commission recalls over 200 products each year; most of the recalls are voluntary.

COMPLIANCE WITH PRODUCT SAFETY STATUTES

Within the *Restatement (Third) of Tort: Product Liability* (1998), there is a section titled "Noncompliance and Compliance with Product Safety." The statutes or regulations contained therein state:

> In connection with liability for defective design or inadequate instructions or warnings:
>
> (a) a product's noncompliance with an applicable product safety statute or administrative regulation renders the product defective with respect to the risks sought to be reduced by the statute or regulation; and
>
> (b) a product's compliance with an applicable product safety statute or administrative regulation is properly considered in determining whether the product is defective with respect to the risks sought to be reduced by the statute or regulation but such compliance does not preclude as a matter of law a finding of product defect. (120)

STATE PRODUCT LIABILITY LAW

Buckley (1993) noted that there are five elements of product liability that are found in most state statutes or case law. These five elements are listed below:

1) The defect must render the product unreasonably dangerous to use.

2) The seller or manufacturer must be in the business of selling products such as the flawed one(s).

3) The product cannot have been substantially changed between the time it left the seller's or manufacturer's hands and the time it reached the ultimate user.

4) The defect must have proximately caused the ultimate user's injuries.

5) The ultimate user must have used the product properly (i.e., in a way that the product was designed to be used).

DEFENSES

Defenses to product liability are contributory negligence, assumption of risk, misuse, and disclaimers. Apportionment of responsibility between and among plaintiffs, sellers, and distributors of defective products considers the contributory negligence of the plaintiff as well as the liability of the defendant.

Contributory Negligence

Contributory negligence means that the user was negligent in his/her use of the equipment. A user who ignores the manual and warranty, assembles the equipment in a faulty manner, or uses a product in a new and unusual way not anticipated by the manufacturer or the retailer is contributorily negligent. Users who fail to discover a defect that a reasonable person should have discovered are contributorily negligent. In states that have comparative negligence, contributory negligence will be used in arriving at the percentage of fault.

Assumption of Risk

Assumption of risk is recognized in most product liability situations. Assumption of risk requires that the plaintiff knew of the risk of danger or should have known of the risk of danger. The user must:

1) Be aware of the danger.

2) Recognize and appreciate the

   a) significance, and

   b) magnitude of the risk associated with the use of the product.

3) Voluntarily take the risk.

Knowledge and appreciation of the danger means that the user must actually have known of the danger rather than should have known of the danger. This means that the injured person was properly informed of the danger. It also means that when an elite athlete is injured, his/her previous experience and observation of others sustaining injury as a result of using a product will serve to inform him/her of potential hazards in the activity.

A person assumes a risk when he/she discovers a product defect, ignores the risk, and uses the product. The courts will examine the owner's liability in ignoring a discovered product defect.

Misuse

Mishandling, abuse, or the use of a product for abnormal purposes is called misuse. The manufacturer, wholesaler, and retailer are liable for warning the user about foreseeable misuse. A product must be used for its intended purpose—the function for which it was designed. Use of a product for a purpose other than that envisioned by the manufacturer is considered misuse and could bar recovery to the injured party. When the manufacturer, wholesaler, and retailer become aware that their products are being used in ways other than the intended purpose, they are to provide warnings to the public and to all new product purchasers. To avoid liability, sport and physical activity professionals, such as fitness center managers, are to demand that participants use equipment only for the manufacturer's intended use. When professionals wish to use equipment in ways other than its intended use, they should seek written permission from the manufacturer and request that reasons be provided for denial of requested use.

Disclaimers

A disclaimer is a defense in breach of warranty lawsuits. A manufacturer and a seller may place disclaimers or statements declaring they are not responsible or liable for the product if the product is used for a purpose or in a manner beyond the limits of those uses recommended by the manufacturer, retailer, etc. These statements explain product use and disclaim responsibility for products used in ways other than those recommended. "As is" and "with all faults" are disclaimers about the quality of the product.

Disclaimers must be conspicuous and unambiguous, and clearly convey their message. An injured party needs to give notice to the defendant of the breach of warranty within a reasonable time after the injury. This enables the defendant to investigate and, when warranted, take action on the product for the benefit of other consumers.

DAMAGES

Product liability damages are usually compensatory. On occasion, punitive damages are awarded. Compensatory damages provide for the expenses directly involved in the injury and rehabilitation. Punitive damages are awards assessed against the party responsible for the harm in an effort to stop the party from continuing to create the harm. Usually, the defendant's level of liability must be reckless before punitive damages are awarded. Prior knowledge of the defective condition and failure to do anything about it may result in punitive damage awards. Failure to inspect or to test may also be reasons for the award of punitive damages.

LITIGATION

In *Ontiveros v. 24 Hour Fitness USA, Inc.* (2008), Susana Ontiveros was a member at a 24 Hour Fitness Center in Los Angeles. This fitness center contained numerous exercise machines and also offered aerobic exercise classes. For an additional fee, Ontiveros received an upgraded membership that gave her access to additional equipment, services, and amenities, such as equipment to test her blood pressure. To obtain this membership, Ontiveros was required to sign a membership agreement containing a release from liability, which included the following stipulation:

> You understand and acknowledge that [defendant] is providing recreational services and may not be held liable for defective products. By signing below, you acknowledge and agree that you have read the foregoing and know of the nature of the activities at [defendant's facilities] and you agree to all the terms of the front and back pages of this agreement and acknowledge you have received a copy of it and the membership policies. (*Ontiveros v. 24 Hour Fitness USA, Inc.*, 2008, 427)

Ontiveros declared that she was familiar with exercise machines and therefore did not need or receive assistance concerning proper use of equipment. Ontiveros was injured while using a stairstep machine, alleging that she fell backwards onto the floor because of the failure of a component of the machine. She brought suit against the fitness center, asserting a product liability claim using strict liability. Ontiveros asserted that the fitness center provided her no services, making them part of the product distribution chain and liable for defective equipment under the strict liability doctrine.

The court ruled in favor of the fitness club, finding that the dominant purpose of the membership agreement she signed was for fitness services. Thus, she had no valid claim under the strict liability doctrine. Had the gym simply made exercise equipment available for her use, the gym could have been held strictly liable for defective equipment. However, the membership agreement between the plaintiff and defendant included aerobics classes, dance classes, yoga, and additional health testing centers which the court concluded was indicative of fitness services. Since it was primarily a fitness service that the plaintiff was provided, the defendant could not be found liable for her injuries using product liability.

When one thinks of product liability in sport, one usually thinks of football. Among the more notable football product liability cases are *Bryns v. Riddell, Inc.* (1976), *Rawlings v. Daniels* (1981), *Hemphell v. Sayers* (1982), *Galindo v. Riddell, Inc.* (1982), *Carrier, et al. v. Riddell, Inc., et al.* (1983), *Fiske v. MacGregor, Division of Brunswick* (1983), *Gentile v. MacGregor Mfg. Co.* (1985), *Lister v. Bill Kelly Athletic, Inc.* (1985), *Austria v. Bike Athletic Co.* (1991), *Rodriguez v. Riddell Sport Inc.* (2001), and *Green v. Schutt Sports Manufacturing, et al.* (2010). Cases involving Riddell include *Byrns, Galindo, Carrier,* and *Rodriguez.*

The eleven football helmet litigations span a period of time from the *Byrns* case of 1976 to *Green*, a 2010 decision. The majority of the cases were litigation on defective design or defective manufacture by high school athletes. A few mentioned failure to warn.

Examples of the litigation are the lawsuits filed by Byrns (1976), Daniels (1981), and Green (2010). Football player Kevin Byrns received an on-side kick, fell to the ground, and was hit by one or more players. The impact resulted in serious head injuries. His suit against Riddell was that the helmet "was defective by design and manufacture and by reason of such defects was inherently dangerous to the user" (1066). The argument was over the helmet's ability to absorb force during impact. The trial court found for the manufacturer. After hearing the views of experts and watching films, the trial court concluded "that the film, as a matter of law, left no reasonable doubt as to the place of impact, thus ruling that the appellant failed to show causation between the impact and the injury" (1069). Byrns appealed the decision and the Supreme Court of Arizona reversed and remanded the case for further proceedings on the issue.

Mike Daniels experienced severe brain injuries that reduced his abilities when his football helmet collapsed as he collided with another player during practice. He sued Rawlings for a defective helmet and for failure "to warn of the protective limitations of the helmet" (437). The district court awarded Daniels $1,500,000. Rawlings appealed. The Court of Civil Appeals of Texas at Waco affirmed the district court's decision.

Green (2010), a high school football player, sued Schutt Sports when he suffered a severe burst—a fracture of a neck vertebra resulting in quadriplegia in a tackle. His suit was for defective helmet design. The Court found that it was the way he executed the tackle rather than the helmet design that caused the injury. The U.S. Court of Appeals for the Fifth Circuit found for the manufacturer.

SUMMARY

Product liability is the liability of the manufacturer, retailer, and seller for placing a defective product on the market. A product is defective under product liability when the defect existed at the time the product left the manufacturer or retailer and the defect caused the injury. Product liability may be negligence, misrepresentation, breach of warranty, violation of a Consumer Product Safety Commission rule, or strict liability in tort. Defenses to product liability include contributory negligence, assumption of risk, misuse, and the Uniform Commercial Code (UCC) disclaimers. In product liability cases, the damages are compensatory and punitive.

DISCUSSION QUESTIONS

1. How should a sport professional implement product warnings?

2. Describe the various kinds of product warranties and give an example of each.

ACTIVITIES

1. Research a recall involving a sport product on the United States Consumer Product Safety Commission website (http://www.cpsc.gov). Identify the risk presented by the product? Why do you think the recall was necessary to protect the public?

2. Locate two cases in sport, one representing a manufacturer defect and one representing a design defect. Contrast the differences between the two.

REFERENCES

Austria v. Bike Athletic Co., 810 P. 2d 1312 (1991).

Bessinger, H. M., & Cade, N. (2010). Who's afraid of the Restatement (Third) of Torts? *Wisconsin Law Journal.* Retrieved from http://wislawjournal.com/2010/09/17/whos-afraid-of-the-restatement-third-of-torts/

Buckley, W. R. (1993). *Torts and personal injury law.* Albany, NY: Delmar.

Byrns v. Riddell Incorporated, 550 P. 2d 1065 (1976).

Carrier, et al. v. Riddell, Inc., et al., 721 F. 2d 867 (1983).

Consumer Product Safety Act, 15 USCA 2051 (2004).

Fiske v. MacGregor Division of Brunswick, et al., 464 A. 2d 719 (1983).

Galindo v. Riddell, Inc., 437 N. E. 2d 376 (1982).

Gentile v. MacGregor Mfg. Co., 493 A. 2d 647 (1995).

Green v. Schutt Sports Manufacturing Co., et al., 369 Fed. Appx. 630; 2010 U.S. App. LEXIS 5482.

Lister v. Bill Kelly Athletic, Inc., 485 N. E. 2d 483 (1985).

Ontiveros v. 24 Hour Fitness USA, Inc., 169 Cal. App. 4th 424 (2008).

Rawlings Sporting Goods Company v. Daniels, 619 S. W. 2d 435 (1981).

Restatement (Third) of Torts: Product liability. (1998). St. Paul, MN: American Law Institute.

Rodriguez v. Riddell Sports, Inc., et al., 242 F. 3d 567 (2001).

Uniform Commercial Code (UCC) Articles 1 through 9. UCC 2010-2011, American Law
   Institute. Retrieved from http://www.law.cornell.edu/ucc/2/2-313.html

Wittenberg, J. D. (1985). *Product liability: Recreation and sports equipment.* New York, NY:
   Lawyers Journal Seminar Press.

RECOMMENDED READING

Mills, B. J. (2001). Football helmets and products liability. 8 *Sports Law J.* 153.

Polinsky, A. M., & Shavell, S. (2010). The uneasy case for product liability. 123 *Harv. L. Rev.*
   1437.

Seiberling, M. (2002). "Icing" on the cake: Allowing amateur athletic promoters to escape
   liability in Mohney v. USA Hockey, Inc. 9 *Vill. Sports & Ent. L.J.* 417.

Part II

— CONSTITUTIONAL LAW —

The United States Constitution is the supreme law of the land. Judges in every state are bound by the Constitution of the United States and by the constitutions of their respective states. The First, Fourth, and Fourteenth Amendments to the U.S. Constitution are the aspects of constitutional law most often affecting participants and managers of sport and physical activity.

Chapter 4 addresses laws associated with the First, Fourth, and Fourteenth Amendments. Only the due process clause of the Fourteenth Amendment is addressed. Chapter 5 addresses gender equity by discussing the Equal Protection Clause of the Fourteenth Amendment, Title IX, and the Civil Rights Acts of 1987 and 1991. The Americans with Disabilities Act (ADA) and related disability laws impacting the sport industry are discussed in Chapter 6.

All constitutions can be amended. An amendment to the United States Constitution may be proposed by a two-thirds vote of those present in each house of Congress, or by a committee of the legislatures of two-thirds of the states. Amendments may be ratified by the legislature of three-fourths of the states or by conventions in three-fourths of the states. There are times when an amendment may be acceptable within a particular state but will not be acceptable to the entire country. The Equal Rights Amendment's success in numerous states and failure at the federal level is such an example.

The Constitution of the United States guarantees—or enforces—individual rights only with reference to the federal government and to state actions as they are incorporated within the Fourteenth Amendment. When a complaint involves a guarantee of a personal right, a court must determine whether the action challenged is a federal or state action. A person challenging a privately owned and operated agency forces the court to determine whether the agency is subject to state protection and regulation.

4

First, Fourth, and Fourteenth Amendments

OBJECTIVES

Upon completing this chapter, you will:

1) understand the constitutional protections afforded to sport participants, spectators, and others;

2) balance individual rights against the rights of the state;

3) identify legal issues associated with regulating speech by students and athletes;

4) design fan code of conduct policies that should withstand constitutional challenge; and

5) analyze when, and under what circumstances, a sport organization can restrict fan speech.

FIRST AMENDMENT

The First Amendment of the United States Constitution states that "Congress shall make no law respecting an establishment of religion, or prohibiting the free exercise thereof; or abridging the freedom of speech or of the press; or the right of the people peaceably to assemble, and to petition the government for a redress of grievances." Historically, the First Amendment applied only to actions of the federal government. However, the courts, through the process of incorporation, have made the First Amendment applicable to state actions. First Amendment rights are the freedoms of religion, speech (including symbolic protest), and press. "The First Amendment provides protection for a wide range of expression ... with the goal of preserving an uninhibited marketplace of ideas and fostering self-expression free of government restraint" (Grady, McKelvey, & Clement, 2005, p. 272). In making a decision about the freedoms of religion, speech, and press, the courts balance the needs of the public against the rights of the individual.

When challenging a denial of First Amendment rights, an individual requests that a court of law examine the facts with respect to the particular situation and balance the personal rights in relation to the authority of the state, federal government, or private agency to effect a particular rule, law, or regulation for the benefit of society. Sport and speech have been described as intersecting American icons (Wasserman, 2004). That intersection often creates collisions between fans, the media, and sport organizations (Grady & Moorman, 2008). While "fan expression is a long-standing and expected part" of modern-day sporting events and is "encouraged by the teams, the players, [and] the cheerleaders," how far does the right to engage in this expression go (Wasserman, 2006, p. 526)? Current application of the First Amendment in sport is seen in cases involving athletes criticizing coaches via social media, fans being ejected from stadiums for wearing T-shirts or holding up signs with offensive messages, and the ongoing debate about the role of prayer in sport.

Freedom of Religion

Freedom of religion is analyzed under the Establishment and Free Exercise of Religion Clauses. The Establishment Clause separates church and state. For example, the United States Supreme Court decision *Santa Fe v. Doe, et al.* (2000) bans prayer at public high school events, including football games. In 1992, the United States Supreme Court found that conducting a religious exercise as part of a high school graduation ceremony was a violation of the First Amendment (*Lee v. Weisman,* 1992). The Court held that "the Constitution forbids the state to exact religious conformity from a student as the price of attending her own high school graduation" (2660).

In the *Santa Fe* case, current and former students at a Texas public high school complained to school administration about the prayer before varsity football games. In response to the complaint, the school adopted a policy of holding a student election to determine whether an "invocation should be delivered at games" (308). If the results of the election approved the invocation, a second vote was to be held to select the person to give the invocation. The election results favored giving an invocation and a student was elected to give the invocation. Current and former students then filed another complaint. Eventually, the Fifth Circuit held that "permitting student-led, student-initiated prayer at football games violated the Establishment Clause" (310). The school district petitioned for review by the U.S. Supreme Court. Their argument was that the facts of the current situation were distinguishable from the prayer policy in the *Lee* case. Graduation was a requirement of all students; a student's attendance at a football game was elective. The Court, however, pointed out that football games were mandatory for some students, including band members and cheerleaders. The Supreme Court found that the delivery of an invocation prior to home football games violated the establishment of religion clause of the First Amendment.

Good News Club v. Milford (2001) was an example of the Free Exercise of Religion Clause. A New York school district opened its facilities for the public's use, specifically for education, recreation, and the welfare of the community. The policy stated that the schools were not to be used for religious purposes. The Good News Club, a private Christian organization for children between the ages of 6 and 12, requested permission to use the school facilities. The request was denied under the school district's public use policy. The Good News Club brought suit, arguing "that denial of the club's request violated the club's free speech rights under the Federal Constitution's First Amendment" (99).

The district court granted the Good News Club's request for a preliminary injunction. The school district could not enforce its public use policy. The Good News Club subsequently held meetings in the school. The district court then decided that exclusion of the club was permissible. The club appealed the decision. The United States Supreme Court reversed, holding that

(1) the district's exclusion of the club constituted viewpoint discrimination in violation of the First Amendment's free speech guarantee, for (a) any group that promoted the moral and character development of children was eligible to use the school building, (b) the club's activities did not constitute mere religious worship that was divorced from any teaching of moral values, (c) there was no reason to treat the club's use of religion as something other than a viewpoint merely because of any evangelical message that the club conveyed, and (d) for purposes of the free speech guarantee, there was no logical difference in kind between the club's invocation of Christianity and the invocation of teamwork, loyalty, or patriotism by other associations to provide a foundation for such associations' lessons; and

(2) the free speech violation was not justified by the district's concern that permitting the club's activities would violate the First Amendment's establishment of religion clause. (99)

Subsequent cases involving freedom of religion have focused on displaying a Ten Commandments monument on the grounds of the Texas state capitol (*Van Orden v. Perry*, 2005) and the required recitation of the Pledge of Allegiance by a school student (*Elk Grove Unified School District and Gordon v. Nedow*, 2004). While not dealing directly with sport, these cases have application and are analogous to the use of religious symbols or pledges in or around sporting events and at other public forums. In *Van Orden* (2005), plaintiffs sued for a declaration finding that the Ten Commandments monument violated the Establishment Clause and an injunction to have it removed. The district court, in denying declaratory and injunctive relief, concluded that the monument did not contravene the establishment of religion clause, because the state had a valid secular purpose in recognizing and commending the donating organization's efforts to reduce juvenile delinquency, and a reasonable observer would not conclude that the monument conveyed a message that the state was seeking to endorse religion. The United States Court of Appeals for the Fifth Circuit affirmed, finding that the monument did not contravene the Establishment Clause. The Supreme Court found that (1) the establishment of religion clause did not bar any and all governmental preference for religion over irreligion; (2) the *Lemon* test was not useful in dealing with the sort of monument in question; (3) although the Ten Commandments had religious significance, they also had an undeniable historical meaning; and (4) the placement of the Ten Commandments monument on the capitol grounds was a far more passive use of those texts than the posting of the Ten Commandments in public schoolrooms, a practice that the Supreme Court had found to have an improper and plainly religious purpose.

Elk Grove Unified School District and Gordon v. Nedow (2004) involved a public school district in California that required each elementary school class to recite daily the Pledge of Allegiance. The father of one of the students filed suit, alleging that the school district's policy requiring the recitation of the Pledge violated the Establishment and Free Exercise Clauses of the First Amendment. The district court dismissed the complaint. However, the United States Court of Appeals for the Ninth Circuit concluded that the father had standing as a parent to challenge a practice that allegedly interfered with his right to direct his child's religious education, and the district's policy violated the establishment of religion clause.

On appeal before the Supreme Court, it was determined that the father lacked standing to bring the case; however, a concurring opinion by Justices William Rehnquist and Sandra Day O'Connor ruled that the school district's Pledge of Allegiance policy did not violate the establishment of religion clause because reciting the Pledge, or listening to others recite it, was a patriotic exercise, not a religious one (99). Justice Clarence Thomas, in a concurring opinion, found the establishment of religion clause was a federalism provision intended to prevent Congress from interfering with state establishments. Thus, it made little sense to incorporate the establishment of religion clause into the Constitution's Fourteenth Amendment so as to be applied against the states. Justice Thomas felt that the school district's policy did not infringe any religious liberty right that would arise from incorporation of the establishment of religion clause; and the Pledge policy did not infringe the Free Exercise of Religion Clause (100). It is easy to see how cases involving team prayer before sporting events could raise similar constitutional challenges as the cases discussed in this chapter.

Freedom of Speech

Freedom of speech is the freedom to speak, remain silent, discuss with others, advocate, and communicate ideas. Freedom of speech does not protect speech that is libelous, slanderous, lewd, or obscene. The possibility of creating a breach of peace or advocating the commission of a crime is also not protected.

Students, athletes, teachers, government employees, and employees of private industry possess all First Amendment rights available to all citizens. Despite these general First Amendment rights, professionals in education are expected to maintain an atmosphere in which all persons can learn at their maximum potential. Sometimes, the First Amendment is perceived to be in conflict with the mandate to maintain the learning environment so that all can achieve at maximum potential.

Speech may be verbal or expressive (e.g., protests and demonstrations). In order to determine whether speech merits protection, the courts will examine and balance the following factors:

- The subject of the speech;
- To whom it was directed;
- The forum in which it occurred; and
- The manner of delivery.

Symbolic gestures have been used to influence and alert the public to new and oftentimes controversial ideas. *Tinker v. Des Moines School District* (1969), the case most often cited in symbolic protest, involved three students who wore black armbands in public protest of the government's participation in the Vietnam War. School authorities, knowledgeable on the proposed armband protest, established a school policy on armbands a few days prior to the event.

The students were asked to remove their black armbands, but they refused. They were suspended from school and told not to return until the armbands were removed. The students sought injunctive relief from the courts but were unsuccessful in their quest. The United States District Court "upheld the constitutionality of the school authority's action on the grounds that it was reasonable in order to prevent disturbance of school discipline" (505). The United States Court of Appeals for the Eighth Circuit reversed and remanded the lower court's decision, stating that the Constitution of the United States did not permit state officials to deny a form of expression which "neither interrupted school activities nor sought to intrude in the school affairs or the lives of others" (514). The court saw the activity as one to stimulate discussion outside of the classroom rather than to disrupt the learning environment.

A more recent case raising similar student speech issues is *Morse v. Frederick* (2007). In 2002, Frederick was a high school student who attended a school-supervised and school-sanctioned event to watch the Olympic Torch Relay as it passed by their high school in Juneau, Alaska, on its way to the Winter Games in Salt Lake City. Students were allowed to watch the Torch Relay on both sides of the street as it passed by, under the supervision of teachers and school administrators. Growing impatient waiting for the torch to pass by, some students became rambunctious, throwing plastic cola bottles and snowballs and scuffling with their classmates (397). As the torchbearers and camera crews passed by, Frederick and his friends unfurled a 14-foot banner bearing the phrase "BONG HiTS 4 JESUS" (397). Upon seeing the sign from the other side of the street which was also easily readable to other students, school principal Morse crossed the street and demanded that the banner be taken down (398). Everyone but Frederick complied. Principal Morse confiscated the banner and told Frederick to report to her office, where she suspended him for 10 days, later explaining that she told Frederick to take the banner down because she thought it encouraged illegal drug use (398). This violated an established school board policy which "specifically prohibits any assembly or public expression that ... advocates the use of substances that are illegal to minors" (398). Frederick appealed his suspension to the school superintendent, who reduced it to 8 days, finding that Frederick "was not disciplined because the principal of the school 'disagreed' with his message, but because his speech appeared to advocate the use of illegal drugs" (398).

Frederick then filed suit under 42 USC §1983, alleging that the school board and Morse had violated his First Amendment rights (398). The district court granted summary judgment for the school board and Morse, ruling they were entitled to qualified immunity and finding that their actions did not violate Frederick's First Amendment right of free speech. The district court noted that "Morse had the authority, if not the obligation, to stop such messages at a school-sanctioned activity" (App. to Pet. for Cert., 37a).

On appeal, the Ninth Circuit reversed the district court's decision, finding that even though Frederick "acted during a 'school-authorized activit[y],' and 'proceed[ing] on the basis that the banner expressed a positive sentiment about marijuana use,'" Frederick's First Amendment rights were violated "because the school punished Frederick without demonstrating that his speech gave rise to a 'risk of substantial disruption'" (2006, 1118, 1121–1123). Furthermore, the court held that "Frederick's right to display his banner was so 'clearly established' that a reasonable principal in Morse's position would have understood that her actions were unconstitutional, and that Morse was therefore not entitled to qualified immunity" (1123–1125). Morse and the school district then petitioned the U.S. Supreme Court to hear the case.

The U.S. Supreme Court granted certiorari on two questions: whether Frederick had a First Amendment right to wield his banner, and, if so, whether that right was so clearly established that the principal may be held liable for damages. The Supreme Court found this was a school speech case, agreeing with the superintendent that the school could supervise students' behavior at a school-sanctioned activity. While Frederick himself claimed "that the words were just nonsense meant to attract television cameras," the high court found that the principal thought that the sign would be widely understood by students and others as referring to marijuana use and that it violated the policy against promoting illegal drug use. As phrased by the Court, "The question thus becomes whether a principal may, consistent with the First Amendment, restrict student speech at a school event, when that speech is reasonably viewed as promoting illegal drug use. We hold that she may" (403). As noted by the Court in *Morse*, "*Tinker* held that student expression may not be suppressed unless school officials reasonably conclude that it will 'materially and substantially disrupt the work and discipline of the school'" (*Morse*, 2007, 403 citing *Tinker*, 1969, 513). While students "do not shed their constitutional rights to freedom of speech or expression at the schoolhouse gate," the First Amendment rights of students must be applied in light of the special characteristics of the school environment (*Tinker*, 506). Thus, consistent with First Amendment principles, the Court held that "schools may take steps to safeguard those entrusted to their care from speech that can reasonably be regarded as encouraging illegal drug use" (*Morse*, 396). The Court therefore concluded "that the school officials in this case did not violate the First Amendment by confiscating the pro-drug banner and suspending the student responsible for it" (396).

Similar to the educational disruption arguments in *Frederick v. Morse,* sport participants and groups, including Olympic athletes, have occasionally engaged in symbolic protest. The courts have permitted such gestures, denying them only when the actions were thought to disrupt the peace or threaten the safety of society.

More frequently occurring instances involving free speech issues in sport include fans wearing T-shirts or holding signs, flags, or banners that contain or convey messages that may be perceived as offensive to some fans, particularly children. These cases, referred to as forms of "cheering speech" by Wasserman (2006), raise fundamental First Amendment issues. "Cheering speech can be oral, symbolic, or written on signs, banners, clothing, and body parts. It can be in good taste or bad, clean or profane, provocative, clever, or otherwise. And it will be loud and obvious" (Wasserman, 2006, p. 528).

These cases are often resolved with the sport facility or athletic department deciding to deny or stop the speech (in the form of a T-shirt, sign, or banner), and typically run afoul of well-established First Amendment case law. Calvert and Richards (2004) analyzed one of the more controversial instances of "cheering speech," which occurred in 2004 at the University of Maryland during the men's basketball game between Maryland and Duke. "Maryland fans chanted and wore T-shirts reading 'F--- Duke' and directed homophobic epithets at Duke's star player" (Calvert & Richards, 2004, p. 2). In reviewing the incident, Maryland officials considered implementing regulation of student cheering speech, and the NCAA responded that screaming obscenities at players was not acceptable (Wasserman, 2006). Furthermore, the university sought the counsel of the Maryland Attorney General, who advised the school that a carefully drafted fan code of conduct would be constitutionally permissible (Wasserman, 2006). Cheering speech is not isolated to collegiate sports by individual fans' crazy signs or shirts. It occurs at all levels of sport, and determinations that regulate speech must be made carefully.

Cheering speech can also occur on sport merchandise produced for entire fan bases to purchase and can also raise trademark infringement concerns. A T-shirt with the phrase "Muck Fizzou" sold by a Kansas retailer, Joe-College.com, containing the same shade of blue as the school colors of Missouri's rival, the University of Kansas, resulted in a lawsuit by the University of Kansas against the retailer (Nystrom, 2007). Plaintiffs alleged the shirts could cause consumers to believe that the shirts were licensed by the University of Kansas to poke fun at their rivals. University of Kansas filed suit alleging that Joe-College.com was infringing the university's trademarks (Nystrom, 2007). The school's athletic director also added that the messages on the shirts were in poor taste and cast the school in a bad light. The retailer cited the First Amendment right of free speech as a defense to trademark infringement and asserted that signs in his store make clear that the merchandise is not licensed by the University of Kansas, in effect a disclaimer. The case resulted in a jury verdict in 2008 for the university (Diepenbrock, 2009). In 2009, the judge ordered Joe-College.com to pay $667,507 in attorneys' fees and costs, which would essentially put the company out of business (Diepenbrock, 2009). The recurring theme in these cases is that many were resolved with the sport organization or university responding with a heavy-handed approach to suppress the speech that, in effect, sanctioned them for speaking (Grady & Moorman, 2008). This approach suggests that sport organizations may resort to using the threat of a lawsuit to stop speech they find offensive or against their commercial interests.

Freedom of the Press

Freedom of the press includes freedom to write, draw, and create models. Ideas may be published and conveyed. Absolute freedom of thought and belief is guaranteed under the First Amendment. In *Marcum v. Dahl* (1981), female basketball players at the University of Oklahoma stated to the press that, if the current coach was hired for the following year, they would not play. Shortly after the press released the statement, the athletes' scholarships were not renewed. The athletes filed suit, stating that their First Amendment free speech rights had been violated in the non-renewal of their scholarships. The court concluded "that the plaintiffs' First Amendment rights were not violated by the defendants' refusal to renew the plaintiffs' athletic scholarships" (485). A person's freedom of speech and of press depends upon the circumstances under which the freedoms are used; certain language is not protected.

Defamation

Defamation is the "holding up of a person to ridicule, scorn or contempt in a respectable and considerable part of the community.... A communication is defamatory if it tends to do harm to the reputation of another as to lower him in the estimation of the community or to deter third persons from associating or dealing with him" (*Black's Law Dictionary,* n.d.). Defamation may be of a living person, a corporation or business, or an association. Defamation does not exist unless the statements are communicated to a third person. If the communication is oral (i.e., spoken), it is slander; if the communication is in print, it is libel. To establish liability for defamation, the following elements must be present:

- a defamatory statement concerning another must be made;
- the statement must be published to a third person (publication can be in writing, spoken to the person, or overheard by the third party);
- the person publishing the statement must intend to publish the statement (there is no need of intention to hurt someone); and
- damage must occur.

The status of a person is a factor in defamation. Whether the person is widely known or known only by a few is a factor in what can be said about a person in a public forum, or what can be revealed about the same individual to a third party. People are classified into two categories: public figures/officials and private individuals. Public figures are people known to the community. Athletes, sports professionals, and administrators may be public figures. Private persons are those not widely known in the community. The decision of whether a person is a public figure or a private person will be determined by the judge and/or jury. A public figure is defamed only when the defamatory statement is false. A private individual is defamed whether the defamatory statement is true or false.

The "public figure"—"private individual" comparison is related to the individual's right to maintain his/her reputation and the public's interest in preserving free speech. A need exists for the public to be informed about its leaders, but at the same time, an individual's personal life should be secure. In *New York Times Co. v. Sullivan* (1964), the court, under the First Amendment, permitted a statement that was true to be made against a public official and public figure.

Private individuals continue to have a cause of action under defamation, even though the statement may be true. A 1974 case, *Gertz v. Robert Welch, Inc.,* extended the idea of a public figure from one who was known by all, to one who voluntarily injected oneself or was drawn into a particular controversy. As a result of being drawn into the controversy, one becomes a public figure for a limited period of time or for a range of issues (345).

Defenses to defamation are truth and privilege. The defendant must establish that what was said was the truth. A defendant may be excused under privilege if his/her conduct was an act in furtherance of some socially useful interest. Privilege is a difficult element to establish. Like truth, it must be established by the defendant.

Damages in defamation may be compensatory and punitive. They may be a result of the damage to one's business or reputation (compensatory) or they may involve punitive damage (awarded to discourage similar actions on the part of the plaintiff or others).

A very public sport-related defamation case was *Curtis Publishing v. Butts* (1967). Curtis Publishing, publisher of the *Saturday Evening Post,* printed an article that alleged Butts—who at the time was the athletic director at the University of Georgia—was involved in fixing a football game between Georgia and the University of Alabama. Butts, a former football coach at Georgia, was a well-known and respected person, and at the time of the defamation was a candidate for a position with a professional team.

> George Burnett, an Atlanta insurance salesman, had accidentally overheard, because of electronic error, a telephone conversation between Butts and the head coach of the University of Alabama, Paul Bryant, which took place approximately one week prior to the game. Burnett was said to have listened while "Butts outlined Georgia's offensive plays … and told … how Georgia planned to defend…. Butts mentioned both players and plays by name." The readers were told that Burnett had made notes of the conversation, and specific examples of the divulged secrets were set out. (136)

The article went on to discuss the game and the players' reactions to the game, concluding that "the Georgia players, their moves analyzed and forecast like those of rats in a maze, took a frightful physical beating" and said that the players and other sideline observers were aware that Alabama was privy to Georgia's secrets. It set out the series of events commencing with Burnett's later presentation of his notes to the Georgia head coach, Johnny Griffith, and culminating in Butts's resignation from the university's athletic affairs for health and business reasons (136–137). In the football game, Georgia was sorely defeated by Alabama.

Butts brought a libel action in federal court for $5 million in compensatory and $5 million in punitive damages. All parties involved conceded that Butts was a public figure. Curtis Publishing Company's only defense was substantial truth. The evidence showed that Butts and the Alabama coach had discussed football, but failed to prove that what had been discussed would have been of value to the Alabama coach. Butts's contention was that the magazine's investigative reporting was reckless and wanton misconduct. The jury returned a verdict of $60,000 in general damages and $3 million in punitive damages. The latter was later reduced to $460,000.

Of particular importance in the *Curtis* case was the fact that what might have appeared as "kidding" could be taken seriously and completely misconstrued by another. One responsible for reporting information must be diligent in checking the accuracy and reliability of all sources used.

Hunter, an orthopedic surgeon and consultant to the University of Minnesota football program, sued Sid Hartman, a sportswriter, for comments made by the writer in his news column and radio show. Hunter had been interviewed on the topic of Lou Holtz's handling of injured athletes. Hunter's statements were specific and negative. Hartman reviewed Hunter's statements but attributed them to the fact that Holtz had replaced Hunter after his first year at Minnesota. The defamatory statement was:

> And, uh, we were talking last night about the great Doctor Hunter, yesterday noon, talking about the great Doctor Hunter who ripped Lou Holtz for firing him. We were talking at lunch at the Marriott Hotel and Joe said in 1982 Mr. Hunter operated on 12 players. Hardly any of them came back to play at all. Some of them never played. Some of them played at, uh, about half their ability. So there was a good reason, Mr. Hunter, why Mr. Holtz discharged ya. (*Hunter v. Hartman,* 1996, 702)

The court noted that "to show actual malice, a defamation plaintiff must demonstrate by clear and convincing evidence that the defendant made defamatory statements either knowing the statements were false or acting recklessly with regard to whether the statements were true" (703). The trial court granted summary judgment for Hartman. The Court of Appeals of Minnesota affirmed the lower court's decision, saying that under the public figure analysis, the plaintiff had to show malice and that, in this instance, he had failed to do so.

In *Sprewell v. NYP Holdings* (2007), plaintiff Latrell Sprewell, a high-profile professional basketball player formerly with the New York Knicks, claimed that he was libeled by statements in articles by sports writer Berman. The articles regarding the cause of Sprewell's hand injury were published in *The New York Post* and were based, in part, on information provided by confidential sources. It was undisputed that at some point in September 2002, Sprewell sustained a fracture to the fifth metacarpal bone on his right (shooting) hand while on his boat at a marina in Milwaukee. He did not inform the Knicks of the injury until he arrived at the team's practice facility on September

30. Berman wrote an article describing the injury and the fact that the plaintiff had not reported it sooner. Berman, who accompanied the team to its training camp, tried unsuccessfully to contact Sprewell's agent, Gist, to inquire about the cause of the injury.

Marvet Britto, Sprewell's publicist, told Berman that Sprewell himself had "no clue" how he had injured his hand, but noted that Sprewell lived and worked out on his boat all summer. Berman reported that conversation in another article. Berman received a telephone call from a sportscaster for a New York cable channel, who stated that he had suffered an injury similar to the plaintiff's as a result of punching a pole on a basketball court in anger and that such an injury is commonly referred to as a "boxer's fracture." Berman then contacted two physician hand specialists, who explained that boxer's fractures are "caused by a punch, usually by punching a hard object like a wall or a pole" (18). Gist, returning Berman's earlier telephone messages, related that plaintiff had told him the fracture occurred while "frantically pulling on a rope" to gain control of his boat in rough waters. *The New York Post's* first two editions of October 4 ran Berman's article recounting those details and the fact that the team's general manager had been "peppered with questions regarding how Sprewell broke his pinkie and was even asked if he may have been in a fight" (18).

The court found that, assuming that Berman's statements regarding how the player injured his hand and his alleged attempt to cover up the incident were false, the news corporation and the writer were entitled to summary judgment. The information was not reported as incontrovertible fact, but rather cautioned the reader that it was based on two confidential witnesses and was denied by the player. The record demonstrated that the writer subjectively believed the sources, whose partial description of the interior of the player's boat provided additional indicia of reliability. The writer's investigative efforts demonstrated that the writer did not deliberately fail to seek confirmatory information or otherwise act with reckless disregard for the truth. Thus, the player had not presented any evidence to raise a triable issue of fact concerning actual malice, let alone sufficient evidence to establish actual malice by clear and convincing evidence.

Invasion of Privacy

Invasion of privacy is closely related to the Fourth Amendment's search and seizure clause. It is often found in drug testing and the reporting of suspicion of drug use. The government's interest in the drug testing of athletes is the athletes' health and the maintenance of a level playing field or the natural competitive qualities of the performers. The athletes' interests are in maintaining their privacy. Invasion of privacy, in violation of the First Amendment, has been raised in the context of pat-down searches conducted as a condition of entry to sporting events.

While balanced against the overall interest in safety of the public at large, individual legal challenges to the routinely used practice of pat-down searches persist. One high-profile case receiving much media attention was *Sheehan v. San Francisco 49ers, Ltd.* (2009). The case was brought by two season ticket holders challenging the constitutionality of the team's implementation of a league policy requiring all fans at the team's home games to submit to a pat-down search before entering the stadium. The season ticket holders argued that the California state constitution's guarantee of privacy was violated by the pat-down searches. The court found that, "presumably, the league, and ultimately the team adopted the patdown policy to enhance spectator safety," but the court could not judge the reasonableness of the policy under the circumstances because the record did not establish the circumstances of, or the reasons for, the policy (992). Furthermore, the team had not yet given any explanation or justification for the policy.

The court provided some interesting guidance in approaching the constitutionality of actions in cases such as these:

> [I]n reviewing a private entertainment venue's security arrangements that implicate the state constitutional right of privacy, the court does not decide whether every measure is necessary, merely whether the policy is reasonable. The state constitutional right of privacy does not grant courts a roving commission to second-guess security decisions at private entertainment events or to micromanage interactions between private parties.... Private entities that present entertainment events, like the 49ers, necessarily retain primary responsibility for determining what security measures are appropriate to ensure the safety of their patrons, subject, when those security measures substantially infringe on a privacy interest, to judicial review for reasonableness. (480)

A related pat-down case claiming a Fourth Amendment violation was *Johnston v. Tampa Sports Authority* (2008). The pat-down searches were upheld on appeal in the Eleventh Circuit Court of Appeals using a consent theory rationale. *Johnston* involved an NFL pat-down search policy that was similar to but slightly different from the one in *Sheehan*. The search policy described in *Johnston* encompassed only "limited above-the-waist pat-down searches" (1323). In *Sheehan*, plaintiffs alleged that the screeners "ran their hands around the [plaintiffs'] backs and down the sides of their bodies and their legs" (996). The court in *Johnston* noted "the government had no role in formulating or mandating the pat-down policy. The policy exists solely because of the NFL's mandate" (1329). "Because the condition for entry was imposed by a private party, Johnston was not forced by the government to choose between his constitutional rights and obtaining a benefit to which he was entitled" (1329). The court ultimately held that, considering the totality of the circumstances, Johnston voluntarily consented to the pat-down searches each time he attended a game.

FOURTH AMENDMENT

The Fourth Amendment to the Constitution states that the "right of the people to be secure in their persons, houses, papers, and effects, against unreasonable searches and seizures, shall not be violated, and no warrants shall issue, but upon probable cause, supported by oath or affirmation, and particularly describing the place to be searched, and the person to be seized."

The system for analyzing Fourth Amendment violations is the same as the system used in analyzing First Amendment facts: balancing of the participant's interest in privacy against the agency's right to maintain order in an environment in which others can safely participate. In order to establish or maintain order, it may be necessary to suspend or discipline a participant; however, valid evidence must be obtained before a complaint can be filed.

Searches

In *New Jersey v. T. L. O.* (1985), a case involving teenage students who lied about smoking in a school bathroom, the United States Supreme Court established that searches could be conducted by persons other than law enforcement officers. The ruling stated that the "Fourth Amendment is applicable to the activities of civil as well as criminal authorities" (740). The Court also attempted to establish a standard that could be used to govern school searches. The question of balance in this situation was identified as an analysis of the individual's expectation of privacy and personal security versus the government's need for an effective method of dealing with breaches of order (741). In this case, order meant to maintain an environment in which learning can occur.

The Court noted that the school setting required restrictions on searches different from those needed by other public authorities.

> The warrant requirement, in particular, is unsuited to the school environment; requiring a teacher to obtain a warrant before searching a child suspected of an infraction of school rules would unduly interfere with the maintenance of the swift and informal disciplinary procedures needed in the schools.

> The legality of a search of a student should depend simply on the reasonableness, under the circumstances, of the search. Determining the reasonableness of any search involves a twofold inquiry: first, one must consider "whether the ... action was justified at its inception." Second, one must determine whether the search as actually conducted was reasonably related in scope to the circumstances which justified the interference in the first place. (743–744)

In *Gruenke v. Seip* (2000), the court was faced with issues related to both the First and Fourth Amendments. A swim coach suspected one of his swimmers of being pregnant and required her to take a pregnancy test. She and her mother sued, claiming that the requirement of a pregnancy test was an illegal search under her Fourth Amendment rights, interfered with her right to familial privacy, and violated her First Amendment free speech and association rights. Swim team members harassed Gruenke about taking a pregnancy test. Then, they ostracized her after she was found to be pregnant. Medical authorities ruled that swimming competition would not be detrimental to a pregnant person.

The District Court granted the coach immunity. Gruenke then appealed. The United States Court of Appeals for the Third Circuit had subject matter jurisdiction over Gruenke's Section 1983 claims. Section 1983:

Imposes civil liability upon any person who, acting under the color of state law, deprives another individual of any rights, privileges, or immunities secured by the Constitution or laws of the United States. This section does not create any new substantive rights but instead provides a remedy for the violation of a federal constitutional or statutory right....

In a typical 1983 action, a court must initially determine whether the plaintiff has even alleged the deprivation of a right that either federal law or the Constitution protects....

If the plaintiff's allegations meet this threshold, we must next determine whether, as a legal matter, the right that the defendant's conduct allegedly violates was a clearly established one, about which a reasonable person would have known. If so, then the defendant is not entitled to qualified immunity. If, in contrast, the plaintiff's allegations fail to satisfy either inquiry, then the defendant is entitled to summary judgment. Until the question of qualified immunity is addressed, a court cannot reach the underlying merits of the case.

It is not sufficient that the right at issue be clearly established as a general matter. Rather, the question is whether a reasonable public official would know that his or her specific conduct violated clearly established rights.

Under a Fourth Amendment analysis, the court held that the swimming coach was not entitled to qualified immunity from the Fourth Amendment, a Section 1983 claim, because the coach should have known that his conduct would violate a clearly established right. The fact that the swim coach, without a medical background, had forced the swimmer to take a pregnancy test was the issue. "His responsibilities can be reasonably construed to include activities related to teaching and training. They cannot be extended to requiring a pregnancy test. Moreover, a reasonable swim coach would recognize that his student swimmer's condition was not suitable for public speculation. He would have exercised some discretion in how he handled the problem" (302). Thus, the court found the swimmer's Fourth Amendment rights were violated.

Drug Testing

Drug testing of athletes continues to be a popular deterrent mechanism utilized in professional, collegiate, and high school sports. Not only can drug use by athletes result in serious health problems, but organizers of athletic events are also interested in maintaining a level playing field or avoiding an unfair advantage to athletes on performance-enhancing drugs. Court decisions involving drug testing programs in industry find the courts upholding pre-employment testing, while random testing has not been upheld. For tests to be upheld among veteran employees, there has to be reason to believe that the employee is on drugs.

Olympic and intercollegiate athletes have challenged the standards used in drug testing, league rules, and university policies in the courts. The classic case of Butch

Reynolds is one of those tests. Reynolds, a world-class runner, was randomly tested for drugs in August 1990 by the International Amateur Athletic Federation (IAAF) following a meet in Monte Carlo. He was suspended from competition for two years, including the 1992 Olympics, for allegedly testing positive for the anabolic steroid Nandrolone. Reynolds appealed his suspension. When he was unable to obtain the information needed to prepare for the appeal hearing, he filed suit to stop The Athletic Congress (TAC) and IAAF from conducting the hearing. Reynolds's evidence was that a similar test, taken seven days later, had no trace of Nandrolone. He concluded that the reported results of the first test had been an error. The court, in its decision to dismiss the case, ruled that Reynolds had failed to use the sport's official appeal processes before going to court.

Reynolds then participated in an arbitration governed by the Amateur Sports Act and the United States Olympic Committee (USOC) Constitution. The arbitrator found that there was strong evidence that the urine sample did not belong to Reynolds. The IAAF refused to accept the arbitrator's decision, saying that the arbitration had not been conducted under international rules. Reynolds appealed the IAAF decision using the procedure required by the IAAF—an appeal to The Athletic Congress (TAC). TAC made the same decision—that there was strong evidence that the urine did not belong to Reynolds. The IAAF again refused to accept the decision even though it was made according to its governing rules. The international sport governing body conducted its own arbitration in London in May of 1992. The IAAF found the drug test to be valid and the federation upheld the two-year competition suspension.

Reynolds filed an action against IAAF in the Southern District of Ohio requesting a temporary restraining order allowing him to compete in the Olympics and to collect money damages. The IAAF refused to appear. The district court, after establishing jurisdiction over the IAAF, issued a temporary restraining order allowing Reynolds to prepare for the Olympic team; this was followed by a preliminary injunction permitting Reynolds to participate in the Olympic trials.

On the day of the above decision, TAC—an organization that no longer supported Reynolds—asked for and was granted a "stay" of the court's decision. Reynolds was stopped from entering the Olympic trials. The next morning Reynolds filed and was granted an emergency motion with the United States Supreme Court asking that the district court "stay" be vacated. Now, Reynolds could compete in the Olympic trials.

The IAAF, aware of the court's decision, ruled that athletes who competed with Reynolds in the United States trials would be barred from the Olympics. TAC filed an application to the Supreme Court barring Reynolds from competing. The application was denied and Reynolds was allowed to compete in the trials. He made the team as an alternate for the 400-meter relay team. The IAAF removed Reynolds from the team roster.

Reynolds filed a supplemental complaint to the district court regarding his elimination from the team. Neither the IAAF nor TAC responded or appeared for the proceedings. Reynolds was awarded $27,356,008. The award included treble punitive damages. In February of 1993, Reynolds began garnishment proceedings against four corporations with connections to the IAAF to obtain the damage award. He also brought a new cause of action against the federation. This time, the Sixth Circuit of Appeals decided that it did not have jurisdiction (authority) over the IAAF. As a result of the Sixth Circuit's decision, the judgment of the district court (for Reynolds, with money damage) was reversed and remanded.

Mary Decker Slaney, a world-class runner accused of a drug doping offense in the 1996 national trials for the Atlantic Olympics, faced a series of confusing decisions similar to Reynolds's experience. Her urine sample was tested for prohibited substances including exogenous testosterone. The court reported:

> Because current technology cannot detect the presence of prohibited testosterone in the body, testing programs measure the ratio of testosterone to epitestosterone ("T/E") in the body. This test, referred to as the T/E test, assumes that an ordinary T/E ratio in humans is one to one, and thus any ratio of above six to one is consistent with "blood doping." The ratio was established at six to one in order to account for non-doping factors that might cause elevated ratios in female athletes. Factors which may influence T/E ratio include an individual changing birth control pills, age, menstrual cycle, bacterial contamination of the urine sample, and alcohol use [Slaney tested significantly higher than the accepted ratio].
>
> Slaney claimed that her elevated level was the result of (1) her menstrual cycle, and (2) her changing of birth control pills. Furthermore, Slaney posited that there was no scientific validity to the hypothesis that a T/E ratio above six to one was not normal for female athletes. Nonetheless ... the IAAF adopted the investigating doctor's recommendation and found Slaney's specimen positive for the prohibited substance testosterone. (586)

The IAAF suspended Slaney just prior to the National Track and Field Championships. The federation also involved the contamination rule used earlier in *Reynolds,* "whereby anyone who competed with a suspended athlete would themselves be suspended." (587)

> The Hearing Board, unpersuaded by the testimony of the IAAF investigating doctor, unanimously determined that no doping violation had occurred. Satisfied with the USATF Hearing Board's finding that the IAAF's rules regarding the use of the T/E ratio test were vague and inconsistent and the six to one ratio was not scientifically proven to be inconsistent with the normal ratio in humans, Slaney withdrew her complaint with the USOC....
>
> The IAAF was unsatisfied with the USATF Hearing Board's findings, and invoked arbitration ... the Tribunal issued an interlocutory decision

upholding the IAAF's interpretation of how to adjudicate a testosterone doping offense, and found that the rules were neither vague nor inconsistent. Thus, once the IAAF showed that Slaney had a T/E ratio greater than six to one, Slaney had to come forth and show by clear and convincing evidence that the elevated ratio was attributable to a pathological or physiological condition. Believing that it was scientifically impossible to prove by clear and convincing evidence that her high T/E ratio was due to pathological or physiological factors, Slaney withdrew from the arbitration ... [and] filed suit. (587)

Slaney filed suit in District Court, Southern District of Indiana, for an extensive list of contract, tort, RICO, and 18 USC 1961 claims. The District Court held that 1) the United Nations Convention on the Recognition and Enforcement of Foreign Arbitral Awards barred her claims against the IAAF, 2) the Amateur Sport Act gave the USOC exclusive right to determine eligibility disputes, and 3) her RICO claims were not adequate. Slaney appealed the ruling. The Court of Appeals for the Seventh Circuit, following a lengthy analysis of each claim, affirmed the decision of the district court. The most important point was that Slaney participated in a valid arbitration with the IAAF which, under the New York Convention, the court was obligated to recognize.

University of Colorado v. Derdeyn (1991, 1993, 1994) involved the constitutionality of the university's drug-testing policy. The policy, created to prepare athletes for NCAA mandatory drug testing, included a range of tests from random testing of athletes' urine samples obtained under direct visual observation to the use of rapid-eye-movement examinations. The trial court found that the program violated the students' Fourth Amendment and Colorado Constitution rights.

Following a bench trial, the court found that "obtaining a monitored urine sample is a substantial invasion of privacy" (*University of Colorado v. Derdeyn,* 1993). Also, "the trial court found that there is no evidence that the university instituted its program in response to any actual drug abuse problem among its student athletes. There is no evidence that any person has ever been injured in any way because of the use of drugs by a student athlete while practicing or playing a sport" (933). The trial court concluded that "CU's random urinalysis drug testing of athletes without individualized suspicion violates the Fourth Amendment's guarantee that persons shall be secure against unreasonable searches and seizures conducted by the government" (934). The trial court's decision was affirmed by the Colorado Supreme Court. The court stressed that when student consent was not voluntary, it could not be used to validate an unconstitutional search. The University of Colorado's petition to the United States Supreme Court for a writ of certiorari was denied in May of 1994 and its petition to the same court for rehearing was denied the following month.

In January of 1994, the Supreme Court of California held in *Hill v. National Collegiate Athletic Association (NCAA)* that the NCAA drug-testing program did not violate the plaintiff's constitutional right to privacy. Student privacy was balanced against the NCAA's need to maintain equitable competition and a safe competitive environment.

In contrast to *Derdeyn,* the NCAA discussed the problems of drug use in athletics. The *Hill* case was the result of a series of complaints in which Hill and earlier parties to the case were successful in the trial and appeals courts. The courts were required to examine the invasion of privacy issue that required the NCAA to prove a compelling state interest and the absence of an alternative method for accomplishing its goal.

The Supreme Court of California (1994) stated that persons choosing to be elite athletes agree to intrusions, including the reporting of medical information to trainers and coaches, dressing in same-sex locker rooms, and frequent physical examinations. Further, the court noted that the

> NCAA's rules contain elements designed to accomplish the purpose, including (1) advance notice to athletes of testing procedures and written consent to testing, (2) random selection of athletes actually engaged in competition, (3) monitored collection of a sample of a selected athlete's urine in order to avoid substitution or contamination, and (4) chain of custody, limited disclosure, and other procedures designed to safeguard the confidentiality of the testing process and its outcome. (637)

Acton v. Vernonia (1995) was the Supreme Court decision that upheld the right of public schools to randomly test athletes for drugs. Vernonia, a small Oregon town, had experienced an increase in drug use among young people; athletes appeared to be the leaders in the drug culture. In response to this change in drug use, the school created a policy. Acton's parents refused to consent to the drug-testing policy, thus denying him an opportunity to play football. His parents filed suit against the school district for declaratory and injunctive relief on the grounds that the Student Athletic Drug Policy violated their son's Fourth Amendment, Fourteenth Amendment, and Oregon Constitutional rights.

The District Court found for the school district; the United States Court of Appeals, Ninth Circuit reversed, finding that the policy violated the Fourth and Fourteenth Amendments and the Oregon Constitution. The Supreme Court of the United States granted certiorari. This court's emphasis was on the reasonableness of the search as it balanced the rights of the individual required to take the test with the interests of the government. The Supreme Court reversed the Ninth Circuit's decision and found the Vernonia School District's Student Athletic Drug Policy constitutional under the Fourth and Fourteenth Amendments. The Court found the search to be reasonable, as student-athletes have a "lesser privacy expectation with regard to medical examinations and procedures than the general population. Student athletes have even less of a legitimate privacy expectation, for an element of communal undress is inherent in athletic participation, and athletes are subject to preseason physical exams and rules regulating their conduct" (2387, 2388).

In the 2002 United States Supreme Court decision in *Board of Independent School District, No. 92 of Pottawatomie County, et al. v. Earls, et al.,* drug testing without suspicion was held not to violate the Fourth Amendment to the United States Constitution. The Student Activities Drug Testing Policy required all middle and high school students wishing to participate in an extracurricular activity to consent to urinalysis testing for drugs. Students' parents sued under 42 USC 1983. They claimed that the policy violated the Fourth Amendment. The District Court found for the School District; the Tenth Circuit reversed, stating that the policy violated the Fourth Amendment. It concluded "that before imposing a suspicionless drug testing program a school must demonstrate some identifiable drug abuse problem among a sufficient number of those tested, such that testing that group will actually redress its drug problem. The court then held that the School District failed to demonstrate such a problem among [the school district's] students participating in competitive extracurricular activities" (824).

The school district's certiorari to the United States Supreme Court was accepted. The Court used *Vernonia* as a model for a number of issues. In reversing the court of appeals' decision, the Supreme Court stated, "Within the limits of the Fourth Amendment, local school boards must assess the desirability of drug testing schoolchildren. In upholding the constitutionality of the Policy, we express no opinion as to its wisdom. Rather, we hold only that Tecumseh's Policy is a reasonable means of furthering the School District's important interest in preventing and deterring drug use among its schoolchildren" (749–750).

FOURTEENTH AMENDMENT: DUE PROCESS

Procedural due process is the opportunity to be heard. It is a system to assure people of fair treatment when a "life, liberty, or property" right is challenged. No right is to be taken prior to due process. The Fifth and Fourteenth Amendments to the United States Constitution guarantee life, liberty, and property rights. Federal rights are embedded in the Fifth Amendment; state rights are in the Fourteenth Amendment. While the "life" right is complex, it does not create the legal confusion that "liberty" and "property" rights create. "Liberty" rights are, for example, privileges essential to the pursuit of happiness and safe working conditions. "Property" rights include claims of entitlement, termination of benefits or status, and exclusion from state or federal opportunities without cause.

Professionals will be called upon to fashion due process systems such as club membership rights, as employment termination agreements, and for various other occasions. A hearing is usually part of the system. The system is to include the written charge or complaint and detailed reasons for the charge or complaint; adequate time for the defendants to prepare for a hearing and to retain representation; an opportunity for the defending party to present evidence and arguments, including witnesses; and ample time for each party to confront adverse witnesses. The hearing and decision should be made by an impartial decision maker with the ruling based on the evidence provided in the hearing. A clear and comprehensive statement giving the reasons for the decision is to be provided to the parties.

Tarkanian v. NCAA (1987, 1989, 1994), *NCAA v. Tarkanian* (1988, 1992, 1993, 1997), and *University of Nevada v. Tarkanian* (1979, 1994) involved a number of legal theories, including the Due Process Clause of the Fourteenth Amendment. Beginning in 1970, the National Collegiate Athletic Association (NCAA) orchestrated an investigation of the University of Nevada, Las Vegas. At the completion of the NCAA's first hearing, after naming the coach—Jerry Tarkanian—in 10 of the 38 violations, the association "directed UNLV to show cause why additional penalties should not be imposed against it if it does not suspend Tarkanian from involvement with the University's Intercollegiate Athletic Program for two years" (*Tarkanian v. NCAA*, 1987, 1347).

In September of 1977, UNLV suspended Tarkanian. After requesting and being granted an injunction, he returned to coaching. The court reversed the injunction, saying that Tarkanian should include the NCAA in his suit. Tarkanian then sued UNLV and the NCAA, arguing that he was suspended from his job without due process. The NCAA does not use a formal due process system in most of its investigations.

In 1987, the Supreme Court held that the NCAA had to use due process. The NCAA petitioned that court. The court reversed the ruling, declaring that the NCAA was not a state actor and thus not required to honor Tarkanian's due process rights. The case was remanded to the Nevada courts, as UNLV was the only agency that could discipline and/or suspend Tarkanian, who was a faculty member. Since 1992, Tarkanian has worked at collecting financial damages.

Fourteenth Amendment claims have also been raised in the school setting by students and parents of students who have been disciplined for some form of speech critical of the school or its personnel. In *J. S. v. Blue Mountain School District* (2011), a high school student was suspended for ten days for "creating, on a weekend and on her home computer, a MySpace 'profile' making fun of her principal, which contained adult language and sexually explicit content" (920).

The high school student and her parents sued the school district, claiming First Amendment free speech violations, unconstitutionally overbroad and vague policies, and violation of the parents' due process rights under the Fourteenth Amendment to raise their child in the manner that they saw fit. Specifically, they argued that, in disciplining J. S. for conduct that occurred in her parents' home during non-school hours, the school district interfered with their parental rights, and punishing the student for out-of-school speech was outside the district's authority.

Under *Tinker,* the court found the school district violated J. S.'s First Amendment free speech rights when it suspended her for creating the profile, citing the fact that "J. S. was suspended from school for speech that indisputably caused no substantial disruption in school and that could not reasonably have led school officials to forecast substantial disruption in school" (920). On the Fourteenth Amendment due process claims, J. S.'s parents alleged that the school district interfered with their ability to determine what out-of-school behavior warranted discipline and what form that discipline took (934). The court, however, found this was not an accurate description of the impact that the school district's actions had upon J. S.'s parents' ability to make decisions concerning their daughter's upbringing because the school district's actions in no way forced or prevented J. S.'s parents from reaching their own disciplinary decision, nor did its actions force her parents to approve or disapprove of her conduct (934). Further, there was no triggering of the parents' liberty interest due to the subject matter of the school district's involvement; a decision involving a child's use of social media on the Internet is not a "matter of the greatest importance" (934). The appellate court thus affirmed that the school district did not violate the parents' Fourteenth Amendment substantive due process rights to raise their child (920).

The decision in *Blue Mountain School District* raises several questions about how the boundaries of student speech, as delineated in *Tinker,* apply in the context of social media. Questions include whether, as a result of the decision, students have the right to make malicious comments about school personnel, so long as the speech takes place off campus (Bemiller & Trendafilova, 2011). Furthermore, the need for schools to create social media policies to apply to (and therefore regulate) comments made by students and student-athletes using social media will need to be explored as decisions involving First Amendment rights in the Internet age continue to be handed down.

SUMMARY

The First Amendment to the United States Constitution includes freedom of religion, freedom of speech, freedom of the press, and defamation. Freedom of religion separates church and state and prohibits the government from enacting laws that aid a church or religion. Freedom of speech is the freedom to speak, remain silent, discuss with others, advocate, and communicate ideas. Freedom of the press is the freedom to write, draw, and create models. Ideas can be published and conveyed. Defamation is influenced by the status of the person—whether he/she is a public figure or an ordinary person. Sport seems to have many cases in defamation; athletes and coaches meet the status of a public figure.

The Fourth Amendment of the Constitution of the United States covers searches and drug testing. It guarantees the rights of people to be secure in their persons and homes against unreasonable searches and seizures. As in the First Amendment, the system for analyzing violations is to balance the rights of the individual with the rights of society.

The Fourteenth Amendment (Due Process Clause) of the United States Constitution is the right of people to be treated fairly when a life, liberty, or property right is challenged. No right can be taken away without providing due process.

DISCUSSION QUESTIONS

1. Many of the student speech cases involved schoolchildren who were minors. Why must colleges and universities be cautious in trying to regulate speech by college students at sporting events? Why are the constitutional issues less of a concern when the speaker is a minor?

2. How can stadiums effectively balance the security needs to protect the general public against terrorism with the constitutional protections guaranteed to each citizen at sport venues in the United States?

ACTIVITIES

1. Locate and review the fan code of conduct policy for your college or university's stadium or arena. Now, locate a similar policy for the venue that hosts an NBA team's games. Are the policies similar? Do you think the policy sufficiently protects the rights of sports fans to "speak" during the event?

2. Locate news articles about the drug testing policies used at the most recent Olympic Games. Are these testing policies effective to ensure fair competition? Now, locate the NCAA policies about drug testing of student-athletes.

REFERENCES

Acton v. Vernonia School District, 66 F. 3d 217 (1995); 23 F. 3d 1514 (1994); 796 F. Supp. 1354 (1992).

Bemiller, J., & Trendafilova, S. (2011). Criticizing the coach, social media, and the First Amendment. *Sport Entertainment and Venues Tomorrow Conference:* Columbia, SC.

Board of Education of Independent School District No. 92 of Pottawatomie County, et al. v. Earls, et al., 536 U.S. 822; 122 S. Ct. 2559 (2002).

Calvert, C., & Richards, R. D. (2004). Fans and the First Amendment: Cheering and jeering in college sports. 4 *Va. Sports & Ent. L.J.* 1.

Curtis Publishing Co. v. Butts, 388 U.S. 130 (1967).

Diepenbrock, G. (2009, Oct. 9). Joe-College.com argues judge's ruling would mean end to T-shirt company. *KU Sports.* Retrieved from http://www2.kusports.com/news/2009/oct/09/joe-collegecom-argues-judges-ruling-would-mean-end/

Elk Grove Unified School District and Gordon v. Nedow, 542 U.S. 1 (2004).

Gertz v. Robert Welch, Inc., 418 U.S. 323, 94 S. Ct. 2997, 41 L. Ed. 2d 789 (1974).

Good News Club v. Milford Cent. Sch., 533 U.S. 98; 121 S. Ct. 2093 9 (2001).

Grady, J., McKelvey, S., & Clement, A. (2005). A new "Twist" for "The Home Run Guys?" An analysis of the right of publicity versus parody. 15 *J. Legal Aspects of Sport* 267.

Grady, J., & Moorman, A. M. (2008). "Muck Fizzou," "Vick 'em," & "I've been ejected!:" Emerging First Amendment issues in sport. *North American Society for Sport Management Conference:* Toronto, Canada.

Gruenke v. Seip, 225 F. 3d 290 (2000).

Hill v. NCAA, 865 P. 2d 633 (1994).

Hunter v. Hartman, 545 N. W. 2d 699 (1996).

J. S. v. Blue Mountain School District, 650 F. 3d 915 (2011).

Johnston v. Tampa Sports Authority, 530 F. 3d 1320 (2008).

Lee v. Weisman, 505 U.S. 577 (1992).

Marcum v. Dahl, 658 F. 2d 731 (1981).

Morse v. Frederick, 551 U.S. 393 (2007).

National Collegiate Athletic Association, et al. v. Tarkanian, et al., 939 P. 2d 1049 (1997); 10 F. 3d 633 (1993); 795 F. Supp. 1476 (1992); 484 U.S. 1058 (1988); 488 U.S. 179 (1998).

New Jersey v. T. L. O., 105 S. Ct. 733 (1985).

New York Times Co. v. Sullivan, 376 U.S. 254, 84 S. Ct. 710, 11 L Ed. 2d 686 (1964).

Nystrom, T. (2007, Aug. 30). Battle over unlicensed T-shirts proceeds. *The University Daily Kansan.* Retrieved from http://www.kansan.com/news/2007/aug/30/Joe_college/

Reynolds v. The Athletic Congress of the U.S.A., Inc., 23 F. 3d 1110 (1994); 841 F. Supp. 1444 (1992).

Santa Fe v. Doe, et al., 530 U.S. 290 (2000).

Sheehan v. San Francisco 49ers, Ltd., 45 Cal. 4th 992 (2009).

Slaney v. The International Amateur Athletic Federation, et al., 244 F. 3d 580 (2001).

Sprewell v. NYP Holdings, 43 A.D. 3d 16 (2007).

Tarkanian, et al. v. NCAA, 114 S. Ct. 1543 (1994); 105 Nev. 1049; 810 P. 2d 343 (1989); 741 P. 2d 1345 (1987).

Tinker v. Des Moines School District, 393 U.S. 503 (1969).

University of Colorado v. Derdeyn, 863 P. 2d 929 (1993); 832 P. 2d 1031 (1991); 114 S. Ct. 1646 (1994); petition for writ of certiorari denied; 61 USLW 3843 (June 20, 1994); petition to U.S. Supreme Court for rehearing denied.

University of Nevada, et al. v. Tarkanian, 879 P. 2d 1180 (1994); 95 Nev. 389; 594 P. 2d 1159 (1979).

Van Orden v. Perry, 545 U.S. 677 (2005).

Vernonia School District v. Acton, 515 U.S. 646; 115 S. Ct. 2386 (1995); 115 S. Ct. 1090 (1995); 513 U.S. 1013; 115 S. Ct. 571 (1994).

Wasserman, H. M. (2006). Fans, free expression, and the wide world of sports. *67 U. Pitt. L. Rev.* 525.

RECOMMENDED READING

Kaufman, C. J. (2009). Unsportsmanlike conduct: 15-yard penalty and loss of free speech in public university sports stadiums. *57 Kan. L. Rev.* 1235.

Klupinski, S. (2010). Getting past the schoolhouse gate: Rethinking student speech in the digital age. *71 Ohio St. L.J.* 611.

Miller, J. J., Wendt, J. T., & Young, P. C. (2010). Fourth Amendment considerations and application of risk management principles for pat-down searches at professional football games. *20 J. Legal Aspects of Sport* 107.

Miller, S. B. (2008). Morse v. Frederick: Did Bong Hits 4 Jesus slam the Tinker schoolhouse gates? *33 Okla. City U.L. Rev.* 879.

Otto, K. A., & Stippich, K. S. (2008). Revisiting Tarkanian: The entwinement and interdependence of the NCAA and state universities and colleges 20 years later. *18 J. Legal Aspects of Sport* 243.

5

Fourteenth Amendment and Title IX

OBJECTIVES

Upon completing this chapter you will:

1) know that constitutional law uses a balancing system that recognizes the rights of the individual in relation to the rights of society;

2) have become aware of the relationship between the Fourteenth Amendment to the United States Constitution, Equal Protection Clause, and Title IX;

3) understand the concept of equity by enrollment;

4) be aware of how the courts view retaliation under Title IX; and

5) be conversant with sexual harassment, hostile environment, and quid pro quo.

INTRODUCTION

Public schools served as the agencies for race integration in the 1970s; collegiate and scholastic athletics became the agencies for sex integration beginning in the 1990s and remain so today. A review of laws, legal theories, governing structures, and court decisions will enable the professional to understand the factors that influence today's gender equity court decisions. This chapter will also consider sexual harassment under Title IX and those cases involving athletes.

LAW AND LEGAL THEORY

Laws governing equity in athletics are the Equal Protection Clause of the Fourteenth Amendment to the United States Constitution, Title IX, the Civil Rights Restoration Act of 1987, the Civil Rights Act of 1991, the Equity in Athletics Disclosure Act, and the 2011 changes in the implementing guidelines of Title IX. Disparate treatment and disparate impact (equity by enrollment) are found in many cases. These laws and theories were strengthened by the *Franklin v. Gwinnett* (1992) decision.

The Equal Protection Clause of the Fourteenth Amendment

The Equal Protection Clause of the Fourteenth Amendment to the United States Constitution states that "no state shall make or enforce any law which shall … deny to any person within its jurisdiction the equal protection of the law." An equal protection challenge must show that groups of people are being treated differently without justification. An equal protection challenge in scholastic and collegiate sport is a complaint by a group of people (women) that its members are being treated differently from others (men) in athletics and that no justification exists to warrant the difference in treatment. One woman or a group of women (class) may retain an attorney and bring a legal action against an educational institution that receives public funds (elementary, secondary, or college) for sex discrimination under the Fourteenth Amendment.

Oregon's Jerry Hunter is believed to have filed the first Fourteenth Amendment discrimination case in sport. Her filing was a defense to the crime of participating in competitive wrestling (*State of Oregon v. Hunter,* 1956). The court denied her constitutional claim, stating "that there should be at least one island on the sea of life reserved for men that would be impregnable to the assault of women" (458).

The following cases paved the way for Title IX of the Education Amendments of 1972. Note that the dates reported for these cases are settlement dates and that the impetus for the original filing occurred prior to the implementation of Title IX. *Brenden v. Independent School District* (1972, 1973), *Hollander v. Connecticut Interscholastic Athletic Conference, Inc.* (1972), *Reed v. Nebraska* (1972), and *Haas v. South Bend Community School Corporation* (1972) were cases that involved high school women requesting an opportunity to participate on men's teams when women's teams were not available. In many of these cases the school district was merely enforcing a league rule. In the *Brenden* case, the Eighth Circuit invalidated the association's policy of prohibiting women from participating in cross-country skiing, running, and tennis when no team existed for women. In the *Connecticut* case, Susan Hollander was denied an opportunity to run on the cross-country team. The court in the *Reed* case granted Debbie Reed's request to play golf. Haas, a golfer, requested and was denied a permanent injunction from the Indiana State League rule that prohibited women from playing on men's teams. The Supreme Court of Indiana reversed the trial court's decision, stating that the regulation, while fair on its face, was discriminating in effect because a women's program did not exist and thus, there was no opportunity for interscholastic competition. It should be noted that the requests were granted in Nebraska, Minnesota, and Indiana while the request in Connecticut was denied.

Morris, a tennis player, brought a similar action against the Michigan State Board of Education (*Morris v. Michigan State Board of Education,* 1973). The trial court issued an injunction; the state court of appeals affirmed. Similar situations were found in Kansas (*Gilpin v. Kansas State High School Activities Association,* 1973), Tennessee (*Carnes v. Tennessee Secondary School Athletic Association, et al.,* 1976), and Nebraska (*Bednar v. Nebraska School Activities Association,* 1976). Following the implementation of Title IX, issues of league mandates continued to be litigated in West Virginia (*Israel v. West Virginia Secondary School Activities Commission,* 1989), Illinois (*Libby v. South*

Inter-Conference Association, 1988, 1990), and Louisiana (*Habetz v. Louisiana High School Athletic Association,* 1988, 1990).

A number of young women attempted to gain membership in Little League Baseball and community recreation programs prior to the advent of Title IX. Ten-year-old Pamela Magill sought injunctive relief to be permitted to participate with males in the sport of Little League Baseball (*Magill v. Avonworth Baseball Conference, et al.,* 1973, 1975). Despite the absence of an alternative program for girls, the court dismissed the case. Success was achieved in a similar situation in which the Essex County National Organization for Women filed a class action suit on behalf of all girls 8 to 12 years of age who wanted to play Little League Baseball (*National Organization for Women v. Little League Baseball, Inc.,* 1974). In another case, "Pookie Fortin" received tremendous publicity as she gained entry to Little League Baseball (*Fortin v. Darlington Little League,* 1974, 1975). Fortin was denied access by the lower court, but the First Circuit reversed the lower court's decision.

Title IX of the Education Amendments of 1972

After considerable debate in Congress, Title IX became part of the Education Amendments of 1972. Title IX states that

> No person in the United States shall, on the basis of sex, be excluded from participation in, be denied the benefits of, or be subject to discrimination, under any educational program or activity, receiving federal financial assistance. (20 USC Section 1681 [a])

Title IX, a federal statute, extended the principles articulated under the Fourteenth Amendment to all schools, public and private, that rely upon federal and/or state funds. Title IX is enforced by the Department of Education. Institutions in violation of Title IX are to have all federal funds withheld. Although there have been threats of withholding federal funds, the authors are not aware of an institution that has lost federal monies as a result of a Title IX violation. The result of a Supreme Court decision in 1979 (*Cannon v. University of Chicago*) enabled individuals to bring a cause of action under Title IX. In addition, Title IX was applied successfully to employment in *North Haven v. Bell* (1982).

In 1978, the Office of Civil Rights prepared a policy interpretation of Title IX. The final interpretation was published the following year. Under the topic of effective accommodations, the policy interpretation provided a three-part test that recommends the following:

1) Whether intercollegiate level participation opportunities for male and female students are provided in numbers substantially proportionate to their respective enrollment; or

2) Where the members of one sex have been and are under-represented among intercollegiate athletes, whether the institution can show a history and

continuing practice of program expansion which is demonstrably responsive to the developing interests and abilities of the members of the sex; or

3) Where the members of one sex are under-represented among intercollegiate athletes, and the institution cannot show a continuing practice of program expansion such as that cited above, whether it can be demonstrated that the interests and abilities of the members of that sex have been fully and effectively accommodated by the present program. (44 Fed. Reg. at 71,418)

In 2005, the Bush Administration recommended that prong three be satisfied by a survey to discover the interests and abilities of the female population. This was considered a good idea in light of the fact that women had been forced into the male sport model by the courts (*AIAW v. NCAA*, 1983, 1984). However, it was discovered that the surveys, in some situations, were used to suggest that women were not interested or did not have the physical skill to participate in the male-designed program and were therefore not interested in sport. Further, questions were raised as to the fact that Olympic Sports and sports such as golf and tennis that could provide professional career opportunities for both men and women were ignored. As of 2011, the United States Department of Education's Office of Civil Rights rescinded the 2005 clarification that allowed institutions to use only an Internet or an email survey to meet effective accommodations. While the survey continues to be used, it must be one aspect, not the exclusive method, of fulfilling prong three. Also, the system of evaluating non-returned surveys as an indication of lack of interest in sport has been stopped.

Complaints in the early days of Title IX were usually resolved within a school district or by an Office of Civil Rights. *Yellow Springs Exempted Village School District v. Ohio High School Athletic Association* (1981), *Gomes v. Rhode Island Interscholastic League* (1979), and *Petrie v. Illinois High School Association* (1979) were among the few complaints filed in the courts. In the *Yellow Springs* case, a school district brought an action against the Ohio High School Athletic Association, claiming that the Association rule prohibiting females from playing contact sports was unconstitutional and in violation of Title IX. When middle-school girls had successfully made the boys' basketball team, the school district was forced by the Ohio High School Athletic Association to eliminate the qualified girls or withdraw from the league. The United States District Court, Southern District of Ohio, ruled under the Constitution for the female student athletes; the court of appeals reversed the ruling. The court refused to rule on Title IX. It should be noted that this case contains a rich history of women's athletics.

Gomes (1979) and *Petrie* (1979) were cases involving men petitioning the courts, under Title IX, to be permitted to play on women's interscholastic volleyball teams. Gomes, a student at Rogers High School in Newport, Rhode Island, brought suit against the Rhode Island Interscholastic League while Petrie's action was against the Illinois High School Athletic Association. The United States District Court, District of Rhode Island, granted Gomes a preliminary injunction allowing him to play. The court established that Gomes, as an average volleyball player, would not disrupt the competitive level of the women's team, and he had successfully argued that his failure to play would cause him irreparable harm. The defendants appealed the ruling. The United State Court of Appeals, First Circuit, addressed the case as rapidly as possible; Gomes was a senior graduating from high school with one volleyball game remaining in the season when the case was heard. The district court's judgment was vacated and the case was remanded for dismissal.

Petrie, a 16-year-old high school junior, was practicing with the volleyball team when he was informed by school officials that the league rules barred him from competition. The trial court "reasoned that the prohibitions against boys were classifications based on sex but were justified because they preserved, fostered and increased athletic competition for girls and prevented unfair competition that would arise from male dominance from the game" (*Petrie v. Illinois High School Association,* 1979, 857).

In an effort to divert attention from athletics, three cases—two in athletics (*Othen v. Ann Arbor School District,* 1981, 1982; *Bennett v. West Texas State University,* 1981, 1983, 1986) and one general college case (*Grove City College v. Bell,* 1982, 1983, 1984)—successfully petitioned the courts to make Title IX "program specific." The phrase "program specific" meant that only those programs receiving direct federal funding were under Title IX. Athletics, seldom financed with federal dollars, would no longer be under Title IX jurisdiction. The *Othen, Bennett,* and *Grove City* rulings brought to a halt the Title IX investigations of athletics and other areas by the Office of Civil Rights.

Disparate Treatment and Disparate Impact

Disparate treatment and disparate impact are employment discrimination legal theories that have influenced "equity in athletics" cases. These theories have been used in court decisions under the Fourteenth Amendment, Equal Protection Clause. They involve practices that appear neutral in their treatment of different groups but fall more harshly on one group than another (*Teamsters v. United States,* 1977). Disparate treatment is identified when evidence exists that there was discriminatory intent or that persons acted pursuant to a policy that is discriminatory on its face. The *Hazelwood* case provides a method of analysis for use in identifying patterns and practices of discrimination under disparate impact. The patterns and practices include history, statistics, procedures, and specific instances. Disparate impact theory in sport is "participation by enrollment" (*Hazelwood School District v. United States,* 1977). Disparate impact theory is the basis for analysis of sport participation legal violations under the Fourteenth Amendment to the U.S. Constitution and prong one of the Title IX statute.

To achieve equity in athletics under the theory of disparate impact, an institution of higher education or secondary school must show that the percentage of females and males given the opportunity to play in sport is the same as the percentage of males and females attending the institution. For example, the figures for an institution with a student body of 16,000 students (9,600 females and 6,400 males) with 600 berths in competition (with 300 under scholarship) are noted in Table 6.1.

TABLE 5.1: Participation Rate Under Fourteenth Amendment and
Prong One of Title IX

	Enrollment	Participation	Berths	Full Scholarships
Males	6,400	40%	240	120
Females	9,600	60%	360	180
Total	16,000	100%	600	300

Under a disparate impact theory, all opportunities are to be equal for the athletes. Budgets are to reflect the cost of supporting teams of equal levels of competition. If it costs less to maintain a synchronized swimming team at an elite level of competition than to maintain a football team at the same level, the budgets required to keep each team at an elite level of competition are considered the comparable budgets. Trainers, choreographers, assistant coaches, and others are to be provided to enable males and females to achieve an elite level of recognition in their respective sports.

The Civil Rights Restoration Act of 1987

The Civil Rights Restoration Act of 1987 restored Title IX to its original strength and removed the "program specific" status. It reversed the rulings of *Othen, Bennett,* and *Grove City*. Title IX was once again applied to an entire institution and to all programs.

The Civil Rights Act of 1991

Disparate impact theory was strengthened by the Civil Rights Act of 1991, which placed the burden of proof on those who practiced discrimination, not on those who suffered discrimination. Founders of the act stated the following: "Plaintiffs must first prove intentional discrimination, then must provide actual injury or loss arising there from to recover compensatory damages, must meet an even higher standard (establishing that the employer acted with malice or reckless or callous indifference to their rights) to recover punitive damages" (House Report, 102 Cong., 1st Session at 72).

For example, when discrimination is alleged in a university athletic department, the athletic department and the university have the burden of proof (or must show evidence) of equitable participation in all forms of intercollegiate, intramural, and club sports. The athletic department and the university, not the person alleging discrimination, must demonstrate that no discrimination occurred or currently exists, and provide victims of intentional discrimination with the right to recover compensatory and punitive damages. Punitive damages are based on recklessness. Attorney fees are to be paid by the losing party.

Many colleges claim that they did not intend to discriminate; however, it should be noted that in January of 1992, the United States Office of Education sent a letter of warning about the Civil Rights Act of 1991 to all educational institutions, informing them of their responsibilities under the law. Failure to heed that warning has been considered intentional discrimination.

The *Franklin* case—a U.S. Supreme Court sexual harassment decision—enables victims of discrimination to be compensated under Title IX (*Franklin v. Gwinnett*, 1990, 1991, 1992). Judges White, Blackmun, Stevens, O'Connor, Kennedy, and Souter "held that a money damage remedy is available for an action brought to enforce Title IX" (208). Prior to this case, civil rights complaints in athletics had requested increases in the number of sports and opportunities for participation, and prohibition from dropping women's sports. Now, plaintiffs could request monetary compensation for lost opportunities.

Equity in Athletics Disclosure Act

The 1994 reauthorization of the federal Elementary and Secondary Education Act contained a provision requiring colleges and universities to collect and disclose information concerning gender equity in intercollegiate athletics. The disclosure component of the act requires schools to publish the male-to-female ratio data for school enrollment and athletic participation on the day of the team's first scheduled contests. Schools are to list varsity team membership, operating and recruiting expenses, and the number and gender of all coaches. All student aid that is provided to athletes, the revenue that is generated by the teams, and the coaching salaries are to be disclosed. These data are to be published yearly. Legislation—introduced in June of 1997 as the Fair Play Act—requires the United States Department of Education to publish financial and other information about sports on the Internet. The information is to be available to students to assist them in making informed choices about athletics in their selection of colleges and universities.

Rule 23, Class Actions

Class action suits are presented to a court of law when groups of people have similar complaints in an effort to suggest the importance of the issue to the court and to provide an efficient method of review for the court. For a group to become a class action suit they must satisfy the Federal Rules of Civil Procedure (2010), Rule 23, which requires that

1) the class is so numerous that joinder of all members is impracticable;

2) there are questions of law or facts common to the class;

3) the claims or defenses of the representative parties are typical of the claims or defenses of the class; and

4) the representative parties will fairly and adequately protect the interests of the class. (Federal Rules of Civil Procedure, 2010, Rule 23[a])

THE IMPACT OF ATHLETIC GOVERNANCE ON EQUITY

Early collegiate and scholastic athletic programs were governed by men's and women's physical education departments. As the scandals in men's collegiate athletics increased and as the National Collegiate Athletic Association (NCAA)—an organization external to the institutions of higher education—began to control participation and competition, colleges created athletic departments to administer men's athletics. Collegiate women's sports remained with women's physical education departments. Athletic directors, the leaders of men's sports, soon answered only to the university or college presidents; leaders of women's athletics remained an integral part of the university or college and answered to department chairs and deans (the regular line of administrators at the university level). In some secondary schools, athletic departments were formed but their ties were always close to the physical education department.

In 1967, the American Alliance for Health, Physical Education, Recreation, and Dance (AAHPERD), Division of Girls and Women in Sport—the agency that had created, interpreted, and disseminated rules for women's sports for years—established a governance system for collegiate women's athletics. This governance system was the Commission on Intercollegiate Athletics. Prior to the organization of the Commission, members of the Division of Girls and Women in Sport (DGWS) met with NCAA officials to ascertain the NCAA's interest in athletics for women. DGWS members were told that

> the NCAA's "jurisdiction and authority" under its organic documents were "limited to male student-athletes;" that women were prohibited from participating in NCAA events; that a women's national governance organization would "consequently … not be in conflict;" and that NCAA stood ready to offer advisory assistance in this important endeavor. (*AIAW v. NCAA,* 1983, 490)

In 1971, the DGWS Commission became the Association for Intercollegiate Athletics for Women (AIAW). The AIAW had 278 members and seven national championships in 1971. By 1980-1981, the membership had grown to 961 colleges and universities, and 39 championships were staged (*AIAW v. NCAA,* 1983, 490). The AIAW played the same role in athletics for women that the NCAA played in athletics for men—with one exception: the AIAW refused to include athletic scholarships in its programs (Hult, 1980). The AIAW members believed that the scandals in men's athletics were a result of scholarships, and the "big business" approach to sport. Two different models for collegiate athletics existed at that point in time: a scholarship ("big business") NCAA male model, and a non-scholarship (educational student-athlete) AIAW female model. For a detailed discussion of today's "big business" male model of athletics, as predicted by AIAW members, see Brake (2007), Kuznik and Ryan (2008), and Koller (2010).

The National Collegiate Athletic Association brought suit against Joseph Califano (Secretary of the United States Department of Health, Education, and Welfare), the AIAW, and AAHPERD for "declaratory and injunctive relief seeking to invalidate regulations promulgated by the Department of Health, Education, and Welfare under the aegis of Title IX of the Education Amendments of 1972" (*NCAA v. Califano,* 1978, 428).

Title IX had become law in 1972. In 1975, the Department of Health, Education, and Welfare (HEW) issued regulations affecting all aspects of education, including sport and athletics. The NCAA's action, filed in 1976, was against the presumed harm that the operating regulations and the named organizations might cause in the future.

The NCAA's complaints were that Title IX should not cover athletics because collegiate athletics was privately funded; that the requirement of treating males and females equally was arbitrary and capricious; that the requirement of providing athletic scholarship equally to men and women violated 20 USC 1681 and the Fifth Amendment to the U.S. Constitution; and that the regulations violated the "due process" requirements of the Fifth Amendment (*NCAA v. Califano,* 1978, 429).

The United States District Court for the District of Kansas found that the NCAA did not have legal standing to represent its membership in a suit against HEW. The court's decision did not consider the Title IX regulations or the NCAA's complaint. The NCAA appealed the decision to the Tenth Circuit, United States Court of Appeals (*NCAA v. Califano,* 1980). The Tenth Circuit studied the issue of standing and remanded for a clear definition; again, the court did not consider the contents of the NCAA's complaint.

The National Collegiate Athletic Association (NCAA), wishing to maintain control of athletics, created sport championships for women. The NCAA permitted colleges and universities to enter NCAA and AIAW events for the first years as the NCAA was offering only a few tournaments to replace the 39 championships sponsored by AIAW (Uhlir, 1982). The NCAA's funding for championships was changed in the early 1980s to make NCAA representation over AIAW representation highly attractive to schools. In the meantime, the AIAW lost members, sponsors, and television interests.

The AIAW then sued the NCAA, alleging Sherman Act violations (antitrust). The court, in ordering judgment for the NCAA, stated that

> even if defendant's conduct were avowedly anticompetitive in purpose, this record would not support a finding that its effect on plaintiff was the product of anything but direct competition. Two plaintiffs, former presidents of AIAW who were also directors of women's athletics at Division I Institutions (the Universities of Texas and Iowa), described the economic incentives to participate in NCAA's women's championships (i.e., the "free dues and travel reimbursement") as "irresistible inducements" which the AIAW could not match. (*AIAW v. NCAA,* 1983, 506)

The AIAW appealed the decision. The United States Court of Appeals for the District of Columbia Circuit affirmed the lower court's decision, "holding that AIAW failed to prove [that the] NCAA's dues policy, proceeds distribution formula, or sale of television rights violated the Sherman Act" (*AIAW v. NCAA,* 1984, 590). With this decision, the NCAA took over women's athletics.

LEADING CASES IN COLLEGIATE AND
SCHOLASTIC ATHLETICS

The leading cases following the implementation of Title IX were *Haffer v. Temple University* (1981, 1982, 1987) at the collegiate level and *Ridgeway v. Montana High School Athletic Association* (1986, 1988) at the scholastic level. Of the thirty-six cases reviewed in this area the following themes appear: women seeking equitable participation;

elimination of sports; athletes seeking membership on opposite-sex teams; facilities; roster management; and the prong three survey. These decisions, and their certioraris to the United States Supreme Court, are to be considered before a defendant institution chooses to incur the expense of a trial.

Collegiate

Haffer v. Temple University (1981, 1982, 1987, 1988) was a class action suit against Temple University by women who were participating in athletics and those who had been deterred from participating in athletics due to sex discrimination. Their claims focused on three basic areas: the extent to which Temple University afforded women students fewer opportunities to compete in intercollegiate athletics; the alleged disparity in resources allocated to the men's and women's intercollegiate athletic programs; and the alleged disparity in the allocation of financial aid to male and female students. Their class action complaint alleged discrimination in opportunities to compete, expenditures, recruiting, coaching, travel and per diem allowance, uniforms, equipment, supplies, training facilities and services, housing and dining facilities, academic tutoring, and publicity. These actions were in violation of the Fourteenth Amendment and the Pennsylvania Equal Rights Amendment. With the exception of meals, tutoring, facilities, and scheduling, the court ruled for the plaintiffs in all areas. The case was in the courts for over 10 years and provides insight into the civil rights changes caused by the *Grove City* decisions.

Blair v. Washington State University (1989) was similar to the foregoing decisions, except that the trial court chose to exclude football in the equity calculation. The plaintiff appealed the football decision; the Supreme Court of Washington reversed the decision, requiring that football be included in all calculations for finance and participation. While this decision is precedent for the State of Washington, it has defined the role of football in equity considerations.

Cases litigated in the 1990s changed somewhat as the courts began to look at the three prong policy of accommodation interpretation of Title IX published in 1979. Often, schools (particularly universities) failed to recognize the significance of prong one that had been taken from the Fourteenth Amendment, Equal Protection Clause analysis, and used in many previous cases. It was and is precedent and is therefore an important issue in legal decisions. Prong two, program expansion for the under-represented gender, and prong three, accommodating the interests of students, are Title IX specific and thus less significant. Prong two was a stop gap for those forced to make radical program changes in a short period of time. However, after forty years those changes had to occur. Prong three, meeting the needs and talent of females, has been redefined to be used only as one factor, not the only factor, in determining compliance. Women faced with conforming to the male model of athletics are beginning to speak out.

Considerable resources have been invested, unsuccessfully, by institutions of higher education in litigating their violations of Title IX with the hope of changing the law. *Cohen v. Brown University* (1992, 1993, 1995, 1996, 1997, 2001, 2003) and *Roberts v. Colorado State Board of Agriculture* (1993[1], 1993[2], 1993[3]) are examples of this effort. *Cohen* was a class action suit against Brown University, its president, and its athletic director for discrimination against women in collegiate athletics. Women's gymnastics and volleyball team members brought suit on behalf of "all present, future and potential Brown University women students who participate, seek to participate, and/ or are deterred from participating in intercollegiate athletics funded by Brown" (*Cohen v. Brown University*, 1996, 161). They alleged violations of Title IX of the Education Amendments of 1972.

The suit was in response to the 1991 demotion of the gymnastics and volleyball teams from varsity to club status; men's water polo and golf were also demoted. Brown was the Ivy League volleyball champion in 1988, and the gymnastics champion in 1990. After 14 days of testimony, the United States Court of the District of Rhode Island issued a preliminary injunction restoring the volleyball and gymnastics teams to varsity status and prohibiting Brown University from eliminating or reducing the status or funding of any existing women's varsity sport pending the resolution of other Title IX claims (*Cohen v. Brown*, 1992). Brown appealed the decision.

In the 1993–1994 school year, 62% of Brown University's intercollegiate opportunities were for men and 38% were for women. Men constituted 48% of the enrollment, while women made up 52%. A 14% disparity existed between enrollment and participation. The trial court determined that they could not meet prong one, the disparate impact standard of the Fourteenth Amendment to the U.S. Constitution. The United States Court of Appeals, First Circuit, affirmed the trial court's decision (*Cohen v. Brown*, 1992). The District Court, after a lengthy bench trial, found Brown University to be in violation of Title IX and ordered that a compliance plan be submitted within 120 days. The plan, as submitted, was inadequate and forced the court to maintain varsity status for women's gymnastics, fencing, skiing, and water polo teams.

Roberts v. Colorado State Board of Agriculture saw current and former members of the women's varsity fast-pitch softball team bring suit against Colorado State University, challenging the elimination of the softball and baseball teams in June of 1992 in response to budget cuts. The court posed the central question as "whether defendant's termination of the women's softball team either caused a violation of Title IX or was the perpetuation of an already existing violation of the defendants" (*Roberts v. Colorado State Board of Agriculture*, 1993[a], 1510). In using "equity-by-enrollment" figures of the undergraduate population for a 14-year period beginning in the 1980-1981 school year, the plaintiffs noted that the university's "average disparity between enrollment and athletic participation rates for women was 14.1%" (*Roberts v. Colorado State Board of Agriculture*, 1993[b], 1512). In response to the university's statement that the percentage was much better than many schools, the court responded "that if defendants are found by the Court to be in violation of Title IX, the fact the CSU's participation statistics are better than those of other schools is of no legal consequence" (*Roberts v. Colorado State Board of Agriculture*, 1993[b], 1513). CSU also failed part two of the three-prong test; no new teams had been added in the past 12 years and a number of teams had been dropped. CSU appealed the decision. The Court of Appeals for the

Tenth Circuit affirmed the trial court's decision that CSU was in violation of Title IX. CSU's petition (certiorari) to the U.S. Supreme Court was denied.

The result of two Louisiana State University cases that were combined by the courts, *Pineda, et al. v. Louisiana State University, et al.* and *Pederson, et al. v. Louisiana State University, et al.* (1996, 2000), provides a review of many gender equity issues. The issue of standing (whether the plaintiffs were among the persons harmed by the law) became apparent in *Pineda*. The plaintiffs were not university athletes; therefore, they could not be considered athletes under equal treatment. To award monetary damages, the court had to find intent on behalf of the defendants. The court noted that it "holds that the violations are not intentional. Rather, they are a result of arrogant ignorance, confusion regarding the practical requirements of the law, and a remarkably outdated view of women and athletics which created the byproduct of resistance to change" (1996, 918). The plaintiffs failed to meet the needs of women athletes. In *Pedersen*, LSU was found to have intentionally violated Title IX (2000, 864).

In *Barrett, et al. v. West Chester University of Pennsylvania of the State of Higher Education, et al.* (2003, 2006, 2009), eight members of the gymnastics team brought suit against the university when the women's gymnastics and men's lacrosse teams were eliminated in response to state budget cuts. In 1998, 25 years after Title IX became law, West Chester University's "Athletic Department created the Sports Equity Committee to obtain a basic and working knowledge of Title IX in order to begin the task of ensuring that the athletic program is in compliance with the law" (2003, 8). They used the three-prong test. Under accommodations, women were 60.8% of the undergraduate student body and 44.6% of the athletes; they fell short of compliance by over 16%. The fact they had not added a team for women for over 10 years meant prong two was violated, and it became evident that if they would keep the gymnastics team it would assist in meeting prong three, the interests and abilities of women. In 2006, plaintiffs requested attorney fees of $207,609.50 and costs of $12,477.82 for a total of $220,087.32. The court awarded a total of $148,472.59 (2006, 59). In 2009, the plaintiffs again filed a motion for the original $220,087.32; the motion was denied (2009, 18).

Heather Mercer, a high school all-state football kicker, tried out as a walk-on player for the Duke University football team (*Mercer v. Duke University*, 1998, 1999, 2001, 2005). Although she failed to make the team, she served as a team manager and practiced with the kickers. Later in the year, she was selected to play in an intra-squad scrimmage game and kicked a field goal that won the game for her squad. She was then named to the team. The media gave Heather a great deal of attention. As a result of the attention, the coach became concerned, tried to discourage her from playing, and finally dismissed her from the team.

Mercer brought suit against Duke University, stating that she was discriminated against. The district court dismissed the case because "Title IX did not require Duke University to give a women an opportunity to play on the men's football team" (2005, 201). Mercer appealed the decision. The United States Court of Appeals for the Fourth Circuit found for Mercer, concluding "that while the contact-sport exemption would have shielded Duke from liability had it refused to allow Mercer to try out for the team, the exception did not give Duke license to discriminate against Mercer because of her sex once Duke decided to allow her to join the team" (2005, 202). Mercer received "one dollar in compensatory damages and two million dollars in punitive damages and attorney fees" (2005, 202). The one-dollar compensatory damage award meant that the court believed that Mercer had not been damaged financially; she had not lost income or potential professional status. The punitive damage award, as explained earlier, was assessed against Duke University with the knowledge of Duke's financial positions, at a level the court hoped would stop Duke from committing such behavior in the future.

In *Brust, et al. v. Regents of the University of California* (2007, 2009), Brust, Bulala, Ludwig, and all other female athletes enrolled in the University of California, Davis filed a class action suit against the university under Title IX, the Fourteenth Amendment to the U.S. Constitution, and other state laws in 2007. Brust and Bulala were skilled field hockey players. Ludwig was a rugby player and a club member wrestler. Discovery revealed that during the 2005–2006 academic year, female enrollment was 55%, while intercollegiate varsity teams enrolled only 50% of the University of California, Davis, undergraduate students. The case is unique in that it published the details of the settlement agreement, including equitable relief, squad size, participation differential, funding, reporting, monetary relief, and attorney fees. A field hockey team was part of the settlement agreement.

Foltz, et al. v. Delaware State University (2010), a class action suit, was prompted by the university's decision to eliminate the women's equestrian team. Plaintiffs requested a temporary restraining order and preliminary injunction. Temporary restraining orders and preliminary injunctions required the university to stop its action; in this case, to stop the elimination of the equestrian team. The suit was for "present, prospective, and future female students and athletes at the university—fulfilling the numerosity requirement of Rule 23" (*Foltz, et al. v. Delaware State University,* 2010, Overview). The case continues. The value of the case is in the detailed explanation of the requirements for a class action suit.

Choike v. Slippery Rock University (2010) provides a supervised and published settlement, something not found in earlier documents. Plaintiffs were 12 members of the women's swim, water polo, and field hockey teams who filed charges against Slippery Rock University for "intentional discrimination for failure to provide equitable athletic opportunities for [SRU's] female students and equitable treatment of its female students, including its announced elimination of three viable women's athletic teams" (2010, 3). In January 2006, the university announced the elimination of eight varsity sports: men's and women's water polo, women's field hockey, men's golf, men's wrestling, and men's tennis. Soon after the announcement, students formed a committee (Save our Sports) and met with the athletic administration without success. An audit conducted in November 2005 showed participant opportunities for 2001 through 2005, with the following disparities between the number of undergraduate women enrolled in the university and the number of university women participating in collegiate

TABLE 5.1. Slippery Rock University Male to Female Sport Participation Disparities

Year	Disparity
2001	12.3%
2002	11.2%
2003	8.7%
2004	8.7%

athletics (Table 5.1). (To be in compliance with Title IX and the Fourteenth Amendment to the U.S. Constitution, the number needs to be as close to zero as possible.)

A formal student survey found that the interests of females had been met. Roster management appeared in this case as a successful means of manipulating Title IX equity. While roster management existed since the first implementation of Title IX, this is the first time it appears as a viable means of addressing equity to a court of law. Roster management is the loading of female teams with all athletes that try out, but only taking a small number of persons on the team to competitions and other events. Some schools have had as many as forty females on a tennis team, but only eight entered competition. At the same time, the males had a team of ten: eight in competition and two substitutes. Roster management is severe, as demonstrated in this and the following cases.

The athletes in *Choike* obtained an attorney and chose to file a class action suit requiring a preliminary injunction to stop the elimination of the women's teams mentioned above. The women sued the university's president and athletic director under Title IX for equal participation and unequal coaching and training, equipment and supplies, publicity, promotional materials, events transportation, uniforms, playing fields, locker rooms, and facilities.

The students' claims were successful and a case management conference was scheduled (*Choike v. Slippery Rock University,* 2006). Since that time, the parties returned to the court in 2007, 2008, and 2010 in an effort to resolve disputes. The case has the contemporary value of the *Temple* case mentioned earlier in this chapter.

In *Mansourian, et al. v. Board of Regents of the University of California, Davis (UCD), et al.,* (2008, 2010, 2011), plaintiffs claimed that the university had a long-standing women's varsity wrestling program that was eliminated. The university says there was a single wrestling program event. It appears that women varsity wrestlers were given the same experience as the men or were members of the men's team, but did not compete with men or follow NCAA rules. In 2000, when the university imposed roster limits on teams, the women were removed from the wrestling team. This removal created a media blitz causing UCD to reinstate the plaintiffs. In the fall of 2001, the women were forced to try out for the men's team using the male rules. "Plaintiffs contend that at practice the head wrestling coach was hostile to the women and did not provide them with any coaching tips, or support" (2010, 10).

Between 1995 and 2005, the University of California, Davis was short of proportionality by over a hundred varsity slots each year (2010, 14). They were warned of the inequity by the Office of Civil Rights, California National Organization for Women, and in numerous memos between collegiate administrators. No steps were taken to add programs. In 2003, plaintiffs filed an action asserting six claims. The claims included violation of Title IX based on unequal opportunities; violation of Title IX based on unequal financial assistance; retaliation in violation of Title IX; violation of 42 USC 1983; violation of the California Unruh Civil Rights Act; and violation of public policy (*Mansourian, et al. v. University of California, Davis, et al.,* 2010, 17). The court denied the motion. The athletes filed a number of complaints without success and then filed a Fourteenth Amendment equal protection claim regarding the removal of plaintiffs from the varsity wrestling program based on gender and the permanent barriers that they faced. Defendants were successful in their motions with one exception. Plaintiffs successfully presented "triable issues of fact with respect to their 1983 claims arising out of the assertion that defendants violated the Equal Protection Clause by maintaining an athletics program that discriminates on the basis of gender" (2010, 50).

In *Equity in Athletics v. Department of Education and James Madison University* (2007, 2008, 2009, 2011), the plaintiff (a nonprofit organization comprised of male student-athletes, coaches, parents, alumni, and fans) challenged the equity by enrollment requirement of Title IX. The appellate court held that the recommended accommodations did not violate the Equal Protection Clause, and therefore it was legitimate. Equity in Athletics also sought relief against James Madison University, challenging their decision to eliminate ten sports. Controversy existed over enrollment and scholarships; the court found that women had not achieved equity. The district court dismissed the Equity in Athletics constitutional, statutory, and procedural claims against the Department of Education and James Madison University.

A class action suit was brought by members of the women's rowing team against the University of Cincinnati under Title IX and the Fourteenth Amendment Equal Protection Clause, for failure to provide the team with a boathouse, minimal equipment, training facilities, coaches, and scholarships (*Miller v. The University of Cincinnati,* 2008). Cincinnati started a women's rowing team but could not afford it. The university decided to discontinue rowing and created a lacrosse team. The university was in compliance with prong one of Title IX accommodations and remained in compliance after eliminating the rowing team. Therefore, the court found for the university.

Another complaint regarding facilities, this time in softball, was *Hess, et al. v. Ramona Unified High School, District, et al.* (2007, 2008). Women softball players filed a complaint for equal facilities; the men had two fields on campus while the women practiced and played on an off-campus facility. The court required the school to build a softball facility on campus.

A decision still in process regarding opportunities for league play is *Barrs, et al. v. The Southern Conference* (2010). The suit against the league was a request to expand post-season sports from four to eight for men's and women's soccer, men's and women's tennis, women's volleyball, and women's softball. They "allege that this decision disproportionately affected female student athletes and contend that the reduction violates Title IX" (1230). The request was for a preliminary and permanent injunction and damages. The court denied the Southern Conference's motion to dismiss the complaint. As the named plaintiffs were graduating, some of the claims became moot; the plaintiffs requested and received the opportunity from the court to expand the plaintiff group to a class action suit. This case addresses many of the complaints brought by athletes against leagues in the early days of gender equity.

Scholastic Athletics

Ridgeway v. Montana High School Athletic Association (1986, 1988), one of the most comprehensive decisions in athletics at the secondary level, was a class action suit brought on behalf of all Montana high school girls against the State Athletic Association. The lawsuit alleged violations of Title IX, the Fourteenth Amendment to the U.S. Constitution, and the Constitution of Montana. The women claimed that discrimination existed in the number of sports, seasons of play, length of seasons, practice and game schedules, and access to facilities, equipment, coaching, trainers, transportation, the school band, uniforms, publicity, and general support. The parties accepted an agreement that provided for equal opportunity and placed a court-appointed facilitator in charge. The settlement gave specific roles of enforcement to the Montana office of public instruction and to individual schools. The entire state of Montana—not just the three schools represented in the class action suit—were included in the settlement. Although the decision is precedent only in Montana, the case provides a formula for secondary schools to use in avoiding discrimination in athletics.

Richard Landow, on behalf of his daughter Kayla, sued over the inequities between women and men in her school softball and baseball programs (*Landow, et al. v. School Board of Brevard County,* 2000, 2001). Among the differences were the quality of uniforms, available equipment, choice of fields for practice and game play, and locker rooms. The District Court for the Middle District of Florida found for the students and ordered the board to take the following measures:

1) Develop a plan that elevates the girls' softball program at Titusville and Astronaut to the level enjoyed by the boys' baseball teams at those schools.

2) Not later than February 1, 2001, counsel for the parties shall meet in person at a mutually convenient location in a good faith effort to determine whether they can agree upon a single plan for remedying the inequalities addressed in this Order.

3) Not later than March 15, 2001, the parties shall both file a joint plan with the Court, or file and serve separate proposed plans. (967)

Another case on behalf of students against a school district found the Court of Appeals for the Second Circuit affirming the district court's holding "that the decision by the School District of Mamaroneck and Pelham to schedule girls' high school soccer in the spring and boys' high school soccer in the fall, which deprives girls but not boys of the opportunity to compete in the New York Regional and State Championships in soccer, violates Title IX" (*McCormick, et al. v. The School District of Mamaroneck and the School District of Pelham,* 2004, 302).

Three of the primary scholastic cases involved scheduling. The plaintiffs in *Horner v. Kentucky* (1994, 2000) and *Alston v. Virginia High School League, Inc.* (1999, 2000) lost. *Communities for Equity v. Michigan High School Athletic Association* (2003), after appearing in court at least nine times between 1998 and 2008, put together an equity plan and established attorney fees. Twelve female high school slow pitch softball players brought suit against the Kentucky State Board of Education for Elementary and Secondary Education and the Kentucky High School Athletic Association for discrimination in sanctioning of sports for women and refusing to sanction fast pitch softball (*Horner v. Kentucky,* 1994). Their claims were under the Equal Protection Clause, Title IX, and state law. The district court granted summary judgment for the defendants; female athletes had not been denied equal athletic opportunity. The school had offered equal opportunities in accordance with the interest and abilities of students (prong three of the Title IX implementing guidelines). Also, the plaintiffs had failed to prove intentional discrimination. Horner appealed the decision. The United States Court of Appeals, Sixth Circuit, reversed the trial court's decision and found for the plaintiffs under the Title IX claim. The court affirmed the trial court's equal protection claim. *Alston v. Virginia High School League, Inc.* (2000) was a challenge of intentional discrimination against women in the scheduling of athletic seasons. The court ruled that the Virginia High School League was not an entity subject to Title IX.

Communities for Equity v. Michigan High School Athletic Association (May, 2001, Sept., 2001, Dec., 2001, Feb., 2002, Aug., 2002, 2003, 2006, 2007, Mar., 2008, Aug., 2008) was a challenge of sex discrimination in the planning and scheduling of sport seasons and sport competitions that began in 1998 and was not resolved for ten years. In the initial court session, the standing of the plaintiffs and defendants, rather than the issue, was the discussion. In 2000, the class action was approved, and in 2001, the court determined that the Michigan School Athletic Association's scheduling of interscholastic athletic seasons violated the Equal Protection Clause of the Fourteenth Amendment to the Constitution (Dec., 2001). A compliance plan was approved in 2003 (9). Plaintiffs continued to return to the court to bring various seasons in either the Lower or Upper Peninsula of Michigan into compliance. During that time, their certiorari to the U.S. Supreme Court in April 2007 was denied. In 2008, the United States District Court for the Western District of Michigan, Southern Division, awarded over $4.5 million in legal fees against the Michigan High School Athletic Association (Mar., 78).

High school female ice hockey athletes suing a league for discrimination was first found in *Mason, et al. v. Minnesota State High School League* (2004), and later, a Minnesota female ice hockey enthusiast asked the U.S. Department of Education to intervene in the league issue in *Cobb & Saly v. United States Department of Education, Office of Civil Rights* (2006). In *Mason,* female ice hockey players requested a state tournament site equal to that provided the males. The men played in Xcel Energy

Center in Minneapolis, while the women played at the State Fair Coliseum, a building dedicated to horse shows. In 2000, the women filed a discrimination complaint with the Office of Civil Rights; the agency explored the difference between the two facilities, identified the University of Minnesota's women's ice hockey team facility as a potential arena, ruled that the women's high school tournament be held in that facility, and closed the investigation. The high school girls decided that the University of Minnesota women's ice hockey facility was not adequate and took their case to the courts, requesting an injunction. In 2003, the United States District Judge denied the requested injunction stating that "plaintiffs had failed to establish a likelihood of success on the merits" (7). On appeal, the defendants were denied summary judgment.

High school girls complained of discrimination in practice and competitive facilities, locker rooms, training facilities, equipment and supplies, travel and transportation, coaches, and coaching facilities, scheduling of game and practice times, publicity and funding (*Ollier, et al. v. Sweetwater Union High School, et al.,* 2008, 2009, 2010). The school failed all three prongs of Title IX: Opportunities were inadequate, a new sport had not been added for years, and while lack of interest was demonstrated for field hockey on a survey, it was noted that the team did not have a coach. They also failed the Fourteenth Amendment to the U.S. Constitution.

Parker and others sued the Indiana High School Athletic Association for violating Title IX and the Fourteenth Amendment by scheduling women's games and competitions on non-preferred days while scheduling men's events on Friday and Saturday (*Parker v. Indiana High School Athletic Association,* 2009, Sept. 2010, Oct., 2010). The school succeeded on immunity.

Schnarrs v. Girard Board of Education (2004, 2006) was a complaint by females that males were used as opponents in practice sessions in an effort to improve the females' game skills and strategies. This arrangement was believed to be causing injuries among the female players. It was recommended that athletes, male or female, be challenged by a person with one or more of the following characteristics: slightly higher skill level, slightly taller, or slightly heavier. The court found that the coaches' decision to use male athletes as competitors was a valid teaching strategy or, as they put it, a "positive exercise of judgment" (1265).

Roster Stacking in Scholastic and Collegiate Sports

Roster stacking or roster management, a system often used by schools insincere in achieving equity by enrollment, was first publicly mentioned in *Biedeger, et al. v. Quinnipiac University* (2009, 2010), but today is the focus of a number of lawsuits. In March of 2009, Quinnipiac University decided to cut three sports: women's volleyball, men's golf, and outdoor track teams. At the same time, the university decided to create competitive cheerleading (*Biediger, et al. v. Quinnipiac University,* 2009). The plaintiffs (members of the volleyball team) requested an injunction to stop the elimination of their team. The court granted the preliminary injunction, holding that the university "managed its varsity rosters—essentially, by setting artificial ceilings for men's varsity teams and floors for women's varsity teams" (July 2010, 63). Quinnipiac's practice of requiring individual female members of the cross-country, indoor, and outdoor track teams to be counted as members of all three teams even though they practiced with only one of the teams, was found to be in violation of Title IX. This case is a classic receipt for analyzing sports for the possibility of roster management by schools and universities attempting to come into compliance with Title IX. One suspect area is the number of athletes on a team that are not included in travel and competition. The court refused to recognize a competitive cheerleading team as a varsity sport for the purposes of Title IX, and therefore refused to count the cheerleaders as female varsity athletes. It was the court's decision to deny cheerleading sport status for the purpose of gender equity that received widespread national visibility; however, the roster management component was equally important to the sport professional.

Males Complaining of University Systems for Attaining Equity

Gender equity laws and policies have encouraged administrators of athletic programs to increase opportunities so that male-to-female participation levels reflect enrollment ratios. Some administrators have made the decision to reduce male participation opportunities in athletics instead of increasing female participation. This practice is acceptable under a strict reading of the law, and its acceptance has been confirmed by the courts. It does, however, become an issue of ethics. An analysis of the nine cases brought by males since 1994 as they lost competitive opportunities include *Kelly v. Board of Trustees of the University of Illinois* (1987, 1990, 1993, 1994), *Gonyo v. Drake University* (1993, 1995), *Cooper v. Peterson* (1995), *Lichten, et al. v. State University of New York at Albany, et al.* (1996), *Boulahanis, et al. v. Board of Regents, Illinois State University, et al.* (1999, 2000), *Neal, et al. v. The Board of Trustees of the California State Universities, et al.* (1999, 2002, 2003), *Chalenor, et al. v. University of North Dakota* (2000, 2002), *National Wrestling Coaches Association, et al. v. United States Department of Education* (2003, 2004), and *College Sports Council v. Department of Education* (2005, 2006, 2007). The *Kelly* case concerned the elimination of swimming, diving, and fencing. The *Lichten* case involved tennis, swimming, and wrestling. The *Boulahanis* case was the elimination of soccer and wrestling.

Five of the cases mentioned above involved athletes who sued their universities because wrestling had been cut in an effort to bring collegiate sport competitive opportunities into compliance with gender equity. In all of the situations, the courts denied the request. In March of 1993, Drake University cut its wrestling program in response to university budget cuts and lack of support in its athletic conference and community. The scholarships of existing wrestlers were honored until each athlete's graduation. Five of the wrestlers brought a cause of action against the university, its president, and its athletic director for violations of Title IX and the Equal Protection Clause of the Fourteenth Amendment (*Gonyo, et al. v. Drake University, et al.,* 1995). Drake's Title IX case was weak, as their 1992–1993 data showed a 75.3% male to 24.7% female participation ratio in an institution with an enrollment of 57.2% females. In finding against this claim, the court stated, "Restricting universities from eliminating men's scholarship sports ... while requiring them to expand opportunities for women in athletics … would make it impracticable to spend less, rather than more, money on their athletic programs. Title IX does not so restrain a university's spending decisions" (1995, 1005). Members of the St. Lawrence University wrestling team—a sport that had been cut during budget constraints—brought claims against the university and its president on breach of contract, fraud, misrepresentation, estoppels, and sex discrimination. Their request for a temporary injunction was denied (*Cooper v. Peterson,* 1995).

In *National Wrestling Coaches Association, et al.,* the sport governing association attempted to stop the Department of Education from enforcing Title IX. "Specifically, plaintiffs maintain that the Department's current enforcement policies lead educational institutions to cut men's sports teams, artificially limiting the number of participants on men's teams, and otherwise impermissibly discriminating against men based on sex in the provision of athletic opportunities, thereby denying male athletes and other interested parties the equal protection of the law" (2003, 85). *College Sports Council, et al. v. Department of Education, et al.* (2005, 2006, 2007), an outgrowth of a number of the above cases involving wrestling, saw the National Wrestling Coaches Association join a number of private university wrestling clubs and others against their original defendant, the Department of Education. In 2005, the case was dismissed by the United States District Court for the District of Columbia for lack of standing, a decision from the same court (*National Wrestling Coaches Association, et al. v. United States Department of Education,* 2003). Plaintiffs then brought suit against the government accountability office for violation of the higher education amendments. The defendants moved to dismiss the lawsuit for failure to state a claim, and the motion was granted (*College Sports Council, et al. v. Government Accountability Office, et al.,* 2006).

In 1993, in the only case not representing wrestling, the University of Illinois announced the elimination of two men's varsity sports (swimming and fencing) and one varsity sport (diving) that had both men's and women's teams. Members of the men's swimming team filed an action against the Board of Trustees of the University of Illinois, alleging that the university violated Title IX and the Equal Protection Clause of the Fourteenth Amendment to the United States Constitution (*Kelly v. The University of Illinois,* 1994). This lawsuit followed an Office of Civil Rights investigation in which Illinois agreed to remedy disparities in opportunities for women in a reasonable period of time. The U.S. District Court for the Central District of Illinois granted summary judgment for the university. The swimmers appealed the decision by the lower court. The court of appeals affirmed the district court's ruling. The plaintiffs were denied certiorari by the United States Supreme Court.

RETALIATION UNDER TITLE IX

The United States Supreme Court's first Title IX case and the first retaliation decision under Title IX was *Jackson v. the Birmingham, Alabama Board of Education* (1998, 2002, 2003, 2004, 2005). *Jackson* tells the story of a young male women's basketball coach who was dismissed from his coaching position for complaining "that his team was not receiving equal funding and equal access to athletic equipment and facilities" (Jackson, 2005, 1503). The District Court dismissed the complaint, ruling that

Title IX did not include a claim of retaliation; the court of appeals confirmed the district court's decision. The U.S. Supreme Court reversed the decision, stating that the "private right of action implied by Title IX encompassed claims of retaliation for complaining about sex discrimination as: (1) such retaliation was (a) by definition an intentional act, (b) a form of discrimination; and (c) 'on the basis of sex'" (*Jackson*, 2005, 1498).

Two collegiate cases decided near the same time as the *Jackson* case, *Wells v. Board of Trustees of the California University, et al.* (2005, 2006) and *Burch v. Regents of the University of California, et al.* (2006), did not seem to be influenced by *Jackson*. Mr. Wells was hired as men's and women's track coach by Humboldt State University in 1980 on a one-year contract. David Wells complained that women's athletics was disproportionally funded in relation to men's. His comments caused the university to appoint a faculty committee to conduct an investigation; the investigation confirmed that the funding for the teams was disproportionate and in violation of Title IX. The violation was ignored. Wells also conducted his own evaluation and further discovered that a large sum of money, $270,000, was unaccounted for in the athletic department. He filed complaints with administrators, the state auditor, and the Office of Civil Rights in 2001.

In April 2003, Wells received a contract for 10 months, rather than 12 months as his previous contracts had been, and his track team's budget was reduced by $104,000. He sued for retaliation under Title IX. He lost; his year-to-year contract did not give him the right to a renewed contract. Thus, his case was not a constructive discharge.

Michael Burch, head wrestling coach for men at the University of California, Davis, was a part-time employee of the athletic department in addition to a lecturing position. Burch made a weak wrestling team successful and received a local coach of the year award. He also complained about the status of wrestling for women. Shortly after the equity complaint, his coaching contract was not renewed.

Burch sued the university for retaliation, claiming he was punished for his "positive advocacy" for the women wrestlers who practiced with his team but could not compete in events. Under a university-imposed roster management system, the wrestling team was capped at 30 and as a result, the women were removed from the roster. Burch was successful against the athletic director, associate athletic director, and assistant chancellor for student affairs. Among the five components of the holding of the court for the plaintiff were: a) the fact issues as to whether reasons given for termination were pre-textual, and b) the coach's claims of gender discrimination affecting wrestlers were protected by the First Amendment. Holdings for the defendant were that: a) the coach's complaint of no separate women's wrestling team did not violate Title IX, b) the university provided gender neutral explanation of termination, c) there were fact issues as to whether the university would have terminated the coach in absence of his statements, and d) the chancellor had no involvement with termination decisions and was not liable for free speech violations (Burch, 2006).

Kiser, the male women's basketball coach on a yearly renewable contract at Clark College, was dismissed. He filed a cause of action against the college for retaliation, stating that his job had been threatened by the athletic director (AD) if he continued to make Title IX allegations (*Kiser v. Clark College,* 2008). He claimed that there existed "a consistent pattern of inequality between the College's men's and women's basketball teams. He said the differences were in budget, travel accommodations, and the AD's hostility toward the women's teams" (2). The college said he was fired for misappropriation of funds. The trial court found for the college; Kiser appealed. The court of appeals reversed and remanded the case for further proceedings. There is a possibility of retaliation, but because the coaching position was under a year-to-year contract, Kiser may have a difficult time succeeding.

Dr. Eve Atkinson was hired as Lafayette College's athletic director in 1989. One of her first responsibilities was to bring the college into compliance with Title IX. The detailed court document of 2009 identifies the rocky road she faced in attempting to satisfy compliance, morale, management, and competitive decisions. She was also faulted for encouraging athletes and coaches to take a stand against the management's suggestion to move athletics from NCAA Division One to Division Three (*Atkinson v. Lafayette College, et al.,* 2002, 2003, 2006, 2009). The college cited poor judgment, poor performance, and insubordination as the bases for her dismissal, while she cited retaliation for her work with Title IX and age discrimination. Following a nine-year battle, the U.S. District Court for the Eastern District of Pennsylvania concluded that Dr. Atkinson "has not met the burden of pointing to evidence that would allow a fact finder to discredit the College's legitimate, non-discriminatory reasons for her termination" (2009, 612).

Following *Jackson,* there appear to be a number of suits among people who had experienced problems in their coaching positions and also had defended equity principles for females. Thus, they sued for retaliation under Title IX for their loss of employment. In many of these cases, particularly among secondary schools, the districts were successful in the courts, claiming incompetence, insubordination, unethical conduct, and poor competitive records. Many of the secondary-school personnel lost their year-to-year contract coaching positions but retained their teaching positions. Obviously, some did not fully understand the rights of the school district in a year-to-year contract.

During that same time, a number of persons who claimed retaliation received successful settlements. Fresno State University of the California University system awarded Linda L. Vivas, the university's volleyball coach, $5.85 million when she sued for sex discrimination and retaliation (Lipka, 2007). "Although individuals can't sue public institutions in California for punitive damages, Vivas was awarded the above sum for past and future economic losses and emotional distress" (Redden, 2007a).

Five months later, a Fresno jury ordered the same university to pay Stacy Johnson-Klein $19.1 million. The former women's basketball coach sued for sex discrimination and retaliation for her advocacy for women's athletics (Redden, 2007b). A similar case was recently settled by Fresno University with Diane Milutinovich, the former associate athletic director, for $3.5 million (Redden, 2007b). Jaye Flood, former head women's volleyball coach at Florida Gulf Coast University, received just under $3 million for her suit filed shortly after she was terminated in January 2008 for speaking out about inequities, and the head women's golf coach at the same university received $500,000 to settle her claim (Funk, 2009).

SEXUAL HARASSMENT

Sexual harassment includes actions of employees, supervisors, teachers, coaches, principals, and students. Litigation has involved same- and opposite-sex relationships. Claims are usually filed under Title IX and 42 USC 1983. In these decisions, courts examine the responsibility of the agency (including knowledge or direct involvement in the incident, a negligent or reckless standard), Title VII standards (for hostile environments), and quid pro quo (a strict liability standard). The two major kinds of sexual harassment are hostile environment and quid pro quo.

Hostile Environment and Quid Pro Quo

Hostile environment usually involves behaviors of continuous harassment of a sexual nature. It involves repeated, unwanted requests for sex, offensive touching, or threats of a sexual nature. Offensive pictures, stories, and jokes are often evaluated in the context of what is considered appropriate behavior in the community. Quid pro quo, a strict or automatic liability standard, means that certain benefits are conditioned on sexual relationships. Business benefits, high grades, or money are among the conditions.

In *Faragher v. City of Boca Raton* (1994, 1996, 1997, 1998), the U.S. Supreme Court found that employers were vicariously liable for a hostile work environment. The employer was liable to the victim whether the employer knew (or should have known) of the harasser's conduct. Faragher resigned her lifeguard position with the City of Boca Raton, Florida, and brought a cause of action against the city and her immediate supervisors, stating that the supervisors had created a sexually hostile environment, "repeatedly subjecting Faragher and other female lifeguards to uninvited and offensive touching, by making lewd remarks, and by speaking of women in offensive terms, and that this conduct constituted discrimination in the terms, conditions, and privileges of her employment in violation of Title VII and the Civil Rights Act if 1964" (*Faragher v. City of Boca Raton,* 1998, Syllabus). The district court found the City of Boca Raton liable for the harassment of its supervisors; the Eleventh Circuit reversed, holding that the supervisors were not acting within the scope of their employment. The U.S. Supreme Court agreed with the district court.

Female soccer players brought an action under Title IX and 43 USC 1983 against a group of University of North Carolina administrators, alleging hostile environment and sexual harassment against the women's soccer coach and others. The graphic descriptions of hostile environment and sexual harassment in this case enables a reader to recognize such actions in a specialized educational environment like sport. Also, administrators will note that the action was brought against the head and assistant coaches, an athletic trainer, the estate of a former chancellor, an assistant to the chancellor, former and current athletic directors, and an assistant athletic director. Each was sued individually and in their official capacity (*Jennings v. University of North Carolina at Chapel Hill, et al.,* 2002, 496). Plaintiffs brought eight claims:

1) 42 USC 1983, violation of constitutional rights under First, Fourth, and Fourteenth Amendments against all defendants;

2) Rights under Title IX against all defendants;

3) Intentional interference with plaintiff one's contractual relationships with the U.S. Soccer Federation against the head coach;

4) For assault by plaintiff one against the head coach;

5) For battery by plaintiff one against the head coach;

6) For constructive fraud by plaintiff two against head coach and University, in general;

7) For negligent retention of head soccer coach by both plaintiffs against the University, in general; and

8) For invasion of privacy by both plaintiffs against the head coach and University. (497)

Defendants stated that all claims should be dismissed for lack of jurisdiction, failure to state a claim upon which relief could be granted, and sovereign immunity (Jennings, 2002, p. 497). The United States Court for the Middle District of North Carolina ruled on each of the above claims as they related to each defendant personally and in their official capacity. The following claims remained following the 2002 decision:

1) 42 USC claim brought by plaintiffs against the head and one assistant coach, estate of former university chancellor, assistant to the chancellor, former and current athletic directors, and assistant athlete director in their personal capacity;

2) Title IX claims against UNC by both plaintiffs;

3) state law claims against head coach by one plaintiff for intentional interference with a contractual relationship; for assault; and for battery; and

4) state law claim brought against head coach by both plaintiffs for invasion of privacy. (515, 516)

In the 2004 decision, the university was denied the privilege of submitting evidence under seal (Jennings, 2004). The 2007 U.S. Court of Appeals ruled on many of the detailed facts identified in 2002. The holding was:

1) Coaches' alleged actions, if proven, constituted sexual harassment based upon sex, as required for liability under Title IX;

2) coach's alleged behavior, if proven, was sufficiently severe or pervasive to create hostile or abusive environment; and

3) player alleged report to university's counsel, if proven, provided university with actual notice of hostile environment, as required for university to be liable under Title IX. (*Jennings, et al. v. University of North Carolina*, 2007, Holding)

In 2007, the United States Court of Appeals, Fourth Circuit, ruled against Jennings on the Title IX and 42 USC 1983 claims, demonstrating the kinds of detailed situations that need to be met to succeed under these laws. The allegations against the coaches for sexual harassment and hostile environment; and against the university for failure to act, if proper notice was given, remained. No further decision has been reported.

Faculty to Student Sexual Harassment

A female student in a Texas public high school had a sexual relationship with her male teacher; however, she did not report the incidents to school officials. Later, the police discovered the couple having sex. The teacher was arrested and the school district terminated his employment (*Gebster, et al. v. Lago Vista Independent School District*, 1998). The student filed suit against the school district for sexual harassment under state law, Title IX, and 42 USC 1983. The trial court dismissed the federal claims and remanded the case to state court as a negligence claim. The appellate court affirmed the trial court's dismissal of the federal claims. U.S. Supreme Court review was sought and received. The Court found that the "student was not allowed to recover for sexual harassment by one of the district's teachers unless an official of the district had actual notice of and was deliberately indifferent to the misconduct" (*Gebster, et al.*, 1998, Overview). For a school district to be held liable under *respondeat superior* or constructive notice, they must be aware of the situation. *Respondeat superior* refers to tort liability of the person in charge; constructive notice requires that the individual must be warned of the situation if he/she is to be held liable. *Respondeat superior* is a tort theory, while constructive notice is a civil rights theory.

In this case, the Supreme Court established a standard for sexual harassment cases in school districts. The plaintiff must prove that the abuse occurred, that the school authorities were properly informed, and that they did nothing about it. In a recent case, *Jane Doe, et al. v. School Board of Broward County, Florida, et al.* (2010), the United States Court of Appeals, Eleventh Circuit, grappled with the issue of who needs to be informed in the school and the actions the informed person is expected to take. In this situation, the principal was informed and requested written notice; hearings were held and the teacher was exonerated. Questions were raised by the court as to the discovery process and who was invited to provide written testimony.

The court stated, "In the case of teacher-on-student sexual harassment, our analysis is governed by the Supreme Court's decision in *Gebser v. Lago Vista Independent School District* (1998).... Title IX liability arises only where an official of the school district who at a minimum has authority to institute corrective measure on the district's behalf, has actual notice of and is deliberately indifferent to, the teacher's misconduct (Id. at 277,118 S. Ct. at 1993)" (*Jane Doe, et al. v. School Board of Broward County, Florida, et al.,* 2010, 1254). Jane Doe filed suit in the Southern District of Florida under Title IX and 42 USC 1983, seeking compensatory and punitive damages. The defendants responded with immunity. The court found that the evidence did not show an indifference to claims presented and that the plaintiff failed to show a causal relationship between the principal's actions and the plaintiff's claims of assault.

Assault by Male Athletes

A female basketball team member alleged sexual assault by three members of the men's basketball team (*Jane Doe v. University of the Pacific,* 2010). She reported the incident to the university, which investigated the incident, expelled one male, suspended the other two males, and suggested that there be no contact between the men's and women's basketball team members. The female basketball player sued the university under Title IX, stating that the institution did not prevent the assault, failed to respond appropriately to the complaint, and retaliated against both teams through the policy limiting unsupervised social action between team's members. The district court ruled for the university on all claims, by granting the university's motion in its entirety (*Jane Doe v. University of the Pacific,* 2010, 4).

The Tiffany Williams story is an incident of gang rape by athletes, this time basketball players from the University of Georgia (*Williams v. Board of Regents of the University System of Georgia, et al.,* 2007). Williams was invited by one of the males to his room for consensual sex. A second and a third male entered the room and engaged in nonconsensual sex with the defendant. About a year after the rapes, the university held a hearing in which it was decided not to sanction the players. Williams sued. The United States District Court for the Northern District of Georgia dismissed the Title IX, 42 USC 1983 claim, and the request for injunctive relief. Ms. Williams appealed. The Title IX claims against the University of Georgia Athletics and Athletic Association were reversed and remanded as it was discovered that appropriate persons had knowledge of previous harassment, and were deliberately indifferent. Her quest for injunctive relief was also reversed and remanded. All other district court rulings were affirmed. No further information was available at the time of press.

Plaintiffs Lisa Simpson and Anne Gilmore were sexually assaulted in Simpson's apartment by football players and high school students on a recruiting visit to the University of Colorado, Boulder (*Simpson, et al. v. University of Colorado, et al.* (2004, 2005, 2007). The Boulder campus officials were aware that sexual assaults could occur on these visits if supervision was not maintained. The local district attorney held a meeting with university officials, warning of such behavior. It was believed that the coaching staff not only knew of but condoned the behavior. Simpson and Gilmore each filed complaints, which were combined. They sought relief under Title IX and 20 USC 1681(a), claiming that the university knew of the sexual harassment of female students by the football recruiting program and failed to take any action to prevent the assault.

The University of Colorado filed a summary judgment, contending that the Title IX claims were not established. The district court granted the motion, stating that "no rational person could find (1) that CU had actual notice of sexual harassment by CU students, by football players and recruits before Plaintiffs' assaults or (2) that CU was indifferent to such harassment" (*Simpson*, 2005, 1235). There was lack of evidence of notice and indifference. The plaintiffs appealed. The U.S. District Court reversed the grant of summary judgment to CU and remanded for further proceedings. They stated that

> the evidence before the district court would support findings that by the time of the assaults on Plaintiffs, (1) Coach Barnett, whose rank in the CU hierarchy was comparable to that of a police chief in a municipal government, had general knowledge of the serious risk of sexual harassment and assault during college-football recruiting efforts; (2) Barnett knew that such assaults had indeed occurred during CU recruiting visits; (3) Barnett nevertheless maintained an unsupervised player-host program to show high-school recruits "a good time"; and Barnett knew, both because of incidents reported to him and because of his own unsupportive attitude, that there had been no change in the atmosphere since 1997 (when the prior assault occurred) that would make such misconduct less likely in 2001. A jury could infer that "the need for more or different training [of player-hosts was] so obvious, and the inadequacy so likely to result in [Title IX violations], that [Coach Barnett could] reasonably be said to have been deliberately indifferent to the need. (2007, 1184–1185)

SUMMARY

Gender equity laws are the Fourteenth Amendment to the United States Constitution, Title IX, the Civil Rights Restoration Act of 1967, the Civil Rights Act of 1991, and the Equity in Athletics Disclosure Act. The Fourteenth Amendment and Title IX identify and give basic rights. The Civil Rights Act of 1987 restored Title IX to its original intent following the "program specific" approach that resulted from the *Grove City* case. The Civil Rights Act of 1991 provides attorney fees and punitive damages, and requires the defendant to take the lead in disproving the charge of discrimination in the civil rights area. The *Franklin v. Gwinnett* (1992) case verified the operation of the 1991 statute. The Equity in Athletics Disclosure Act provided society with factual information on which of its members could make decisions.

Disparate treatment and disparate impact (equity by enrollment) have become the bases of many court decisions. Court cases have come from athletes and their parents, coaches, athletic personnel, and others. Note should be made that no school that has been sanctioned by the Office of Civil Rights or the courts under Title IX has lost its federal or state funding. Court decisions have been provided under the impact of athletic governance, collegiate and scholastic women seeking equity, roster stacking, complaints by male athletes, retaliation, and sexual harassment.

DISCUSSION QUESTIONS

1. What is the difference between a constitutional provision and a statute? Thus, what is the difference between the 14th Amendment, Equal Protection Clause to the U.S. Constitution and Title IX?

2. Are the majority of high schools and institutions of higher education in compliance with the 14th Amendment and with Title IX?

3. What is roster stacking? Is it legal or illegal?

ACTIVITIES

1. Obtain a current NCAA Manual and identify the information on scholarship requirements. Design a program for a typical undergraduate institution of higher education with an enrollment of 60% female and 40% male. Identify sports, numbers of participants or berths on teams, and scholarships. You must include football; no other sport is required. The program must be equitable.

2. Locate gender equity court decisions in LexisNexis completed in the last two years. Contrast the facts, the law, and theories found in the recent cases with those published ten years ago.

3. Compare and contrast the Fourteenth Amendment Equal Protection Clause with prong one under Title IX, implementing guidelines.

4. Read *Jackson v. Birmingham Board of Education* and *Faragher v. Boca Raton*. Explain the differences, if any, between the cases settled by the Supreme Court of the United States and those settled by federal courts.

REFERENCES

AIAW v. NCAA, 735 F. 2d 577 (1984); 558 F. Supp. 487 (1983).

Alston v. Virginia High School League, Inc., 108 F. Supp. 2d 543 (2000); 144 F. Supp. 2d 526 (1999).

Atkinson v. Lafayette College, et al., 653 F. Supp. 2d 581 (2009); 60 F. 3d 227 (2006); 2003 U.S. Dist. LEXIS 13951; 2002 U.S. Dist. LEXIS 1432.

Barrett, et al. v. West Chester University of Pennsylvania of the State System of Higher Education, et al., 636 F. Supp. 2d 439 (2009); 2006 U.S. Dist. LEXIS 15332; 2003 U.S. Dist. LEXIS 21095.

Barrs, et al. v. The Southern Conference, 734 F. Supp. 1229 (2010).

Bednar v. Nebraska School Activities Association, 531 F. 2d 922 (1976).

Bennett v. West Texas State University, 799 F. 2d 155 (1986); 698 F. 2d 1215 (1983); 525 F. Supp. 77 (1981); and West Texas v. Bennett, cert. to U.S. Supreme Court denied, 104 S. Ct. 1677 (1984).

Biediger, et al. v. Quinnipac University, 728 F. Supp. 2d 62 (July, 2010); 2010 U.S. Dist. LEXIS 50044; 616 F. Supp. 2d 277 (2009).

Blair, et al. v. Washington State University, et al., 740 P. 2d 1379 (1989).

Boulahamis, et al. v. Board of Regents, Illinois State University, et al., cert to U.S. Supreme Court denied 120 S. Ct. 2762 (2000); 98 F. 3d 633 (1999).

Brake, D. L. (2007). Title IX as pragmatic feminism. 55 *Clev. St. L. Rev.* 513.

Brenden v. Independent School District, 477 F. 2d 1292 (1973); 342 F. Supp. 1224 (1972).

Brust, et al. v. Regents of the University of California, 2009 U.S. Dist. LEXIS 124980; 2007 U.S. Dist. LEXIS 91303.

Burch v. Regents of the University of California, et al. 433 F. Supp. 2d 1110 (2006).

Cannon v. University of Chicago, 103 S. Ct. 1254 (1983); 99 S. Ct. 1946 (1979); 99 S. Ct. 715 (1978).

Carnes v. Tennessee Secondary School Athletic Association, et al., 415 F. Supp. 569 (1976).

Chalenor, et al. v. The University of North Dakota, 291 F. 3d. 1042 (2002); 142 F. Supp. 2d 1154 (2000).

Choike, et al. v. Slippery Rock University of Pennsylvania of the State System of Higher Education, et al., 2010 U.S. App. LEXIS 23791; 2010 U.S. Dist. LEXIS 118131; 2010 U.S. Dist. LEXIS 122218; 297 Fed. Appx. 138 (2008); 2007 U.S. Dist. LEXIS 57774; 2007 U.S. Dist. LEXIS 4284; 2006 U.S. Dist. LEXIS 49886.

Civil Rights Act of 1991, 42 USC 1981.

Civil Rights Restoration Act of 1987, 20 USC 1687 (1994).

Class Action, Rule 23, Federal Rules of Civil Procedure.

Cobb & Saly v. United States Department of Education, Office of Civil Rights, 487 F. Supp. 2d 1049 (2006).

Cohen, et al. v. Brown University, et al., cert. to the U.S. Supreme Court denied, 117 S. Ct. 1469 (1997); 101 F. 3d 155 (1996); 879 F. Supp. 185 (1995); 991 F. 2d 888 (1993); 809 F. Supp. 978 (1992).

College Sports Council, et al. v. Department of Education, et al., 2007 U.S. App. LEXIS 1420; 2007 U.S. App. LEXIS 1410; 2006 App. LEXIS27899; 465 F. 2d 20 (2006); 2006 U.S. pp. LEXIS 1839; 2005 U. S, App. LEXIS 21742; 357 F. Supp. 2d 311 (2005).

College Sports Council, et al. v. Government Accountability Office, et al., 421 F. Supp. 2d 59 (2006).

Communities for Equity, et al. v. Michigan High School Athletic Association, et al., 2008 U S. Dist. Lexis 62298; 2008 U.S. Dist. LEXIS 25640; 459 F. 3d 676 (2006); 2003 U.S. Dist. LEXIS 2872; 2002 U.S. Dist. LEXIS 3575; 2002 U.S. Dist. LEXIS 14220; 178 F. Supp. 2d 805 (2001); 2001 U.S. Dist. LEXIS 14718; 2001 U.S. Dist. LEXIS. 16014; 2001 U.S. Dist. LEXIS 5806; 80 F. Supp. 729 (2000); 26 F. Supp. 2d 1001 (1998).

Cooper v. Peterson, 626 N.Y.S. 2d 432 (1995).

Equity in Athletics, Inc., et al. v. Department of Education, et al., 2011 U.S. App. LEXIS 4493; 685 F. Supp. 2d 660 (2009); 291 Fed. Appx. 517 (2008); 504 F. Supp. 2d 88 (2007).

Equity in Athletics Disclosure Act of 1994, 20 USC 1092.

Faragher v. City of Boca Raton, 118 S. Ct. 1115 (1998); 118 S. Ct. 2276 (1998); 111 F. 3d 1530 (1997); 76 F. 3d 1155 (1996); 864 F. Supp. 1552 (1994).

Federal Rules of Civil Procedure (2010). Washington, DC: Government Printing Office.

Foltz, et al. v. Delaware State University, 269 F.R.D. 419 (2010).

Fortin v. Darlington Little League, 376 F. Supp. 514 F. 2d 344 (1975); 376 F. Supp. 473 (1974).

Franklin v. Gwinnett, 111 S. Ct. 949 (1991); 111 S. Ct. 2795 (1991); 112 S. Ct. 1028 (1992); 11 F. 2d 617 (1990).

Funk, A. (2009, June/July). Firing back. *Athletic Management.* Retrieved from http://www.athleticmanagement.com/2009/06/10/firing_back/index.php

Gebser, et al. v. Lago Vista Independent School District, 118 S. Ct. 1206 (1998); 118 S. Ct. 1989 (1998).

Gilpin v. Kansas State High School Activities Association, 377 F. Supp. 1233 (1973).

Gomes v. Rhode Island Interscholastic League, 604 F. 2d 733 (1979); 469 F. Supp. 659 (1979); 99 S. Ct. 2401 (1979).

Gonyo, et al. v. Drake University, et al., 879 F. Supp. 1000 (1995); 837 F. Supp. 989 (1993).

Grove City v. Bell, 104 S. Ct. 1211 (1984); 104 S. Ct. 521 (1983); 687 F. 2d 684 (1982).

Habetz v. Louisiana High School Athletic Association, 915 F 2d 164 (1990); 842 F. 2d 136 (1988).

Haffer v. Temple University, 524 F. Supp. 678 F. Supp. 517 (1988); 115 Fed. Rules Decision 506 (1987); 688 F. 2d 14 (1982); 524 F. Supp. 531 (1981).

Hass v. South Bend Community School Corporation, 289 N. E. 2d 495 (1972).

Hazelwood School District v. United States, 97 S. Ct. 2736 (1977).

Hess, et al. v. Ramona Unified School District, et al., 2008 U.S. Dist. LEXIS 102743; 2007 U.S. Dist. LEXIS 67687.

Hollander v. Connecticut Interscholastic Athletic Association, Inc., 164 Conn. 654 (1972).

Horner v. Kentucky High School Athletic Association, cert. to U.S. Supreme Court denied, 121 S. Ct. 69 (2000); 206 F. 3d 685 (2000); 43 F. 3d 265 (1994).

House Report, 102 Con., 1st Session at 72.

Hult, J. S. (1980). The philosophical conflicts in men's and women's collegiate athletics. *Quest, 32*(1), 77–94.

Israel v. West Virginia Secondary School Activities Commission, 388 S. E. 2d 480 (1989).

Jackson v. Birmingham Board of Education, 125 S. Ct. 1497 (2005); 125 S. Ct. 457 (2004); 124 S. Ct. 365 (2003); 309 F. 3d 1333 (2002); 695 F. Supp. 1164 (1988).

Jane Doe, et al. v. School Board of Broward County, Florida, et al., 604 F. 3d 1248 (2010).

Jane Doe v. University of the Pacific, 2010 U.S. Dist. LEXIS 130099.

Jennings, et al. v. University of North Carolina at Chapel Hill, et al., 482 F. 3d 686 (2007); 444 F. 3d 255 (2006); 340 F. Supp. 2d 679 (2004); 240 F. Supp. 492 (2002).

Kelly v. Board of Trustees of the University of Illinois, 35 F. 2d 265 (1994); 832 F. Supp. 237 (1993); 559 N.E. 2d 196 (1990); 826 F. 2d 1068 (1987).

Kiser v. Clark College, 2008 Wash. App. LEXIS 703.

Koller, D. L. (2010, Dec.). Not just one of the boys: A post-feminist critique of Title IX's vision for gender equity in sports. 43 *Conn. L. Rev.* 401.

Kuznick, L., & Ryan, M. (2008, Summer). Changing social norms? Title IX and legal activism comments from the Spring 2007 Harvard Journal of Law and Gender Conference. 31 *Harv. J. L. & Gender* 367.

Landow, et al. v. School Board of Brevard County, 2001 U.S. Dist. LEXIS 7156; 2001 U.S. Dist. 7155; 132 F. Supp. 958 (2000).

Lederman, D. (1982). U.S. draft memo on sex equity in college sports. *The Chronicle of Higher Education, 38*(22), 1.

Libby v. South Inter-Conference Association, 728 F. Supp. 504 (1990); 704 F. Supp. 142 (1988).

Lichten, et al. v. State University of New York at Albany, et al., 223 A. D. 2nd 302 (1996).

Lipka, S. (2007). Jury orders Fresno State U. to pay ex-coach $5.85-million in discrimination case. *The Chronicle of Higher Education, 53*(46), A30.

Magill v. Avonworth Baseball Conference, et al., 516 F. 2d 1328 (1975); 364 F. Supp. 1212 (1973).

Mansourian, et al. v. Regents of the University of California, University of California at Davis, et al., 2011 U.S. Dist. LEXIS 4315; 2010 U.S. Dist. LEXIS 130020; 602 F. 3d 957; 2008 U.S. Dist. LEXIS 75014.

Mason, et al. v. Minnesota State High School League, 2004 U.S. Dist. LEXIS 13865.

McCormick, et al. v. The School District of Mamaroneck and the School District of Pelham, 370 F. 3d 275 (2004).

Mercer v. Duke University, et al. 401 F. 3d 199 (2005); 181 F. Supp. 2d 525 (2001); 90 F. 3d 643 (1999); 1998 U.S. Dist. LEXIS 20164.

Michigan High School Athletic Association v. Community for Equity, 125 S. Ct. 1973; 127 S. Ct. 1912.

Miller v. The University of Cincinnati, 2008 U.S. Dist. LEXIS 4339; 2007 U.S. Dist. LEXIS 70484; 241 F. R. D. 285 (2006).

Morris v. Michigan State Board of Education, 472 F. 2d 1207 (1973).

National Collegiate Athletic Association (NCAA), v. Joseph Califano, Secretary of the U.S. Department of Health, Education and Welfare, 444 F. Supp. 425 (1978).

National Organization for Women v. Little League Baseball, Inc., 338 A. 2d 198 (1974); 318 A. 2d 33 (1974).

National Wrestling Coaches Association, et al. v. United States Department of Education, et al., 366 F. 3d 930 (2004); 263 F. Supp. 82 (2003).

Neal, et al. v. The Board of Trustees of California State University, et al., cert denied, 124 S. Ct. 226 (2003); 51 Fed. Appx. 736 (2002); 198 F. 3d 763 (1999).

North Haven v. Bell, 102 S. Ct. 1912 (1982).

Ollier, et al. v. Sweetwater Union High School District, et al., 251 F. R. D. 267 F.R.D. 338 (2010); 735 F. Supp. 2d 1222 (2010); 604 F. Supp. 1264 (2009); 251 F. R. D. 564 (2008).

Othen v. Ann Arbor School District, 699 F. 2d 309 (1982); 507 F. Supp. 1376 (1981).

Parker, et al. v. Indiana High School Athletic Association, 2010 U.S. Dist. LEXIS 103432 (Sept., 2010); 2010 U.S. Dist. LEXIS (Oct., 2010); 2010 U.S. Dist. LEXIS 107497; 2009 U.S. Dist. LEXIS 113395.

Pederson, et al. v. Louisiana State University, 213 F. 3d 858 (2000); 912 F. Supp. 892 (1996).

Petrie v. Illinois High School Athletic Association, 394 N. E. 2d 855 (1979).

Redden, E. (2007a, July 11). Big payday for Title IX advocate. *Inside Higher Ed.* Retrieved from http://www.insidehighered.com/news/2007/07/11/fresno

Redden, E. (2007b, Dec. 10). Fallout from Fresno State's multi-million dollar case(s). *Inside Higher Ed.* Retrieved from http://www.insidehighered.com/news/2007/12/10/fresno

Reed v. Nebraska Athletic Association, 341 F. Supp. 258 (1972).

Ridgeway v. Montana High School Association, 858 F. 2d 579 (1988); 633 F. Supp. 1564

(1986); 638 F. Supp. 326 (1986).

Roberts v. Colorado State Board of Agriculture, 998 F. 2d 824 (1993[a]); 814 F. Supp. 1507 (1993[b]); and Colorado State Board of Agriculture v. Roberts, cert. to the U.S. Supreme Court denied 114 S. Ct. 580 (1993[c]).

Schnarrs, et al., v. Girard Board of Education, et al., 858 N. E. 2d 1258 (2006); 220 F. R. D. 354 (2004).

Simpson, et al. v. University of Colorado, 500 F. 3d 1170 (2007); 372 F. Supp. 2d 1229 (2005); 20 F. R. D. 354 (2004).

State of Oregon v. Hunter, 300 P. 2d 455 (1956).

Teamsters v. United States, 431 U.S. 324 (1977).

Title IX of the Education Amendments of 1972, 20 USC. Section 1681–1688 (1990).

Uhlir, A. (1982). The wolf is our shepherd: Shall we not fear? *Phi Delta Kappa, 64*(3), 172.

Well v. Board of Trustees of the California State University, et al., 2006 U.S. Dist. LEXIS 68260; 393 F. Supp. 2d 990 (2005).

Williams v. University of Georgia, 477 F. 3d 1282 (2007).

Yellow Springs Exempted Village School District v. Ohio High School Athletic Association, 647 F. 2d 651 (1981).

RECOMMENDED READING

Anderson, P. (2008). A historical review of Title IX litigation. 18 *J. Legal Aspects of Sport* 127.

Hefferan, J. (2007). Changing seasons, changing times: The validity of nontraditional sports seasons under Title IX and the Equal Protection Clause. 9 *Vand. J. Ent. & Tech L.* 861.

McCart, W. R. (2008). Simpson v. University of Colorado: Title IX crashes the party in college athletic recruiting. 58 *DePaul L. Rev.* 153.

Mitten, M. J., Musselman, J. L., & Burton, B. W. (2010). Targeted reform of commercialized intercollegiate athletics. 47 *San Diego L. Rev.* 779.

6

Americans with Disabilities Act (ADA)

OBJECTIVES

Upon completing this chapter, you will:

1) understand the relationship between various laws applicable to accommodating people with disabilities in sport settings;

2) be able to explain what a plaintiff is required to establish to bring a claim for violation of the ADA;

3) be able to apply the steps necessary to make a determination about modifying sport rules or eligibility for people with disabilities;

4) understand the detailed requirements for stadium accessibility; and

5) know how to conduct an individualized inquiry assessment of a person with a disability who has requested a modification of policies and procedures.

INTRODUCTION

Providing equal opportunity for people with disabilities is the fundamental principle of the Americans with Disabilities Act (ADA) of 1990 (U.S. Department of Justice, 2011). Sport opportunities for people with disabilities have expanded since passage of the ADA. With the enactment of the ADA, efforts have been focused on including people with disabilities in sport, as both participants and spectators. Historically, full participation and equal opportunity in sport and recreation services have been a challenge for people with disabilities (Fay & Wolff, 2000). This can be attributed to physical barriers to participation, such as inaccessible sport and recreation facilities, as well as a fundamental lack of understanding of the needs of people with disabilities while participating in sport or while attending sporting events.

Today, providing a barrier-free and inclusive environment for people with disabilities has become an emerging priority in sport management and "is now (or should be) an integral part of any discussion when making programming decisions or facility renovations" (Grady & Andrew, 2003, p. 231). Despite the substantial progress made in enhancing access to sport for people with disabilities, sport managers continue to face challenges in implementing the provisions of the ADA into their facilities (Grady & Andrew, 2003). While the ADA is the most-recognized law mandating access for people with disabilities in the United States, the legal precursors to the ADA are also relevant to certain segments of sport management.

SECTION 504 OF THE REHABILITATION ACT

As public awareness of the need to educate children with disabilities grew, the United States Congress enacted federal legislation and provided funding to assist school districts in educating children with disabilities. In 1973, Congress passed the Rehabilitation Act. Section 504 of the act states that

> No otherwise qualified handicapped individual in the United States, as defined in section 7(6), shall solely by reason of his handicap, be excluded from the participation in, be denied the benefit of, or be subjected to discrimination under any program or activity receiving Federal financial assistance. (45 CFR 84)

The scope of Section 504 of the Rehabilitation Act includes schools which educate children as well as entities which receive federal funds. This includes colleges and universities as well as cultural venues, such as performing arts centers, which may rely on federal funds to support their operations. While similar to the goals of the ADA in ensuring access to programs and services, knowledge of the specific requirements of Section 504 of the Rehabilitation Act may be required depending on the type of sport program or service being offered.

AMERICANS WITH DISABILITIES ACT (ADA)

President George H. W. Bush signed the Americans with Disabilities Act (ADA) into law on July 26, 1990. The ADA was enacted to provide a national mandate to eliminate discrimination faced by people with disabilities on a day-to-day basis (42 USC 12101[b]). Discrimination includes "denial of services, aids, or benefits, provision of different service or in a different manner, and segregation or separate treatment" based on disability status (U.S. Department of the Interior, n.d.). The ADA supplements existing federal and state statutes designed to accommodate persons with one or more disabilities. The ADA is a remedial statute (meaning its goal is to remedy the effects of past discrimination) and is modeled after the Civil Rights Act of 1964 and the Rehabilitation Act of 1973. It provides civil protection in employment, in government services (including transportation and schools), and in public accommodations to people with disabilities. To establish a prima facie case of discrimination under the ADA, the plaintiff must prove: (1) that she has a disability, (2) that she is a qualified individual, and (3) that she was subject to unlawful discrimination because of her disability (*Morisky v. Broward County*, 1996).

ADA Titles

The ADA contains five titles which detail legal rights provided to persons with disabilities.

Title I: Employment

Title II: Public Services

Title III: Public Accommodation

Title IV: Telecommunications

Title V: Miscellaneous Provisions

Title I protects people with disabilities from employment discrimination in businesses with 15 or more employees. Businesses that fall within the scope of ADA are required to provide reasonable accommodation so that the individual with a disability may perform the required tasks of his/her job. For example, an arena that provides a ticket taker who has chronic back pain with a chair to take periodic breaks while taking tickets may constitute a reasonable accommodation.

The key provisions of the ADA applicable to sport, physical activity, and recreation services are Title II and Title III (Grady & Andrew, 2003). Title II mandates that public entities, including state and local governments, give people with disabilities an equal opportunity to benefit from all of their programs, services, and activities (42 USC 12132). Title II incorporates aspects of Section 504 of the Rehabilitation Act. Title II is enforced in schools and is a factor when sport and physical activity facilities are municipally owned. Title II is important in creating individualized educational programs (IEPs) for students with disabilities that include or should include physical activity and aquatics.

Educational components of Title II are also addressed under the Individuals with Disabilities Education Act (IDEA). IDEA "requires public schools to make available to all eligible children with disabilities a free appropriate public education in the least restrictive environment appropriate to their individual needs" (U.S. Department of Justice, n.d.). IDEA requires public schools to develop an Individualized Education Program (IEP) for each child that reflects his/her needs (U.S. Department of Justice, n.d.).

Title III provides protection for individuals with disabilities seeking access to places of public accommodation (42 USC 1282). Title III specifically mentions sport, recreation, and play facilities and is usually the area of greatest concern in sport and physical activity. "Title III of the ADA outlaws not just intentional discrimination but also certain practices that have a disparate impact upon persons with disabilities even in the absence of any conscious intent to discriminate," also known as de facto discrimination (*Indep. Living Res. v. Oregon Arena Corp.*, 1169). With respect to de facto violations, places of public accommodation under Title III are only required to "take remedial measures that are (a) effective, (b) practical, and (c) fiscally manageable" (*Ass'n for Disabled Am., Inc. v. Concorde Gaming Corp.*, 1362).

Title IV addresses telecommunication and telephone services with the FCC and individual states working on complaints. Title V involves retaliation, nondiscrimination in service benefits, and attorney fees for prevailing parties in actions brought to enforce the ADA. The Equal Employment Opportunities Commission (EEOC) is responsible for providing technical assistance for Title I. The Department of Justice (DOJ) is to provide technical assistance for Titles II and III.

Definition of Disability

The term "disability," for the purposes of the ADA, means that an individual has:

A) a physical or mental impairment that substantially limits one or more of the major life activities of such individual;

B) a record of such an impairment; or

C) being regarded as having such an impairment. (42 USC 12101, Section 3[2])

A physical or mental impairment is "any physiological disorder or condition, cosmetic disfigurement, or anatomical loss affecting one or more of the following body systems: neurological; musculoskeletal; specific sense organs; respiratory, including speech organs; cardiovascular; reproductive; digestive; genito-urinary; hemic and lymphatic; skin; and endocrine or any mental or psychological disorder" (29 CFR 1630.2[h]). Major life activities are caring for oneself, performing manual tasks, walking, seeing, hearing, speaking, breathing, learning, and working (29 CFR 1630.2[I]).

Purpose of the ADA

The purpose of the act is:

1) To provide a clear and comprehensive national mandate for the elimination of discrimination against individuals with disabilities;

2) To provide clear, strong, consistent, enforceable standards addressing discrimination against individuals with disabilities;

3) To ensure that the Federal Government plays a central role in enforcing the standards established in this act on behalf of individuals with disabilities; and

4) To invoke the sweep of congressional authority, including the power to enforce the Fourteenth Amendment and to regulate commerce, in order to address the major areas of discrimination faced day-to-day by people with disabilities. (42 USC 12101, Section 2[b])

Title I

Title I is "an anti-discrimination statute that requires that individuals with disabilities be given the same consideration for employment that individuals without disabilities be given" (29 CFR 1630.1[a] Purpose). It reaffirms Title VII of the Civil Rights Act of 1964 and Section 504 of the Rehabilitation Act of 1973. The phrase "qualified individual with a disability" refers to a person who is able to perform the essential functions of a job with or without reasonable accommodations. Under the ADA and Section 504, no employer can discriminate against a qualified individual with a disability in the application and interview process, hiring, assignments, evaluation, promotion, and termination. Compensation, training, disciplinary action, leaves, in-service opportunities, and other terms, conditions, and privileges of employment must be the same. Employers have the same obligations to current employees who become disabled while employed.

The ADA requires that reasonable accommodations for the physical or mental limitations of a qualified applicant be made. Reasonable accommodations include facility access, restructuring job tasks with accommodations in mind, modifying work schedules, and providing readers, special computers, and interpreters. While the ADA's role is to remove barriers and to force employers to examine perceived barriers, the ADA does not relieve an employee or applicant with a disability from the obligation to perform the essential functions of the job. The purpose is to enable persons with disabilities to compete in the workplace and be measured on the same performance standards as all employees.

Accommodations are required unless the accommodation places an undue hardship on the employer. Factors to be considered in determining undue hardship are:

- nature and cost of accommodation;
- overall financial resources of agency;
- size, budget, and profitability of business; and
- financial impact of the recommended accommodation.

An undue hardship defense is also available under Title II (discussed below). These decisions are made by the Equal Employment Opportunity Commission (EEOC) on a case-by-case basis.

The ADA does not require an employer to hire an applicant or retain an employee who poses a "direct threat" to the health or safety of other employees or clients. A "direct threat" means a significant risk to the health or safety of others that cannot be eliminated by reasonable accommodations. Direct threat situations in sport and physical activity nearly always involve safety (i.e., the safety of the clients, participants, and employees). In these situations, safety requirements are based on real risks—not speculations, stereotypes, or generalizations about persons with disabilities.

Title I enforcement is similar to the enforcement of Title VII of the Civil Rights Act of 1964. The investigation is conducted by the EEOC. Furthermore, a right to file a lawsuit exists.

Title II

Title II of the ADA, Nondiscrimination on the Basis of Disability in State and Local Government Services, prohibits discrimination in services, programs, and activities provided or made available by state and local governments or their instrumentalities. The receipt of federal financial assistance is not required for the enforcement of Title II. The statute extends the provisions of Section 504 of the Rehabilitation Act of 1973 to state and local governments, including schools and municipal recreation facilities.

The sport professional employed in Title II environments is to inform clients and students of their rights. In addition, the professional must analyze facilities, programs, policies, and procedures for physical and psychological barriers. Lastly, the professional is to assess for violations and retain written documentation.

Title III

With Title III of the ADA (public accommodations and services operated by private entities), sport and physical activities are specifically covered in Section 301(7). Included in this section are the following:

I) a park, zoo, amusement park, or other place of recreation;

J) a nursery, elementary, secondary, undergraduate, or post-graduate private school, or other place of education;

K) a daycare center, senior citizen center, or other social service center establishment; and

L) a gymnasium, health spa, bowling alley, golf course, or other place of exercise or recreation. (Title III, Section 301[7])

Title III requires that all privately operated, non-residential buildings become accessible to and usable by individuals with disabilities. Title III prohibits discrimination against persons with disabilities in the full and equal enjoyment of goods, services, facilities, privileges, and advantages of any public accommodation provided by private individuals or organizations. Discrimination under Title III would include provision of different services or benefits to people with disabilities than are provided to able-bodied patrons, as well as providing services and benefits in a different manner to people with disabilities. A place of public accommodation is a facility operated by a private entity whose operations affect commerce and fall into one of the following categories: lodging, eating, entertainment, recreation, service, and education. Public accommodations include restaurants, hotels, shopping malls, grocery stores, museums, and recreation centers, among others.

Under Title III, facilities must comply with the required approach, entry, and use standards. Use standards are programs, policies, and procedures. Accommodations for people with mobility impairments, visual impairments, hearing impairments, and mental capacity issues are to be made. When strict compliance is not possible, minor deviations are permitted. However, no deviation that is a safety risk is allowed.

The Department of Justice (DOJ) recommends a detailed written plan that establishes a good faith effort to be prepared. Plans are to include goals, objectives, programs, services, evaluations (including assessment tools), and methods of integrating results. The U.S. Attorney General, Office of Civil Rights, investigates violations of the ADA. When violations are identified, a compliance review is initiated.

The DOJ's Civil Rights Division is responsible for Titles II and III compliance reviews and complaints. The Equal Employment Opportunities Commission (EEOC) is responsible for Title I complaints. States with laws similar to the ADA and cities with building codes that mirror the ADA standards also play a role in the resolution of violations of the ADA.

DEFENSES TO DISABILITY DISCRIMINATION

While the ADA creates numerous obligations for the sport business, there are several defenses available to a service provider that can be used to deny a policy modification request or to protect the health and safety of other patrons (Grady & Andrew, 2003). Under Title II, a public entity is not required to take actions that would result in undue hardship, including undue financial and administrative burdens (U.S. Department of Justice, 2005). Undue hardship refers to "an action requiring significant difficulty or expense" when considered in light of several factors (42 USC 12111[10]).

The factors considered are the same as an undue hardship defense under Title I in the employment context and include the nature and costs of the accommodation requested, the overall financial resources of the facility providing reasonable accommodation, the number of employees at the facility, the effect on expenses and resources resulting from providing the accommodation, the overall financial resources of the covered entity, and the type of operation of the covered entity (42 USC 12111[10, A]). Under Title II, the public entity is "required to make reasonable modifications to policies, practices, and procedures where necessary to avoid discrimination, unless the service provider can demonstrate that doing so would fundamentally alter the nature of the service, program, or activity being provided" (U.S. Department of Justice, 2002). The fundamental alteration defense was raised by the PGA, where the Supreme Court held that allowing Casey Martin to use a golf cart during PGA qualifying tournaments would not fundamentally alter the nature of the golf tournaments (*PGA Tour v. Martin,* 2000, 690).

Similarly, Title III requires "reasonable modification of policies, practices, or procedures of a public accommodation unless doing so would fundamentally alter what is offered" (*PGA Tour v. Martin,* 2000, 668).

Title III also requires the removal of architectural or structural barriers that prevent access to public accommodations, when their removal is readily achievable (42 USC 12182[b]). If barrier removal is not readily achievable, the public accommodation must make its goods or services available to people with disabilities through alternative methods, if such alternative methods are readily achievable (42 USC 12182[b]). For example, if a stadium only sells tickets online, the facility must establish an alternative sales method, such as calling on the telephone or buying tickets in person at the box office, to accommodate patrons who, because of their disability, cannot purchase tickets online.

While Title III does not allow for an undue hardship defense for the failure to construct new facilities in accordance with the ADA's implementing regulations and ADA Accessibility Guidelines (28 CFR 36.406, Appendix A), an undue hardship defense can still be raised related to policies and procedures using an administrative burden theory (Grady & Andrew, 2003). In *PGA Tour v. Martin* (2000), discussed below, the PGA asserted that if their organization had to review numerous appeals by other golfers with disabilities requesting accommodations, the administrative process would constitute an undue hardship (1002). The court referred to *Washington v.*

Indiana High Sch. Athletic Ass'n (1999, 852) where the Seventh Circuit analyzed the individualized assessment requirement for a learning-disabled student athlete waiver from an eight-semester limit on competition. The court in *Washington* stated that the few case-by-case analyses that the athletic association "would need to conduct hardly can be described as an excessive burden" (852). Citing this rationale, the Ninth Circuit in *Martin* rejected the undue burden argument, finding that an individualized determination would not impose an intolerable burden on the PGA (*PGA Tour v. Martin,* 2000, 1002).

As mentioned earlier in the context of Title I, the "direct threat" exception can be raised as a defense when there is concern about health or safety of others given the nature of the person's disability or due to the auxiliary aid that the person uses, such as a wheelchair. "Direct threat" is often an issue in the context of emergency evacuation of people with disabilities (Grady & Andrew, 2007). For example, seating patrons in wheelchairs in a path designated as the emergency evacuation route used by able-bodied patrons would raise "direct threat" concerns, as other patrons may not be able to evacuate quickly and efficiently in an emergency due to the presence of the wheelchairs, as well as the potential inability of patrons in wheelchairs to evacuate quickly. To utilize the direct threat defense, the service provider must conduct an individual assessment of the risk to the health and safety of others (McGovern, n.d.). "The assessment must include a consideration of how reasonable accommodations such as rule changes or adaptive equipment would eliminate or minimize the risk and enable participation in the activity" (McGovern, n.d.).

CASES

The following are examples of cases that have examined the application of the ADA in sport: *Martin v. PGA Tour,* 2000; *Anderson v. Little League Baseball, Inc.,* 1992; *Bowers v. the National Collegiate Athletic Association, et al.,* 2003; as well as several cases discussed below involving age eligibility issues of interscholastic athletes with learning disabilities.

Modifications of Rules and Policies

Casey Martin's decision from the United States Supreme Court is the most often mentioned court decision in sport related to the Americans with Disabilities Act. The Professional Golf Association (PGA) uses a three-stage qualifying tournament as the most popular means of gaining entry into its tour. Stages one and two permit a participant to use a golf cart while playing; players must walk the course in the third stage. Martin, a professional golfer, has Klippel-Trenaunay-Weber Syndrome, a degenerative circulatory disorder that meets the ADA definition of a disability. He petitioned the PGA, with comprehensive medical support, requesting an accommodation under Title III to use a golf cart during the third stage of qualifying. Martin was denied the accommodation.

Martin filed an action against the PGA under Title III of the ADA. The District Court of Oregon entered a preliminary injunction permitting him to enter the tournament. After a trial, the injunction became permanent. An underlying issue was whether Title III, which includes public accommodations, could be applied in professional sport. The United States Court of Appeals for the Ninth Circuit affirmed the lower court's decision, stating that the golf course was a place of public accommodation and that the use of a cart during the tour would not fundamentally alter the tournament. The United States Supreme Court affirmed.

In another high-profile case, Judge Lawrence Anderson of Phoenix, Arizona, a wheelchair user, was selected to coach a 1992 All-Star National Little League competition (*Anderson v. Little League Baseball, Inc.,* 1992). However, the president and CEO of Little League Baseball adopted a policy stating that a coach in a wheelchair could coach from the dugout but not from a coach's box. The safety of the players was the rationale for the decision.

Judge Anderson had been an on-field coach of his son's team for three years. Coach Anderson saw the policy as a way to eliminate him from coaching if his team made the finals. In 1991, Judge Anderson's team was eliminated early in the competition. During 1992, the local branch of Little League Baseball allowed him to continue to assume his preferred coaching position on the field. When it appeared that his 1992 team was going to be successful in the national tournament, he filed an injunction to stop enforcement of Little League's policy (or, in the alternative, asked the court to allow him to participate fully by coaching on the field). The injunction requested that he be "involved to the full extent of his responsibilities as a coach" (344). He asked the court to stop Little League Baseball from intimidating or threatening players, parents, coaches, officials, umpires, and other participants in the game. Anderson also requested that the court forbid Little League Baseball from attempting to induce a boycott of the game. The restraining order was granted. Anderson coached his team in the national tournament.

Eligibility

Bowers v. the National Collegiate Athletic Association, et al. (2003) involved a high school football player who had been recruited by Temple University, the University of Iowa, Delaware State University, the University of Massachusetts, and the University of Memphis. The player was denied eligibility to play by the NCAA Clearinghouse. This intercollegiate athletics clearinghouse had a rule that in order for athletes to be eligible to play at the collegiate level, they must have satisfactorily completed 13 core courses in secondary schools. A diagnosed learning disability prevented Bowers from taking several of the core courses and instead, he took special education classes which did not satisfy the core courses requirement.

Bowers's action was against the NCAA, its clearinghouse, and others for violation of the ADA and the Rehabilitation Act. His request for a preliminary injunction to be declared eligible to play was denied. He then added the universities to the complaint. The district court granted summary judgment for the clearinghouse and, in part, for the NCAA and a number of the individual colleges and universities. Claims were subsequently made against other universities. The universities and colleges claimed Eleventh Amendment and sovereign immunity. The United States Court of Appeals for the

Third Circuit dismissed the appeals of the Universities of Iowa, Memphis, and Massachusetts. The appellate court also found that Temple University had a valid claim for contribution against the University of Massachusetts and Delaware State University. Thus, the court remanded the case to the district court. The protracted litigation in *Bowers,* which lasted over a decade and produced twelve court opinions, demonstrates the complex issues raised by these cases, often involving numerous defendants. The case also highlights the need to provide a clearinghouse system that better protects the rights of student-athletes with learning disabilities.

McPherson v. Michigan High School Athletic Association, Inc. (1996); *Reaves v. Mill, et al.* (1995); *University Interscholastic League v. Buchanan and Bomar* (1993); *Pottgen v. The Missouri High School Activities Association* (1994); and *Sandison and Stanley v. Michigan High School Athletic Association* (1995) involved scholastic athletic association rules denying eligibility to students over 19 years of age. These rules originated as safety measures. Buchanan, Bomar, Pottgen, Sandison, and Stanley each had learning disabilities, and as a result lost two or more years in completing elementary school. Reaves lost only one year. Each sought an injunction to permit them to play interscholastic sports in his/ her 19th year. All were successful in the lower courts. The Missouri State High School Activities Association appealed the *Pottgen* case to the United States Court of Appeals for the Eighth Circuit. The court of appeals reversed the decision, denying Pottgen the opportunity to play another year, arguing that the issue was the passage of time. Thus, he was not able to meet the age requirement in spite of his disability. Rhodes's denial of a request for an extension of Ohio High School Athletic Association's eight-semester eligibility rule so he could play high school football was influenced by the *Pottgen* decision (*Rhodes v. Ohio High School Athletic Association,* 1996).

A novel case which even the court admitted "push[ed] the margins of federal disability discrimination laws" was *Shepherd and Hollonbeck v. USOC* (1075). The consolidated case was filed by elite Paralympic athletes who challenged "the USOC's purported failure to provide them with the services, benefits and financial and other support routinely provided to their Olympic counterparts" (2006), in violation of the ADA as well as the Rehabilitation Act. The plaintiffs claimed that "it is discriminatory for the USOC to provide them programming, privileges, and financial support inferior to that provided non-disabled athletes under the Olympic program" (1075–1076). The district court ruled against the Paralympic athletes, finding it "irrelevant that the USOC chooses to provide Olympic programming only to Olympic athletes as long as the gateway to that program operates in a nondiscriminatory manner.... Plaintiffs are afforded a participation opportunity defined by their disability, the benefits of which are lesser based not an additional layer of discrimination but by operation of eligibility criteria beyond the reach of the ADA and Rehabilitation Act" (1095). The court effectively concluded that "Paralympic athletes' expectations for the equitable allocation of benefits between Paralympians and Olympians competing on behalf of the United States under the auspices of the USOC is not a matter which courts, through the ADA, may mandate or enforce" (1095). The Court of Appeals affirmed.

Stadium Accessibility

Stadium accessibility is an area that has experienced much high-profile litigation and required complex interpretations about what level of accessibility is required in sport facilities. Guidelines and standards used in meeting the laws related to accessibility include the Americans With Disabilities Act Accessibility Guidelines for Buildings and Facilities, the Uniform Federal Accessibility Standards, as well as the 2010 Standards for Accessible Design. Two distinct standards related to accessibility exist, depending on the year of construction and date of first occupancy. For "existing" facilities (those constructed prior to 1993), Title III requires the removal of existing architectural barriers in facilities considered places of public accommodation, where removal is "readily achievable," meaning without much difficulty or expense. Facilities intended for first occupancy and building alterations started after January 1993 (referred to as "new" facilities) are required to be in full compliance with all accessibility requirements. A comprehensive listing of "Stadium accessibility" requirements is published by the Department of Justice (U.S. Department of Justice, n.d.).

As large-scale renovations to old college stadiums are contemplated, such as adding luxury suites or expanding the existing seating bowl, when do such renovations trigger additional obligations under the ADA (Grady & Andrew, 2008)? There are specific rules set forth in the ADA and related standards for facilities that undergo renovations. Under Title III, renovations (referred to as "alterations" in the ADA) made by places of public accommodation after January 26, 1992, must be "readily accessible to and useable by individuals with disabilities" to "the maximum extent feasible" (42 USC 12183[a]; 28 CFR 36.402). The facility must also ensure that the area of modification or alteration or expansion complies with the ADA Accessibility Guidelines (ADAAG) for new construction (Hymas & Parkinson, 2003). For facilities that fall within the scope of Title II, public entities must ensure that the altered portions of the facility are accessible but have a choice in applying either the ADAAG or the Uniform Federal Accessibility Standards (UFAS) to the altered portion of the facility (28 CFR 35.151).

"Alterations" refer to any additions, programmatic changes, or major renovations (not routine painting and decorating). These alterations include exterior approaches, entries, and uses of buildings. "A public entity that undertakes alterations … must take that opportunity to make the facilities accessible" (*Association for Disabled Americans v. City of Orlando,* 2001, 1319). In addition, the sport facility must ensure that the area of modification or alteration or expansion complies with the ADAAG for new construction (Hymas & Parkinson, 2003).

Determining whether a renovation is significant enough to trigger the accessibility guidelines for new construction was the main issue in dispute in a lawsuit brought by the Michigan Paralyzed Veterans of America against the University of Michigan regarding a planned $226 million renovation of Michigan Stadium, more commonly known as "The Big House." The plans, announced in 2007, called for increasing the seating capacity to over 108,000, including adding 28 luxury boxes and 3,200 indoor and outdoor club seats, while only increasing the number of accessible seats from 90 to 282. The University of Michigan classified the extensive and costly project as necessary to "repair" severe crumbling of the concrete base of the bowl, not to change or alter the stadium or its seating.

The U.S. Department of Education Office of Civil Rights (OCR), which joined as a co-plaintiff in the case, believed the scope of the project constituted a "renovation." If deemed a renovation, this would trigger the updating of various sections of the stadium, including the seating bowl, to meet the 1% of accessible seating requirements for "new" sport facilities (U.S. Department of Justice, n.d.). In defense of its position, the university phrased the issue as follows: "The principal issue in this case presented by OCR is whether a phased concrete project ... constitutes an 'alteration' of the Stadium which would trigger ... the establishment of a percentage of wheelchair places (of all seats) in the alteration, as well as a requirement for dispersion of these places" ("University's Response," 2007). The university's position was that, as a public institution, the university is required to provide accessibility to wheelchair users to the stadium "when viewed in its entirety" which they argued had consistently been done ("University's Response," 2007).

The university argued that its efforts plainly satisfied the "program accessibility" requirement, which assesses whether a program or activity is readily accessible to and usable by individuals with disabilities, and that no patron with a ticket had been denied access to accessible seating. The Department of Education disagreed, finding that the changes to the physical structure of the stadium constituted an alteration. The university entered into a settlement with the Michigan Paralyzed Veterans of America and the federal government in exchange for dropping the lawsuit. Under the settlement, the university agreed to implement a plan for enhancing access for people with disabilities, including providing at least 329 wheelchair-accessible seats when the renovation project concluded in 2010, at a cost of about $2 million (Nelson, 2008).

As ADA litigation has evolved and become more nuanced, so has the nature of the claims raised by plaintiffs. In *Feldman v. Pro Football, Inc.,* plaintiffs included deaf people and people with hearing impairments who regularly attend Washington Redskins football games. Plaintiffs argued that the Washington Redskins and FedEx Field failed to provide them with equal access to the information and announcements broadcast over the stadium's public address system, in violation of the ADA (699). The Redskins and FedEx Field offered fans with hearing impairments assistive listening devices; however, these devices did not benefit the plaintiffs. In 2003, plaintiffs requested that the Redskins make all announcements on the JumboTron available with closed captioning. By 2006, when the case was filed, the only captioning that occurred was an emergency evacuation video. Some aural content also began to be captioned, but not all that the plaintiffs requested. The captioning was placed on LED boards that were not within the line of sight of the JumboTron, making it difficult to both watch the JumboTron and the captioning. Also, the music played in the stadium was not captioned.

The district court ruled in favor of plaintiffs' motion for summary judgment, holding that the ADA requires defendants to provide auxiliary aids for the aural content broadcast over FedEx Field's public address system, including music lyrics (709). The court found that the Redskins could provide auxiliary access to the music lyrics without undue burden. However, because the ADA does not dictate a particular aux-iliary aid be used, the appellate court declined to require captioning as the means of access for the music lyrics. Defendants appealed the district court's summary judgment ruling and asked the appellate court to decide "whether the deaf and hearing-impaired game spectators require access to music lyrics in order to fully and equally enjoy defen-dants' goods, services, privileges, and facilities" (383).

The appellate court agreed with the district court that Title III required the Red-skins to provide fans equal access to the aural information broadcast over the public address system, including "music with lyrics, play information, advertisements, referee calls, safety/emergency information, and other announcements" (390). Furthermore, the court found that the music played over the public address system during Redskins home games "is part of the football game experience that defendants provide as a good or service" (384). In fact, the court stated that "defendants 'provide more than a foot-ball game.' They provide an entertainment experience. This experience includes aural and visual components that, although not part of the game action, play an important role in generating support for the game and promoting spectator attendance" (391). Thus, while the ADA requires full and equal access to the music lyrics, the court did not require the auxiliary aids and services take a particular form, such as through cap-tioning. The appellate court noted, "When an auxiliary aid of some kind is required, the regulations acknowledge (1) that the type of aid necessary for effective communi-cation inevitably will vary with context and (2) that the auxiliary aid requirement is a flexible one" (392). The court further stated that "full and equal enjoyment is not so capacious as to mean that an individual with a disability must achieve an identical result or level of achievement as persons without a disability" (392). The district and appellate courts' opinions in *Feldman* suggest that the courts appear to be more willing to balance what the ADA requires with the practical realities of providing accessibil-ity to a modern-day sporting event with an excess of 70,000 spectators. This case also suggests that with increased ADA requirements, future courts may be willing to adopt a broader application of the ADA to all aspects of managing accessibility at sport and entertainment events.

2010 REVISIONS TO THE ADA

Significant changes to the ADA that have application to sport facilities were enacted in 2010. The requirements provide specific guidance for sport facilities in the follow-ing areas: ticket sales for wheelchair spaces, ticket prices, ticket transfers, hold and release policies, the secondary ticket market, and the number of accessible and com-panion seats that must be sold together. According to guidance provided by the De-partment of Justice, "as of March 15, 2011, venues that sell tickets for assigned seats must implement policies to comply with the new ticketing requirements" (U.S. De-partment of Justice, 2011, p. 1). According to the U.S. Department of Justice (2011), the new regulations were necessary because "over the past 20 years, some public and private venues, ticket sellers, and distributors have not provided the same opportu-nity to purchase tickets for wheelchair-accessible seats and non-accessible seats" (p. 1).

These regulations were designed to offer guidance to sport facilities in terms of ticket sales and seating for wheelchair users. The 2011 regulations apply to selling tickets for assigned seats at events such as concerts, plays, and sporting events (U.S. Department of Justice, 2011). The requirements are identical for Title II and Title III entities and apply to tickets sold for single events and those sold for a series of events (e.g., subscriptions or season tickets; U.S. Department of Justice, 2011).

SUMMARY

The ADA has five titles, three of which have a direct connection to and impact on sport and physical activity professionals. Title I covers employment discrimination. Title II prohibits state and local governments from discriminating against people with disabilities. Title III, the public accommodations and services area provision, mandates access to sport facilities and impacts how stadiums and other sport facilities provide access to patrons and participants with disabilities.

DISCUSSION QUESTIONS

1. How can the legal requirement to provide accessibility become an opportunity for a sport facility to reach out to new customers or enhance the stadium experience for current fans? Explain your ideas in the context of a response to the general manager of a medium size sport facility who claims that complying with the ADA is just "too costly".

2. How do the defenses provided in the ADA legislation give sport organizations sufficient protection to operate without fundamentally altering the nature of sport competition?

ACTIVITY

1. Review the 2010 ADA regulations (http://www.ada.gov//ticketing_2010.htm). Design a ticket sales policy for a sporting event that complies with the 2010 ADA requirements related to ticket sales.

REFERENCES

Americans With Disabilities Act of 1990, Public Law No. 101-336, 104 Stat. 327 (Codified at 42 USCA 1202–1213).

Anderson v. Little League Baseball, 794 F. Supp. 342 (1992).

Association for Disabled Americans v. City of Orlando, 153 F. Supp. 2d 1310 (2001).

Association for Disabled Americans, Inc. v. Concorde Gaming Corp., 158 F. Supp. 2d 1353 (2001).

Bowers v. National Collegiate Athletic Association, et al., 346 F. 3d 402 (2003).

Fay, T., & Wolff, E. (2000). Critical change factors model: Understanding the integration process of sport opportunities for athletes with disabilities into national governing bodies and the United States Olympic Committee. *Proceedings of the 2000 Pre-Olympic Congress: International Congress on Sport Science, Sports Medicine and Physical Education.*

Feldman v. Pro Football, 579 F. Supp 2d 697 (2008); 419 Fed. Appx. 381 (2011).

Grady, J., & Andrew, D. P. S. (2003). Legal implications of the "Americans with Disabilities" Act on recreation services: Changing guidelines, structures, and attitudes in accommodating guests with disabilities. 13 *J. Legal Aspects of Sport* 231.

Hymas, R. D., & Parkinson, B. R. (2003). Architectural barriers under the ADA: An answer to the judiciary's struggle with technical non-compliance. 39 *Cal. W. L. Rev.* 349.

Indep. Living Resources v. Oregon Arena Corp., 1 F. Supp. 2d 1159 (1998).

Individuals With Disabilities Education Act (1996), 20 USC 1400–1491.

Morisky v. Broward County, 80 F.3d 445 (1996).

McGovern, J. N. (n.d.) Recreation access rights under the ADA. Retrieved from http://ncaonline.org/ncpad/rights.shtml.

McPherson v. Michigan High School Athletic Association, Inc., 77 F. 3d 883 (1996).

Mills v. Board of Education for the District of Columbia, 348 F. Supp. 866 (1972).

Nelson, G. (2008, March 9). University reaches settlement in Big House lawsuit. *The Michigan Daily.* Retrieved from http://www.michigandaily.com/content/university-reaches-settlement-big-house-lawsuit

PGA Tour, Inc. v. Martin, 532 U.S. 661 (2001).

Pottgen v. The Missouri High School Activities Association, 40 F. 3d 926, 1994; 857 F. Supp. 654 (1994).

Reaves v. Mills, et al., 904 F. Supp. 120 (1995).

Rhodes v. Ohio High School Athletic Association, 939 F. Supp. 584 (1996).

Sandison and Stanley v. Michigan High School Athletic Association, 863 F. Supp. 483, 1994; 64 F. 3d 1026 (1995).

Shepherd and Hollonbeck v. United States Olympic Committee, 464 F. Supp. 2d 1072 (2006); 513 F.3d 1191 (2008).

University Interscholastic League v. Buchanan and Bomar, 848 S. W. 2d 298 (1993).

U.S. Department of the Interior. (n.d.). Redress for people outside DOI.

U.S. Department of Justice (n.d.). Accessible stadiums. Retrieved from http://www.ada.gov/stadium.pdf

U.S. Department of Justice (2005). A guide to disability rights laws. Retrieved from http://www.ada.gov/cguide.htm#anchor65310

U.S. Department of Justice (2011). Ticketing sales. Retrieved from http://www.ada.gov//ticketing_2010.htm

RECOMMENDED READING

Fay, T., & Wolff, E. (2009). Disability in sport in the twenty-first century: Creating a new sport opportunity spectrum. 27 *B.U. Int'l L. J.* 231.

Grady, J., & Andrew, D. P. S. (2007). Equality of access to *emergency services for people with disabilities under the Americans With Disabilities Act. 17 J. Legal Aspects of Sport* 1.

Race, P. A., & Dornier, S. M. (2009). ADA Amendments Act of 2008: The effect on employers and educators. 46 *Willamette L. Rev.* 357.

Part III

— THE BUSINESS OF SPORT —

Law in the business of sport includes contracts, business organizations, labor and antitrust, intellectual property, and risk management. Sales agreements, leases, warranties, employment contracts, physician statements, and releases are addressed in Chapter 7. Chapter 8 separates employment into the two categories: self-employment and working for others. Independent contractor status is explained as are the various models one needs to investigate before selecting a business organization. Chapter 9 reviews Article One of the United States Constitution. The chapter also covers four major acts (Sherman, Clayton, Norris LaGuardia, and National Labor Relations) in the context of professional sport players and owners. Antitrust's limited impact on amateur sport will also be reviewed.

Trademarks, service marks, patents, copyrights, and right of publicity are the topics of Chapter 10. Trademarks, service marks, copyrights, and patents may be licensed, sold, loaned, or given to others. An athlete has property rights to his/her personal character, which is referred to as right of publicity. Chapter 11 is concerned with risk management, a growing area of importance to sport managers. This subject relates to the identification, evaluation, and control of loss to personal and real property, clients and students, employees, and the public. A risk management program includes a systematic analysis of all aspects of a business and a strategic approach to mitigating identified risks, while disaster management involves facing, surviving, and recovering from a disaster.

7

Contracts and Representation

OBJECTIVES

Upon completing this chapter, you will be able to:

1) analyze a contract to determine if there has been an offer, acceptance, and consideration;

2) understand the process of forming a contract in sport contexts;

3) recognize the significance of various provisions commonly included in contracts in sport; and

4) understand the importance of contracts in establishing and maintaining business relationships in sport between teams, athletes, and ticket holders.

INTRODUCTION

A contract is a legally enforceable promise or set of promises between two or more people. A breach of the promise or set of promises results in a remedy, usually money, or a demand for performance. Contracts in sport include employment agreements, vendor agreements, sponsorship, naming rights agreements, leases, and warranties. Furthermore, releases and hold-harmless documents may be contracts. An important element of athlete representation is the contract.

Contracts can be express or implied. Express contracts are written or oral agreements, while implied contracts result from conduct. Courts do not distinguish between express and implied contracts. The court's role is to assist the parties in retaining the original or intended agreement. Written agreements are easier to prove than oral agreements. Implied contracts can be difficult to prove. Only adults may enter into contracts; minors are not held to such agreements. The Uniform Commercial Code (UCC) and state and federal regulations require that certain agreements be in writing.

Contract law and how courts interpret agreements differ from state to state. Contracts should be drafted and reviewed or updated annually by legal counsel.

CONTRACTS

A contract is an agreement between two or more parties in which at least one party has made a promise, a second party has accepted the first party's promise, and the element of consideration has been determined. Elements of a contract are:

Offer

Acceptance

Consideration

The offer is a promise, or expression of intent. The offer, as made, must be accepted by another person to whom it was made to constitute an acceptance. An offer may be withdrawn prior to acceptance unless the offer contains exact dates or a period of time in which the offer is open. The offer must be accepted within the period of time designated or within a reasonable period of time if no specific period of time has been designated. Consideration is the third component of the contract. While consideration is often the payment of money, consideration can also be an agreement to do something or not to do something. For example, I offer you a position as a head lifeguard for $65,000 for one year. You accept the position and agree to begin work on January 1, 2012. The offer was the offer of the position and the acceptance was your stating that you would take the position. The consideration was the $65,000. Additional terms of the contract that may also serve as consideration could include the fact that you are required to not pursue other full-time employment during the term of the contract (so, in effect, you are agreeing to not do something that you would otherwise legally be entitled to do). This entire process is often referred to as manifestation of mutual assent. When the agreement is put in writing, it becomes a written contract. Oral contracts are also enforceable, but establishing the existence of a contract and the terms of the contract becomes more difficult for the party trying to enforce an oral contract.

A contract may also be accepted with conduct that amounts to acceptance of the offer. An example of this would be if I offer you $20 to mow my lawn. When I arrive home from work, I notice that the lawn has been mown. Your conduct of mowing the lawn, rather than directly accepting my offer to mow the lawn, constituted acceptance of the offer. Twenty dollars was the consideration.

Consideration may be required before the accepting party carries out the task or is paid following completion of the work. The timing of the consideration is to be understood by both parties in written and oral agreements. If the accepting party (the offeree) refuses to accept the promise exactly as the promise was made by the offeror and requests that the offer be altered, the original offer is "dead" and cannot be accepted. Changing the original terms is a counteroffer, not an acceptance. When a counteroffer is made, the entire process is repeated with the parties exchanging positions (the original offeror now becomes the offeree; the original offeree becomes the offeror by making a counteroffer).

Agreements with Merchants

When the agreement is with a merchant, contract concepts and negotiation processes can be altered to meet the unique needs of the industry. Agreements with merchants usually fall within the scope of the Uniform Commercial Code (UCC) and are described in the law of sales. The offer may be through a wide range of marketing documents, such as through television, newspaper, and Internet advertisements, with the formal bill of sale being the element most resembling the offer. Advertisements and circulars are not offers but invitations to the public to make an offer. Preliminary negotiations are not offers. Advertisements, circulars, and preliminary negotiations become important, however, when the accepting party relies on their content in entering into a deal.

Consideration in a contract with a merchant is the price. If the price is acceptable to the industry, the price can be stated or left open until the date of delivery. The ability to leave the price open is important for orders placed three to six months in advance of delivery in a market where prices shift rapidly.

Shipping and designation of the time of the product's transfer from the manufacturer (or vendor) to the purchaser are unique to sales, including the sale of sport equipment such as would be necessary in starting a fitness center. Depending on the terms of the contract, the purchaser takes ownership at the time the product leaves the manufacturer's (or retailer's) loading dock or at the time the product arrives at the door of the purchaser. The payment of freight, insurance coverage, and obligation to trace lost products are the responsibilities of the owner. Purchasers who have agreed to pay freight on delivery often ignore other potential aspects of ownership until problems occur. Transfer of ownership needs to be clearly understood by all parties at the time of contract formation.

Acceptance of a product often includes inspection prior to acceptance. Although most freight handlers require a signature of acceptance, the signature merely records the location of the product on a particular day. If, after inspection of the product, the purchaser finds that the product does not meet the expectations of the agreement, the purchaser must notify the manufacturer or seller. Alterations in the product, substitutions, and any other changes not acceptable to the purchaser are to be rejected immediately. Contracts should contain the period of time the purchaser has to inspect and accept (or reject) the product, and a designation of freight and insurance coverage of a returned product.

Manufacturers and sellers of products should become familiar with the laws regulating commercial paper or negotiable instruments. These transactions (shipping, inspecting, accepting, and paying for merchandise) are governed by the Uniform Commercial Code (UCC). While the contents of negotiable instruments are beyond the scope of this book, manufacturers and sellers need to be aware that what they believe to be a contract may have additional meaning and obligations in sales.

Breach of Contract

A contract is breached when one of the parties fails to live up to one or more of the promises within the agreement, or fails to perform the expected service. A failure to perform or to live up to an agreement is not legally excused. When a party breaches a contract, the non-breaching party may take the breaching party to court. The court will determine whether the agreement or contract was valid as drafted. If the agreement is found to be valid, the court has a number of choices, including directing the parties to carry out the agreement or providing a damage award to the person harmed. Specific performance is directing the parties to carry out the agreement. Courts will assess damage awards to the breaching party in order to restore the injured party to the position the injured party held prior to the agreement.

Contracts can specify liquidated damages to be paid in the event of a breach of contract. For example, renovations to a stadium could contain financial penalties for the contractors for every day beyond the promised date of completion of all construction. Also, a financial penalty or a form of punitive damages can be specified in the written agreement. Making the elements of a breach of contract part of the written agreement enables parties and the court to understand the ramifications of a breach. On occasion, it may become impossible to carry out a contract. For example, if the building necessary to carry out the activities is destroyed by fire or a natural disaster, employment and participant contracts may be breached. If the promise or service has not begun, money may easily be returned. When the disaster occurs after the event has commenced, it may be difficult to ascertain the appropriate return and payment of monies.

Reliance

In addition to express and implied contracts, there are times when a party can enforce an agreement because he/she relied on a promise. Although a formal agreement is incomplete, courts will consider the fact that one of the parties relied on the agreement, usually to their detriment. When one party to the agreement has relied on the agreement to their detriment or has been harmed because of reliance on the promises made, the courts will consider the following in examining the agreement: What kind of loss has the party experienced? How can that loss be quantified in dollar figures? A promise is binding as a contract when it has been relied upon by one of the parties and when the reliance has caused substantial harm to that party. A promise is also binding when the promisee can foresee the harm created by a breach of promise. An agreement in which one party has been unjustly enriched as a result of the contract may be examined by the courts to remedy the injustice.

Written Agreements

When the contract is in writing and the parties have agreed to the written statements, the courts will use a standard interpretation of the agreement. The standard is the ordinary meaning of the writing to the parties at the time and place of the initial agreement, and under the circumstances of its construction. Contracts may be vague, containing only broad general agreements, or be drafted in greater detail. A court will interpret a vague contract with emphasis on what the parties thought they were agreeing to at the time of the agreement and will interpret a detailed contract using the exact wording of the agreement.

All agreements are to be made in good faith. When the contract's terms involve terminology or practices of a specific industry or business, the court will examine the contract in light of the customs in that industry and in terms of expected performance. Fraud, misrepresentation, and non-disclosure are factors that do not meet the good faith element and can cause a contract to be void. In some situations, the agreement may be so unfair to one of the parties that, even though the parties signed the contract, the court may choose not to enforce the contract.

Merchant forms are forms created by sellers to be used in ordering equipment and arranging for service contracts. If changes are made in the forms, the changes must be in writing and be identified in the first page of the form.

Employment contracts usually list starting and completion dates. Wages, major job duties and responsibilities, and the kind of relationship that will exist between the employer and employee are listed in the agreement. Employee handbook policies and regulations are often incorporated into written and verbal employment agreements. When an employment contract requires a party to have certain licenses or certificates and the person signing the contract does not have the required credentials within a specified period of time, the contract is not binding.

Misunderstandings about employment contracts are frequent in schools and universities, in which contracts must be ratified by a board. For example, when a teacher signs an offered contract that has not been signed by the school district, and returns it to the school system, he/she assumes the agreement is complete. For the agreement to be complete, however, the returned contract must be approved or ratified at the next school board meeting. On occasion, the school or university may choose not to ratify the agreement. If this decision is made, the person no longer has a contract or a job. When prospective employees have sued, the courts have maintained that the agreement signed by the employee was not a valid contract until it was ratified by the appropriate board.

Agreements in spas, sport and fitness clubs, team or individual sports (e.g., part-time coaching positions), and any other sport or physical activity environment may establish the employee as an independent contractor. Chapter 8, Legal Entities and Employer-Employee Relationships, contains a discussion on the subject of independent contracting and reviews the system for analyzing such a contract.

Minors

A person must be 18 years of age, or the age of majority, to enter into a contract. Contracts cannot be negotiated with minors. If a minor enters into a contract, the minor may ratify or accept the agreement once the minor turns 18. The supposed contract, entered into with a minor, is also voidable by the minor but not by the party contracting with the minor. There is no obligation to ratify a contract entered into as a minor.

Warranties

Warranties were discussed in detail in Chapter 3, Product Liability. The failure of a warranty is the failure of an agreement or contract. Warranty failure requires proof of injury that the warranty was made, that goods did not conform to the warranty, that the injury was the real cause of the failed warranty, and that damage exists. Disclaimers to warranties are also contracts and are treated as contracts by the courts.

Physician Statements as Agreements

A physician's statement to a sport professional is an agreement. It should delineate the role and duties of the person who is making the statement. According to Gallup (1995), "A letter of agreement that sets forth the [team] physician's duties and responsibilities, rather than a formal contract, is sufficient to create contractual obligations and protection" (p. 11).

Leases

According to the Statute of Frauds, leases are required to be in writing. Agencies should consider negotiating written leases with groups that use their facilities. In addition to the routine agreements about duration of the rented space, keys, and opening and closing schedules, the elements of safety, maintenance, and insurance are to be identified. The retaining of a positive image for the facility is to be considered when drafting a lease. For example, will the leasing party supply its own lifeguards on the 1-to-75 participant ratio that satisfies the local health code or will it maintain the leasing agency's more stringent ratio of 1-to-25? The building owner may require that the building safety or security personnel be named as part of the lease agreement.

Releases

A release, waiver, or consent form is a contract when it is signed by an adult and meets the elements (offer, acceptance, and consideration) of a valid contract. A release used with a minor or a release that does not meet elements of a contract is a document used to inform patrons of the risks involved in participation. While such a document should more properly be called a risk information form, many people call it a release. The following checklist is to be used in identifying the elements of a release for adults:

1) Terminology of release, waive, covenant not to sue, forever discharge, etc., is used in the construction of the release.

2) The company, officers, directors, etc. and anyone else who might be sued are listed in the release.

3) The release clearly states what is to be released.

4) Releases can be drafted for negligence only, and some negligence releases with adults may not be upheld by the courts. Courts seldom honor a release that is considered against fair public policy.

5) The release must be for both death and injury.

6) The party executing the release must not only release himself/herself but release any and all parties, including creditors, dependents, etc., that might have a cause of action.

7) The release is to acknowledge the risk of the activity. The risk is described so that an ordinary person understands the chances one takes in participating in the activity. These statements are best created by the professional in physical skills.

8) The signing party must clearly acknowledge an understanding of the risk, a willingness to accept the risk, and proof that no pressure existed to force the person to accept the agreement.

The verbiage of offer, acceptance, and consideration is to be part of the written statement. For example, in consideration of being allowed to participate in rafting, an individual would agree to ("I accept...") all the requirements of the release. The courts will look at the release to determine that it is clear, explicit, and unequivocal.

INFLUENCE OF COURT DECISIONS

The acceptance of a release as a contract differs from state to state. In *O'Connor v. The United States Fencing Association* (2003), the level of acceptance of such releases in California, Colorado, and New York is compared. Erin O'Connor, a fencer with aspirations for national recognition, severely injured her knee while performing in a competition held in California. O'Connor reported that "she lost her footing when executing this maneuver because the [fencing] strip was not properly anchored" (548). The injury required surgery and extensive rehabilitation. O'Connor's suit alleged a severe injury as a result of a negligently prepared competitive surface.

The United States Fencing Association (USFA) requested summary judgment on the basis of the following waivers. The first one was signed by O'Connor and her mother, as she was a minor at the time. She was an adult at the time she signed the second waiver. The first waiver states:

> YOU MUST SIGN WAIVER OF LIABILITY OR MEMBERSHIP WILL BE NULL AND VOID
>
> Upon entering events sponsored by the USFA and/or its member Division, I agree to abide by the rules of the USFA, as currently published. I understand and appreciate that participation in a sport carries a risk to me of serious injury, including permanent paralysis or death. I voluntarily and knowingly recognize, accept, and assume this risk and release the USFA, its sponsors, event organizers, and officials from any liability. (547)

ALL PARTICIPANTS MUST READ AND SIGN EACH OF THE FOLLOWING STATEMENTS

Waiver of Liability: Upon entering this tournament under the auspices of the USFA, I agree to abide by the current rules of the USFA. I enter this tournament at my own risk and release the USFA and its sponsors, referees, and tournament organizers from any liability. The undersigned certifies that the birth date of the individual is as stated on the entry form and that the individual is a current competitive member of the USFA. (548)

The USFA reported that it was not responsible for the incident as it did not provide the fencing strips. A third party, Illinois Fencing, was responsible for the placement of the strips on the floor.

When the waiver became the primary point of contention, the state law to be used became significant. The plaintiff was a resident of New York, while the incident occurred in California, and the USFA had its principal place of business in Colorado. "New York had a longstanding policy disfavoring contracts [waivers]…. Indeed, the New York legislature passed a statute specifically disclaiming the legitimacy of exculpatory contracts in the context of recreational activities" (549). In New York, waivers are considered against public policy. California, in contrast, favored waivers of liability and, when the waivers met the requirements of a contract, they were considered valid and were enforced. Colorado law, while not as specific as New York law, appeared to be closer to New York than California. Colorado law spoke to the issue of a "contract of adhesion." A contract of adhesion is one in which the person accepting the agreement has no alternative to accomplish his/her goal but to sign the contract. If O'Connor wanted to compete in a competition sponsored by the USFA, she had no other option than to sign the release. If her ambition were to be an Olympic fencer, no other form of fencing competition would prepare her for that goal. "In this case, Ms. O'Connor was not in a position to negotiate a less onerous contract with [the] USFA, as the waiver of liability was a prerequisite to participation in the National Championship Competition" (552).

The court mentioned that the release was broad and failed to identify specific risks that she was waiving. Therefore, "it is difficult to see how a person signing the agreement involved in this case would have been able to foresee the risk of inappropriate or defective flooring materials. This is not a risk inherent to fencing nor would it be particularly obvious to an inexperienced amateur like Ms. O'Connor, who was competing in her first national tournament" (553).

The United States District Court for the Eastern District of New York denied the United States Fencing Association's summary judgment and motion to dismiss. O'Connor was successful.

On occasion, minors participate in activities unaccompanied by their parents or guardians. Usually the agencies sponsoring such activities obtain blanket releases from the parents prior to the trip. When an event on a trip requires the signature of a parent or guardian, the persons chaperoning the young people usually sign.

Johnson, et al. v. New River Scenic Whitewater Tours, Inc. (2004) identifies the problems that can occur in such a situation. Fourteen-year-old Lindsey Gillespie traveled to Charleston, West Virginia, with a church-sponsored youth group to perform mission work. The culminating activity was a whitewater rafting trip on the New River. The associate pastor of the Fort Johnson Baptist Church planned and accompanied the group on the trip. On the day of the rafting event, he was asked to sign the following releases for each of the minors:

> In consideration for Lindsay Gillespie ("minor") being permitted by NEW RIVER SCENIC WHITEWATER TOURS to participate in its recreational events and activities, I agree to this WAIVER, RELEASE, AND INDEMNIFICATION; the undersigned parent and/or guardian of the minor, for themselves and on behalf of the minor, join in the foregoing WAIVER AND RELEASE and stipulates and agrees to SAVE AND HOLD HARMLESS, INDEMNIFY, AND FOREVER DEFEND NEW RIVER SCENIC WHITEWATER TOURS from and against any claims, actions, demands, expenses, liabilities (including reasonable attorneys' fees), and NEGLIGENCE made or brought by the minor or by anyone on behalf of the minor, as a result of the minor's participation in NEW RIVER SCENIC WHITEWATER TOURS sponsored recreational events and activities and the use of the facilities of NEW RIVER SCENIC WHITEWATER TOURS.
>
> I understand this rafting trip, which has been arranged by NEW RIVER SCENIC WHITEWATER TOURS, INC. is a participation sport which involves certain hazards and risks. The risks and hazards involved may include, but are not limited to, traveling in rough waters in a rubber raft, having medical emergencies in remote areas, unexpected weather conditions, as well as risks involved in transportation by cars, buses, and other vehicles.
>
> By signing this form, I indicate I am aware of the above dangers and that, furthermore, I release NEW RIVER SCENIC WHITEWATER TOURS, INC. from liability, claims, debts, and actions of all kinds both now and in the future, as a result of my participation in this trip. It will also serve as a release for my heirs, executors, administrators, and any minor accompanying me (Parents or Guardian must sign for all persons under age 18).
>
> I hereby assume all risks and dangers and all responsibility for any losses and/or damages whether caused in whole or in part by the negligence or other conduct of the owners, agents, officers, or employees of NEW RIVER SCENIC WHITEWATER TOURS, INC., or by any other person.

I, on behalf of myself, my personal representatives and my heirs hereby
voluntarily agree to release, waive, discharge, hold harmless, defend, and
indemnify … and its owners, agents, officers, and employees from any
and all claims. (624–625)

During the trip, Gillespie's raft flipped over and "she was pinned against a rock
beneath the water and drowned before she could be rescued" (625). Gillespie's mother,
Ms. Johnson, filed suit against the rafting company, claiming the "raft operator's conduct was reckless, intentional, and in contravention of the standard of care imposed
by the West Virginia Whitewater Responsibility Act" (627). New River, the rafting
company, filed a third-party complaint against the church and the associate pastor,
"alleging that the two documents the [pastor] signed operate as indemnity agreements,
requiring the third party defendant to pay any damages for which New River Scenic
or Scott [employee] may be held liable" (625). Fortunately for the parties involved,
the court could not find language in the release to support a conclusion of third-party
indemnification. West Virginia law was the controlling law. The court found for the
plaintiff, as the whitewater rafting company had violated the West Virginia Whitewater Responsibilities Act.

CONTRACTS INVOLVING STUDENT-ATHLETES

As colleges and universities engage in competitive recruiting of top high school athletes, certain promises (either oral or written) are likely to be made by the coaching
staff or university representatives. When relied upon by the student-athletes, these
promises can form the basis of a lawsuit for breach of contract. *Giuliani v. Duke University* (2010) involved a case focused on representations made during recruiting by the
former golf coach at Duke. As a junior in high school, Andrew Giuliani was recruited
to play varsity golf at Duke University by then-head varsity golf coach Rod Myers.
During the recruitment, Myers told Giuliani that if he came to Duke, he would be
given "life-time access" to Duke's "state-of-the-art" training facilities as an alumnus of
the Duke Golf Program, as well as "have the opportunity to compete with his teammates to earn spots in the most competitive tournaments against the most talented
players in the NCAA" (2). Giuliani alleged that these inducements were material to
his decision to enroll at Duke (2). He further alleged that, in exchange for roughly
$200,000 in tuition and fees, as well as forgoing numerous opportunities at other col-
leges and universities, Duke "promised to provide [Mr. Giuliani] with various educational services, lodging, and a right of access to the Athletic Department's Varsity
program and facilities" (3).

In the spring of 2007, Coach Myers passed away, and Coach O. D. Vincent took
over Duke's golf program. Coach Vincent cut the size of the golf squad in half and
"announced to the team that he was unilaterally cancelling [Giuliani's] eligibility to
participate in the University's Athletics Program immediately and indefinitely," citing several incidents involving Mr. Giuliani that allegedly occurred in early February. Coach Vincent indicated that Mr. Giuliani's suspension would become permanent

unless all twelve of his teammates wrote a letter supporting his reinstatement to the team. Giuliani alleged that his teammates generally supported his return to the team, but that Coach Vincent instructed players to "back off" and "was instilling new fears in his teammates that their positions on next year's roster were also in jeopardy." Coach Vincent required Giuliani to participate in a qualifier to rejoin the team for the upcoming season even though Coach Vincent had indicated earlier that those who participated as a member of the varsity team in a 2007-2008 tournament, as Giuliani had done, had already qualified for the team (4). The coach then told Giuliani that he could maintain his status on the team without re-qualifying if he agreed to certain "parameters" that were included in a written agreement. Giuliani refused to agree to these conditions. He alleged the coach then retaliated against him and did not inform him that he had been kicked off the golf team.

In July 2008, Giuliani sued Duke and Coach Vincent for breach of contract, breach of the covenant of good faith and fair dealing, and tortious interference with contract. The United States Magistrate Judge for the United States District Court for the Middle District of North Carolina recommended that the defendant's motion be granted because Giuliani failed to establish the elements of a breach of contract claim. Giuliani filed objections to the recommendations. Duke and Coach Vincent then filed a motion to dismiss Giuliani's claim.

In analyzing the breach of contract claim, Giuliani argued, in part, that Coach Myers' oral recruiting statements were contractual terms "binding on Duke by operation of ordinary principles of contract law" (14). He specifically alleged that Coach Myers's recruiting offer included an opportunity to compete, a promise of a right of access to the Athletic Department's programs and facilities while he was a student, and life-time access to Duke's training facilities. Giuliani further alleged that when he enrolled at Duke, the recruiting offer was converted into a binding promise enforceable under long-held principles of North Carolina contract law. Duke and Coach Vincent, meanwhile, argued that Myers had not alleged facts that establish the elements of an oral agreement between Coach Myers (on behalf of Duke) and Mr. Giuliani. They pointed to the fact that in his complaint, Giuliani identified four documents rather than the oral communications between Coach Myers and himself as the specific provisions of the contract at issue. The four documents were the Duke University Student-Athlete Handbook, the Duke University Athletic Department Policy Manual, the Duke University Student Bulletin, and the NCAA Division I Manual.

The court stated that a valid contract is formed when two parties manifest an intent to be bound. "A contract does not exist if 'one party simply believes that a contract exists, but there is no meeting of the minds'" (17). In addition, the terms of the contract must be "definite and certain or capable of being made so" such that the parties "assent to the same things, in the same sense" (17). In analyzing his breach of contract claim, the court found that Coach Myers's oral statements made during recruiting did not constitute a valid contract because the statements did not show a meeting of the minds, nor did they establish definite and certain terms (17). Rather than manifesting an intent to be bound, Coach Myers's statements to Mr. Giuliani described the potential benefits available if Mr. Giuliani enrolled at Duke, earned a spot on the golf team, and maintained that spot on the team (17–18). The court found that the statements were, at best, ambiguous as to the circumstances under which Mr. Giuliani would acquire any rights. In the court's view, the statement regarding inclusion in tournaments was framed as an "opportunity to … earn spots" to compete, and the statement regarding life-time access was conditioned on Mr. Giuliani being an "alumnus of the Duke Golf Program" (18). These statements are not certain and definite as to what constitutes an "opportunity" or how one may become an "alumnus of the Duke Golf Program" (18). Therefore, the court held that the alleged representations of Coach Myers did not create an enforceable contract (20).

On Giuliani's claims that the handbooks and policy manuals established a valid contract, the court found that "although plaintiff has alleged the statements of Coach Myers and the existence of the handbooks, plaintiff has not produced or alleged a contract specifically incorporating Duke's handbooks and policy manuals into a contract." Thus, this claim for breach of contract was also denied.

More recent interpretations of contracts involving student-athletes have focused on the use of image and likeness in video games. One argument, under contract law, is that requiring amateur student-athletes to waive certain rights, specifically their right of publicity, in order to be eligible to compete under NCAA rules is unconscionable. For a detailed discussion of the unconscionability arguments and how consent theory could cure some of these issues for member institutions and the NCAA, consider Baker, Grady, and Rappole (2012). Significant cases, including *Keller v. NCAA,* are discussed in further detail in Chapter 10, Intellectual Property.

APPEARANCE CONTRACTS

Litigation related to athlete appearance contracts for promotional purposes has become more frequent as celebrity athletes build their own unique commercial brands. *Front-Line Promotions & Mktg., Inc. v. Mayweather Promotions, LLC* (2009) involved a promotional appearance by Floyd Mayweather during the 2008 NBA All Star Weekend in New Orleans. In January of 2008, Insights and Front-Line entered into a partnership agreement to produce two events at the Sugar Mill in New Orleans on February 16 and February 17, 2008. They each agreed to procure the attendance of certain celebrities and musicians to appear at the events; Front-Line agreed to secure Mr. Mayweather to host the Sunday-night event. A representative of Front-Line purporting to be Mayweather's talent representative signed an agreement for Mayweather to appear at the NBA All Star Weekend event in exchange for a $25,000 fee, half of which was to be paid within twenty-four hours of executing the contract. At the top of the agreement is the heading "Mayweather Promotions, LLC." The "Talent" is identified as "Floyd Mayweather of Mayweather Promotions, LLC." The final paragraph stated, "This agreement is confidential between the promoter named Front-Line Promotions and the talent named Floyd 'Money Mayweather' of Mayweather Promotions, LLC." A second page of the fully executed version of the agreement contains signature lines for "Promoter" and for "Talent Representative." Mayweather did not appear at the event.

Plaintiffs subsequently filed a lawsuit seeking damages for financial loss and reputational injury due to defendants' alleged breach of the agreement, as well as consequential damages for defendants' bad faith failure to perform under the agreement. Defendants filed a motion seeking dismissal of all claims against Mr. Mayweather and dismissal of all claims by Insights. The defendants argued that Mayweather was not a party to the contract and, therefore, he could not be liable for any breach of that contract. The plaintiffs, however, contended that Mayweather was a proper defendant for three reasons. First, they argued, Robinson-White was his agent and she bound him to appear at the event when she signed the contract on his behalf. Second, the plaintiffs argued that Mayweather's obligation to appear was strictly personal, under the Louisiana civil code, and that he could not escape personal liability. Third, the plaintiffs contended that the contract was vague and ambiguous as to the identity of the obligor and that it should, therefore, be construed against the drafter, Mayweather Promotions.

12 Louisiana Civil Code article 1766 states that

> An obligation is strictly personal when its performance can be enforced only by the obligee, or only against the obligor.

> When the performance requires the special skill or qualification of the obligor, the obligation is presumed to be strictly personal on the part of the obligor. All obligations to perform personal services are presumed to be strictly personal on the part of the obligor.

> When the performance is intended for the benefit of the obligee exclusively, the obligation is strictly personal on the part of that obligee.

The district court ruled that since "[a] party cannot breach a contract to which it is not a party," determining whether Mayweather was indeed a party to the contract was key. The district court found that "In construing contracts, it is well established that … the contract itself is the best evidence of the relationship existing between the parties and the true intention of the parties is to be sought and determined by the language of the contract when the wording is clear" (9). The court found that the agreement identified two parties to the contract: 1) Front-Line, as promoter; and 2) "Floyd 'Money Mayweather' of Mayweather Promotions, LLC" as talent. This plain text suggests that this agreement intended to make Mr. Mayweather a party. Defendants still stressed the fact that Mr. Mayweather did not sign the agreement; it was initialed and signed by Robinson-White as "Talent Representative." Robinson-White testified she had signed similar agreements as talent representative of Mr. Mayweather which were a part of her duties for Mayweather Promotions.

The plaintiffs, meanwhile, argued that Robinson-White was acting as Mayweather's agent when she signed the agreement, and that under Louisiana law, Mr. Mayweather was bound to perform the obligations that Robinson-White, acting on his behalf, agreed he would perform. There was also conflicting testimony about whether Robinson-White was indeed his agent with authority to book appearances on his behalf. Mayweather himself, however, testified that Robinson-White lacked the "ability to sign appearance agreements" on his behalf, notwithstanding what actually happened in this case. Because of the conflicting testimony about whether Robinson-White was indeed acting as Mayweather's agent, the district court denied Mayweather's claims.

CONTRACTS INVOLVING TICKETS

As personal seat licenses become the norm and season ticket holders gain ownership rights to seats and season tickets at professional and college sporting events, litigation involving tickets becomes inevitable.

In *Brotherson v. Professional Basketball Club, LLC* (2009), former season-ticket holders of the Seattle Supersonics sued after the team moved to Oklahoma City. Plaintiffs' claims for breach of contract involved the "Emerald Club Contract." The contract, which the team ownership group, Professional Basketball Club (PBC), offered to virtually all Sonics 2007 season-ticket holders, let them renew their tickets for the 2008 season at 2007 season prices, and, notably, gave them the option to renew at the same price for the 2009 and 2010 seasons. The contracts were allegedly formed in the spring of 2007, although there was a high probability the team would leave Washington. As noted by the court, the Emerald Club was created out of "concern that uncertainty over the team's future would hurt ticket sales" (1276).

In the meantime, PBC described the Emerald Club in several publications, most notably in a brochure mailed to 2007 season-ticket holders. The brochure provided details of an "unprecedented offer" to Sonics season-ticket holders and an "unprecedented commitment" to provide "three-year cost certainty through the 2009-10 season" (1280). While the brochure did include a message about uncertainty in reaching an agreement with the state and local government to finance a new arena, "nowhere in the Brochure did PBC suggest that the Sonics might play home games at a location other than Key Arena before the 2011 season" (1281). The court found that "PBC deliberately declined to acknowledge the possibility of relocation before 2010 in the Emerald Club Brochure or any other communication sent to potential Emerald Club members" (1281). Furthermore, "whatever uncertainty surrounded the team, PBC marketed the Emerald Club to 'move forward with business models and business practices to promote and sell the team in a go-forward basis in Seattle.' Even when the chairman of Professional Basketball Club, the owners of the Seattle Supersonics, learned that the NBA itself was concerned with PBC's 'messaging relative to renewals,' PBC made no change to the Emerald Club terms" (1281).

In analyzing the breach of contract claims, the court found the existence of a contract. On the question of whether the parties mutually assented to a contract, the court found that the brochure sent by PBC and season-ticket holders had "all the hallmarks of an offer," including 1) containing the word "offer," 2) stating a fixed price and material terms, and 3) giving the option to purchase future tickets at a set price (1284). PBC instead claimed that the brochure was not an offer, relying upon cases holding that certain advertisements are not offers. The court found PBC's argument that the brochure was not an offer "mystifying," ruling that "the brochure itself was an explicit promise that it could provide seats for all renewing season ticket holders" (1284). The court went on to find that "having received the Emerald Club offer, there is no dispute that each Plaintiff accepted PBC's offer by paying the price stated in accordance with the Brochure's instructions. Moreover, no one disputes that Plaintiffs' payments were adequate consideration for the Emerald Club Contract" (1284).

The court then considered whether PBC breached the contract as a matter of law by refusing to honor the option to renew tickets for 2009, and would breach the contract again as a matter of law by not honoring the option for the 2010 season. According to the court, "nowhere in the Emerald Club Contract does PBC mention that the tickets it was selling are revocable, much less revocable at will. Given this omission, PBC finds no support for the notion that the revocable nature of the tickets is disclosed within the four corners of the Contract. Any reasonable person entering the Emerald Club Contract would have understood that the tickets were licenses, in the sense that he or she would have understood that the tickets did not create a property interest in a seat or access to Key Arena" (1286–1287). The court opined, "if a reasonable consumer understood that he or she was buying nothing other than the right to be subject to the unfettered whim of PBC, the court queries why anyone would have entered the Emerald Club Contract" (1287). Thus, the court found that PBC had no absolute right to revoke tickets it sold to Emerald Club members, and thus could not avoid damages on that basis (1285). Furthermore, the court determined that uncertainty over PBC's future in Seattle or its decision to move to Oklahoma City created a condition precedent which would relieve PBC of its contractual obligations to Emerald Club season-ticket holders (1289).

In analyzing the option to purchase tickets for the 2009 season and 2010 season, the court was unable to determine as a matter of law whether plaintiffs had exercised their option in a timely manner. If it was found that PBC breached the Emerald Club option, then plaintiffs had the right to prove expectation damages. Plaintiffs also sought specific performance of the option to purchase 2010 season tickets. Specific performance would compel the sale of the tickets under the agreed-upon terms. They asked the court to order PBC to sell tickets to them on the terms of the option. The court found they were not entitled to specific performance and dismissed these claims. "Even if specific performance were available as a matter of law, the court would not exercise its equitable power to award Plaintiffs tickets that they do not want" (1294).

Other pending cases involving rights owed to season-ticket holders include a suit by the Rosen family against the University of South Carolina (Shain, 2011). The Rosen family claimed they were promised free parking near the football stadium if they became lifetime Silver Spur members of the Gamecock Club, the university's booster organization. The family said they were told when they agreed to become lifetime members in 1987 that they would not have to pay for parking. But the university, as part of a wide-ranging effort to raise more money to improve facilities, started charging for parking around the stadium. Richland County, South Carolina Judge Joseph Strickland dismissed the Rosens' case in 2009 after ruling that the University of South Carolina did not breach the written contract because it did not promise that parking would be free. The Rosen family appealed. A three-judge panel of the South Carolina Court of Appeals agreed with the Rosens.

Another pending lawsuit was filed by a fan who sued her sister over their family's season tickets for Duke basketball (Brooks, 2011). Katina Dorton, the daughter of a longtime Duke basketball season-ticket holder, is seeking unspecified damages and asking the Wake County (North Carolina) Superior Court to invalidate the "fraudulent transfer" of a pair of Cameron Indoor Stadium season tickets to her sister, Sophia, and her sister's husband. Dorton's father, John Dorton, a Duke graduate and dentist who treated athletes and coaches, paid his dues over the years, earning season tickets through contributions to the Iron Dukes booster club. When Sophia Caudle's then-fiancé, Gordon Caudle, transferred the tickets into his name in July 2008, John Dorton, who died in January 2010, was "ill and unable to act for himself" (1). The lawsuit alleges Caudle was not a member of the Dorton family at the time of the transfer and therefore had no authority to repossess the tickets.

EMPLOYMENT CONTRACTS

Bires v. WalTom, LLC, involved a complaint between an auto-racing team that runs a rookie development program and NASCAR Nationwide Series driver Kelly Bires. In 2005, Bires signed an agreement that prohibited him from negotiating for a driving position on another team for a period of forty-five days. He claimed that he had no choice but to sign the agreement based on the surrounding circumstances and as a result, forfeited opportunities to secure other employment. Later that month, Bires received a telephone call from the team's owner that purportedly included a formal offer to drive for the team the following season. He claimed that later conversations solidified the terms of that offer, and altogether resulted in an oral contract to drive in the LMS in 2006, in which he was paid a salary, bonuses, and a percentage of race winnings. According to Bires, the team never indicated that its promises would not be binding until a written agreement was signed, or that he would have to make future royalties payments.

He then claimed he was subsequently forced to enter into a written agreement with substantially different terms. Specifically, he challenged enforceability of a royalty clause that required the driver to pay the team 25% of his gross race earnings for 10 years. The court held that the royalty provision was not a wage assignment covered by the Illinois Wage Assignment Act. In addition, paying the driver for less than one year of employment constituted insufficient consideration by the team to support the royalty clause. On the issue of adequacy of consideration, the court stated, "Any act or promise that benefits one party or disadvantages the other is sufficient consideration to support the formation of a contract" (1028). Bires asserted that the agreement fails for lack of consideration because while WalTom agreed to pay Bires a salary and to pay certain expenses, "the Agreement makes these purported payment obligations entirely optional to WalTom to perform or not perform" (1028). Bires argued that WalTom's promises were illusory and that because it could terminate the contract at its sole discretion, the agreement lacked mutuality (1028). Bires further argued that while WalTom may have performed by paying Bires his salary and other payments owed him based on Bires's performance under the contract, the relevant question was whether there was sufficient consideration for the ten-year royalties provision, which Bires referred to as a restrictive covenant. The court agreed with Bires that the royalties provision at issue, while not stated expressly as a covenant not to compete, is subject to the same analysis as restrictive covenants under Illinois law.

Construing the royalty clause as a non-compete covenant, the court found the following to be unreasonable: a) the 10-year duration; b) the lack of geographic limitation; and c) the application to all the driver's gross earnings, including those derived from racing-related activities such as entertainment and publishing. Thus, the court deemed the royalty clause an illegal restraint of trade. Judgment was entered for the driver on the lack of consideration and illegal restraint of trade counts, but fact issues remained about whether the contract was procedurally or substantively unconscionable or violated the Illinois consumer fraud statute.

ATHLETE REPRESENTATION

In general, athlete representation is similar to representation in the business world in that it requires the representative to understand the person or project and the environment in which the person or project exists. That foundation is in contract, accounting, labor, and intellectual property law.

What is complicated about athlete representation is the understanding of the business of sport. It involves a thorough knowledge of the sport, including the business of a particular sport (i.e., it is essential to understand the rules of the National Collegiate Athletic Association [NCAA]). The agent is expected to understand the particular sport's collective bargaining agreement and bylaws, draft system and other means of gaining entry to a team, salary caps, and value of a particular playing position. The athlete's situation in terms of rules related to interscholastic and intercollegiate governance must be understood. A sincere respect for the athlete is a must.

Representation of athletes in organized team sports and in individual sports varies considerably. In organized team sports, the athlete is usually selected through a draft and is governed by league rules; the collective bargaining agreement and bylaws govern the job. The representative's first task is to explain the collective bargaining agreement and contract to the athlete. At the same time the agent negotiates all additional terms (beyond the collective bargaining agreement) that will meet the needs of the athlete. This combination of accepting the collective bargaining agreement and negotiating contractual terms is unlike any other type of employment. Employees are either members of a union and work under the union's collective bargaining agreement or are management and bargain for the terms of their individual contracts. The team sport athlete has both.

Representation of the team sport athlete may be full support, partial support, or only contractual assistance. In addition to the contract, the full-term support includes obtaining a portfolio of sponsorship and speaking engagements, intellectual property, financial and investment advice (including trusts and wills), real estate guidance, and any support agreed to in the representative/athlete agreement. Partial support usually includes contract, sponsorship, and intellectual property representation. Contract negotiation is the third area.

Individual sport representation is different in that one of the representative's biggest tasks is the identification, selection, and obtaining of the athlete's acceptance to a range of tournaments or events. These tournaments or events must meet the athlete's goals and schedule, yet bring the greatest revenues and future opportunities possible.

The logistics of travel, car rentals, applications, and hotels are among the basic tasks. Training, practice, equipment maintenance, and schedules at home and in tournaments are arranged. Player contracts are usually agreements for individual performance and events.

Athlete representatives or agents are required to have state licenses and league certifications. They are also expected to have experience in contract negotiations and leads for endorsements. They will help the athlete obtain equipment for the athlete's use, equipment and product endorsements, personal appearances (i.e., speeches, autograph sessions), select volunteer and charitable opportunities, summer camp presentations, trading cards, and other opportunities. Financial guidance is extremely important as an athlete usually makes considerable money in a very short period of time. A representative's skill in guiding the athlete in understanding how that large sum of money can enable the athlete to be financially secure for life is paramount.

The scandals that have plagued professional athletes created a need for licensing of sport agents. Many states have statutes requiring agents to be licensed and post a substantial security bond. Often, this legislation has been in response to specific state problems. As the number of states that licensed agents grew, confusion existed among agents as to the merits of seeking licenses in multiple states. There was a cry for reciprocity across state lines, which is the recognition of an agent's license in one state by another state. This prompted the creation of the Uniform Athlete Agent Act (UAAA). The UAAA has been passed in 40 states, the District of Columbia, and the U.S. Virgin Islands. In most cases, the UAAA requires an athlete agent to register with a state authority, typically the Secretary of State, in order to act as an athlete agent in that state. During the registration process, an athlete agent must provide important background information, both professional and criminal in nature. It also provides reciprocity of registration across state lines for an agent certified in a neighboring state. Penalties and remedies for violation of components of the act are provided.

Cases in Representation

Cases that describe two very typical situations in the representation of athletes include the provision of cars and other impermissible benefits to NCAA athletes (*Black, et al. v. National Football League Players Association, Inc.,* 2000) and the problems that athletes might encounter with financial advisors (*Clark v. Weisberg, et al.,* 1999).

The National Football League Players Association (NFLPA) brought disciplinary proceedings against Black for allegedly providing NCAA athletes with cars, stocks, and bribed coaches. Black brought suit against the NFLPA, describing the disciplinary proceedings as unlawful and affecting his livelihood. Specifically, his complaint was an antitrust conspiracy. The NFLPA then revoked Black's contract advisor certificate for three years. Black filed an amended complaint. He removed the antitrust complaint and added new claims:

> That NFLPA's initiation of the disciplinary proceedings was based on race discrimination in violation of Section 1981; and that NFLPA tortuously interfered with Mr. Black's business relations (and those of his corporate entity Professional Management, Inc.) by invoking disciplinary action. Mr. Black continues to claim that the arbitration process established by the regulations is illegal under the FAA. (*Black, et al. v. National Football League Players Association, Inc.*, 2000, 3)

Black had signed the following agreement to become certified as an NFLPA advisor:

> In submitting this Application, I agree to comply with and be bound by these Regulations ... I agree that if I am denied certification or if subsequent to obtaining certification it is revoked or suspended pursuant to the Regulations, the exclusive method for challenging any such action is through the arbitration procedure set forth in the Regulations. In consideration for the opportunity to obtain certification and in consideration of NFLPA's time and expense incurred in the processing of this application for such certification, I further agree that this Application and the Certification, if one is issued to me, along with the NFLPA Regulations Governing Contract Advisors shall constitute a contract between NFLPA and myself. (2)

The United States District Court for the District of Columbia ruled that the plaintiff could take discovery (gather additional evidence) on the discrimination claims, but that the defendant was entitled to judgment as a matter of law on the claims of tortuous interference and violation of the Federal Arbitration Act (2). In 2001, William (Tank) Black was sentenced to nearly 7 years in prison followed by three years' probation and a fine of $15,000 for money laundering charges (Suhr, 2001).

In *Clark v. Weisberg, et al.* (1999), Clark, a former professional football player, sued his accountant. He alleged conversion, breach of fiduciary duty, and negligence. He requested that a special master be named to conduct an accounting of his money. Clark's salary from the National Football League (NFL) team he had played for had been automatically transferred to the accountant. The accountant was to pay his bills, provide him an allowance, maintain his insurance and taxes, and place the residual in investments. Clark suffered a career-ending injury and asked the accountant for an accounting of his investments. The accountant said that Clark was broke and that he had spent his money foolishly.

Clark brought an action, alleging that the accountant invested Clark's money in the accountant's family financial interests, failed to disclose the location of Clark's assets when asked to do so, and did not inform Clark of his insurance and tax status. As Clark retired, he discovered that the accountant had not maintained his injury insurance policy. Clark's motion for the appointment of a special master (person to oversee his accounts) was denied because the issues in the case were not more complicated than those in a usual case such that it required appointment of a special master.

SUMMARY

Contracts are legally enforceable agreements containing a promise (or set of promises) accepted by another (through signature, verbal agreement, or conduct) for consideration. Consideration can be either a promise to do something, a promise not to do something, or money. Sales agreements, leases, warranties, employment contracts, and releases may be contracts. Contracts can be express or implied. Express contracts are facilitated either verbally or in writing. Implied contracts are agreements accepted as a result of the conduct of the accepting party.

DISCUSSION QUESTIONS

1. How can contract law be used to protect the rights of a range of sport businesses? Under what circumstances would a lawsuit for breach of contract become necessary?

2. Given the evolution of the Internet and digital communications, how can professional athletes protect their commercial interests using contract law?

ACTIVITIES

1. Retrieve the coaching contracts of the head coach in any sport at your college or university, if publicly available. Determine what provisions of the contract are included and analyze whether the specific provision benefits the coach or the school, or both.

2. Do an Internet search for a personal appearance contract. Review the terms of the agreement. Now, consider what terms would be necessary for a similar appearance contract between a professional athlete and a sponsor, such as a beverage company.

REFERENCES

Bires v. WalTom, 662 F. Supp. 2d 1019 (2009).

Black, et al. v. National Football League Players Association, 87 F. Supp. 2d 1 (2000).

Brooks, M. (2011, July 15). Duke basketball family lawsuit: Fan sues sister, school over Blue Devils season tickets. *Washington Post.* Retrieved from http://www.washingtonpost.com/blogs/early-lead/post/duke-fan-files-lawsuit-against-family-members-university-over-blue-devils-basketball-tickets/2011/07/15/gIQAsbZaGI_blog.html

Brotherson v. Professional Basketball Club, L.L.C, 604 F. Supp. 2d 1276 (2009).

Clark v. Weisberg, et al., 1999 U.S. Dist. LEXIS 11341.

Front-Line Promotions & Marketing Inc. and Insights Marketing & Promotions, Inc. v. Mayweather Promotions, LLC and Floyd Mayweather, Jr., 2009 U.S. Dist. LEXIS 27136 (2009).

Gallup, E. M. (1995). *Law and the team physician.* Champaign, IL: Human Kinetics.

Guliani v. Duke University, 2010 U.S. Dist. LEXIS 32691 (2010).

Johnson, et al. v. New River Scenic Whitewater Tours, Inc., et al., 313 F. Supp. 2d 621 (2004).

Keller, et al. v. Electronic Arts, Inc.; National Collegiate Athletic Association; and Collegiate Licensing Company, 2010 U.S. Dist. LEXIS 10719; consolidated as In re NCAA Student-Athlete Name & Likeness Licensing Litigation, 2010 U.S. Dist. LEXIS 139724.

O'Connor v. The United States Fencing Association, 260 F. Supp. 2d 545 (2003).

Ruxin, R. M. (2010). *An athlete's guide to agents* (5th ed.). Boston, MA: Jones & Bartlett.

Shain, A. (2011, July 7). Court: Gamecock fan family can continue fight for free parking. *The State*. Retrieved from www.thestate.com

Shropshire, K. C., & Davis, T. (2008). *The business of sports agents* (2nd ed.). Philadelphia, PA: University of Pennsylvania.

Suhr, J. (2001, June 14). Tank Black jailed 6+ years. *CBC News*. Retrieved from http://www.cbc.ca/sports/story/2001/06/14/black010614.html

Uniform Athlete Agent Act (2000). Retrieved from http://www.law.upenn.edu/bll/archives/ulc/uaaa/aaa1130.htm

RECOMMENDED READING

Baker, T. A., Grady, J., & Rappole, J. M. (2012). Consent theory as a possible cure for unconscionable terms in student-athlete contracts. 22 *Marq. Sports L. Rev.*

Carfagna, P. A. (2009). *Carfagna's representing the professional athlete*. Eagen, MN: Westlaw.

Deubert, C. (2011). What's a "clean" agent to do? The case for a cause of action against a players association. 18 *Vill. Sports & Ent. L.J.* 1.

Nagel, M. S. (2011). Changing attitudes regarding ticket "rights." *Journal of Venue and Event Management, 3*(2). Retrieved from http://www.hrsm.sc.edu/jvem/index.shtml

Wong, G. M., Zola, W., & Deubert, C. (2011). Going pro in sports: Providing guidance to student-athletes in a complicated legal & regulatory environment. 28 *Cardozo Arts & Ent. Law J.* 553.

8

Legal Entities and Employer-Employee Relationships

OBJECTIVES

Upon completing this chapter you will:

1) know a number of ways to organize a business;

2) be confident in comparing the status of an independent contractor with a regular employee;

3) be able to explain vicarious liability; and

4) be competent to implement the Fourteenth Amendment of the United States Constitution, Equal Protection Clause, procedural due process, in terminating an employee.

INTRODUCTION

Sport managers have responsibilities that require an understanding of a wide range of business-related laws. Independent contractors play a significant role in sport and physical activity; coaches are often independent contractors. This chapter begins with a description of business organizations, including sole proprietorships, partnerships, "C" and "S" corporations, and limited liability companies and partnerships. Self-employment or working for others becomes a legal concern as the reader compares regular and leased employees with independent contractors. Vicarious liability is the liability of administrators for the torts of their employees. Procedural due process is the major legal theory in employment, evaluation, and termination of personnel.

BUSINESS ORGANIZATIONS

A person starting his/her own business has a number of decisions to make in selecting the organization most appropriate to his/her needs. Businesses are organized under state law. Liability and tax consequences play a primary role in the decision-making process.

Sole Proprietorship

A sole proprietorship is a business owned and operated by one person. The business is started by opening a bank account and obtaining requisite licenses and permits. The sole proprietor is liable for the debts of the business and pays them from the business or personal resources. When the business needs credit or the ability to obtain a loan, a sole proprietor uses his/her personal credit to obtain resources. If the business hires employees, the owner is personally liable for their wages, and for federal and state employment taxes. The sole proprietor's personal assets will be used to satisfy debts the business encounters, including a judgment following litigation. Income from the business—after deductions for money spent to make the income—is taxed at the sole proprietor's individual income tax level. If the business goes bankrupt, the owner covers the bills. If the owner cannot cover the bills, the owner goes bankrupt. Should the owner die or not be able to work, the business may fail.

The advantages of a sole proprietorship are its informality and ease of establishment. Decisions can be made in a short period of time, and the individual is not required to share profits. Profits and losses are part of the owner's personal income tax statement. Sole proprietorships are popular with people starting a business. Often, persons who start as sole proprietors move to a more sophisticated organization as the business grows.

Partnership

The Uniform Partnership Act (UPA) defines partners as two or more co-owners in a business for profit. A written agreement is recommended but not required. Partners need to identify the financial, material, and managerial contributions of each partner. The law considers all partners equal. If partner contributions are not equal, the differences must be identified in writing. The death of a partner is a problem to be addressed in the agreement. Will the partnership fold, with the assets going to the next of kin of the deceased partner, or will the partnership go to the living partner with no assets to the deceased partner's family and/or next of kin? Often, insurance is used to offset the damage that might occur to the business and/or the partner's next of kin at the time of death.

Advantages of a partnership are ease of creation, direct award of profits, more capital than the sole proprietorship, freedom from direct government control, and flexibility in decision making. If people work together effectively, partnerships can provide a business with little bureaucracy. The disadvantages of a partnership are that one partner can be liable for the expenses of both partners, that one partner can speak and/or obtain credit or loans for both partners without the other partner's knowledge, and that capital is difficult to obtain.

Corporation

A corporation is a business formed by the authority of state government through the filing of Articles of Incorporation with the Secretary of State. In addition to obtaining a charter from the state, a corporation must hold annual meetings and adhere to government regulations. Regular "C" and subchapter "S" are the two basic types of corporations. A corporation is a legal entity that is separate and distinct from the shareholders who own the corporation. A corporation can be sued and can sue. It has the same rights and privileges as a person. Shareholders indirectly control corporation activities by electing a board of directors, which in turn elects the officers responsible for the day-to-day operations of the business. All assets are owned by the corporation, not by the shareholders. Owners of the corporation are stockholders and can be held liable only for the extent of their investment in the corporation. The legal ramifications are that shareholders in a corporation can lose only the investment they have in the corporation; their personal assets cannot be attached for corporate debts unless the court can find that the corporation was a sham. Stocks and bonds issued by the corporation must satisfy the federal Securities Act of 1933, the Securities and Exchange Act of 1934, and the policies of the Securities and Exchange Commission (SEC). A corporation pays taxes at a predetermined level. Shareholder dividends are taxed at the shareholder's personal tax rate. Shareholder profits are taxed twice, at the corporation level and at the personal income level.

Subchapter "S" Corporation

A subchapter "S" corporation has all of the characteristics of a corporation. The difference is that profits and losses pass through to the shareholders—as they do in the sole proprietorship and partnership—and become a part of each shareholder's individual taxable income. Thus, shareholders pay taxes once on the profits of the corporation. Limitations of a subchapter "S" corporation are that shareholders are limited to 75 shareholders. Shareholders have only one class of stock and must be United States citizens; corporate status has to be attained as well. The advantages of a subchapter "S" corporation are the limited liability of stockholders to their investment, the status as a legal entity, and the ease of ownership and transfer; in addition, the organization is not affected by the death of participants, and it has a base for securing capital from investors. The disadvantages are governmental control, laws, charter activities, and expenses associated with the forming of a corporation.

Limited Liability Company (LLC)

A Limited Liability Company (LLC) is an organization that is accepted in most states and treated as a partnership for federal (not state) income tax purposes. The LLC has the limited liability of a corporation. It is formed by two or more persons who file Articles of Organization with the Secretary of State. Business elements, including management systems, are in the agreement. The number of partners is unlimited, which permits other corporations and partnerships to become shareholders. The LLC operating agreement resembles a partnership agreement. A limited liability company is not as complex as a subchapter "S" corporation. An advantage is that owners have the liability of a corporation as it is a separate entity. Owners are called members, not partners, and no formal minutes or resolutions are required. Disadvantages are that an LLC is dissolved when members die or file for bankruptcy, whereas corporations go on forever.

Limited Liability Partnership (LLP)

Limited Liability Partnerships (LLPs) are often public service partnerships that retain partnership tax benefits while obtaining corporate liability benefits. Again, similar to the information noted above concerning the LLC, each state is unique in its requirements for an LLP. Therefore, the regulations for an LLP differ from state to state.

Not-for-Profit Corporation

A not-for-profit corporation is a corporation that does not distribute income to its members, directors, or officers. It is organized for charitable, benevolent, educational, religious, social, athletic, scientific, or trade association purposes. The basic organization is the same as any other corporation. It is only the purpose of the organization that differs. While members of the board are not paid, the organization has a staff that is paid.

EMPLOYER-EMPLOYEE RELATIONSHIPS

Employment relationships are regular employee (working for another); independent contractor; self-employed; or leased employee (a combination of regular employee and independent contractor). The leased employee is a regular employee of a business that serves as an independent contractor on the work site. Labor unions are addressed in Chapter 9, Antitrust and Labor Law. The major differences in these relationships are in the various parties' responsibilities for legal, financial, and social obligations.

Regular Employees

A regular employee works directly for the employer. The worker answers to the employer or to a person in the employer's chain of command. In a regular employment relationship, the employer has the right to control the employee and to direct the employee's work. How and what the work will be is controlled by the employer. Employers are responsible for the actions of their employees. In regular employment, the employer has an equitable hiring process and safe working environment, evaluates only the tasks of the job, and provides a due process hearing—if appropriate—prior to termination. Employers have financial responsibilities to the employee for wages, unemployment insurance, worker's compensation, benefits, and other negotiated services. Employers also provide supplies and equipment. The employer is legally responsible for all work-related torts committed by the employee. The relationship in the law is often referred to as master/servant.

Independent Contractors

In an independent contractor relationship, the employer has a contract right to the completed task or project. The employer has no control over selection, training, or the means used by personnel to accomplish the tasks. Independent contractors are usually paid in lump sums. The employer is not liable for the torts of independent contractors or their employees. An employer becomes liable for independent contractors and their employees only if the work environment is hazardous or the independent contractor's status is violated as explained in the Test of Independent Contractor Status below.

Independent contractors are responsible for their own actions and those of their employees. Independent contractors pay wages, federal and state taxes, and insurance. They are liable for their own injuries.

Even though an employer has created an independent contractor relationship through a written agreement, the employer can—by accident—assume control sufficient to end the status. To avoid this situation, the parties should identify, in writing, the party responsible for worker's compensation, withholding taxes, adhering to civil rights legislation (including age, race, and sex discrimination), wage and labor laws, and employee safety. Employers may be personally liable for selecting a contractor with a history of carelessness, permitting a hazardous situation to exist, failing to perform required legal duties, and allowing persons to engage in inherently dangerous work.

When an employer chooses to use an independent contractor, the employer must be confident that the independent contractor understands his/her status. Asking a person to sign an independent contractor agreement may be insufficient. If challenged, the employer must prove that the independent contract was not signed under duress, federal and state taxes were paid, and legal liability was recognized.

An employer with both regular employees and independent contractors must treat each according to their status. An independent contractor supplies his/her own materials and equipment; the business supplies materials and equipment for regular employees.

Test of Independent Contractor Status

Over the years, the courts have arrived at a number of questions to guide a party or the court in distinguishing between a regular employee and an independent contractor. It is not necessary to fulfill all of the requirements listed below. However, a majority of affirmative responses is expected.

1) *Control.* Who is in charge? What is the extent of their control? Who hires, evaluates, and fires? Who determines method of work and when the work will be completed? In an unforeseen situation, who becomes the leader? If the independent contractor controls the above, independent contractor status will be retained.

2) *Is work unique?* Does the job require special certificates or licenses? What is the level of specialization of the employees? When the level of specialization is sufficiently unique that few people can control the day-to-day tasks of the employees, the situation lends itself to the independent contractor status. For example, when the administrator of a sports facility is unable to supervise the swimming pool, the pool manager could easily be an independent contractor.

3) *Custom.* Is the selected relationship—regular employee or independent contractor—the one used most often in the industry?

4) *Skills.* Are requisite skills so unique or so advanced that it is difficult to control or supervise employees? A company claiming independent contractor status

must avoid all but minimal orientation, in-service training, or other forms of employee control. Requirements that specific progressions be used could void the independent contractor status. Note that an employer who wishes to retain an independent contractor status can, for example, require in the contract that all employees possess an American Red Cross certificate; however, they cannot demand the use of a specific program in accomplishing the task.

5) *Period of employment.* Independent contractors are hired to do specific tasks for an identified period of time. Continuous employment will be examined for violation of an independent contractor status.

6) *Compensation.* Compensation is a lump sum. The money is paid only to the contractor. Employer payments directly to independent contractor employees may void the independent contractor agreement.

Leased Employees

According to Clement (2004), leased employees "are a combination of the regular employee and the independent contractor. The leasing firm serves as the independent contractor to the employer. The employee becomes an employee of the leasing firm and is given salary, fringe benefits, and liability coverage by the leasing firm. Leasing firms also hire, fire, and evaluate employees. The employer merely creates a contract for a specific task to be accomplished, and the leasing company provides the service" (p. 101). Under the Equal Employment Opportunity Commission (EEOC), leased employees, temporary, seasonal, and part-time employees are considered contingent or temporary workers. Interns and volunteers are not covered.

Interns and Volunteers

The United States Department of Labor, Fair Labor Standards Act, requires that an unpaid internship in the for-profit or private sector meet the following requirements:

1) The internship, even though it includes actual operation of the facilities of the employer, is similar to training which would be given in an educational environment;

2) the internship experience is for the benefit of the intern;

3) the intern does not displace regular employees, but works under close supervision of existing staff;

4) the employer that provides the training derives no immediate advantage from the activities of the intern; and on occasion its operations may actually be impeded;

5) the intern is not necessarily entitled to a job at the conclusion of the internship; and

6) the employer and the intern understand that the intern is not entitled to wages for the time spent in the internship. (Internship Programs under The Fair Labor Standards Act, fact sheet, April 2010)

If the above criteria are not met, the intern is to be paid a minimum wage with overtime, as appropriate. Higher education, including athletics, is covered under the act whether they are operated for profit or not for profit (U.S. Department of Labor, Wage and Hour Division, WH Publication 1282, September 2010, p. 2). Of primary importance is that the job be similar to that provided in an educational institution and that it be for the benefit of the intern.

VICARIOUS LIABILITY

Vicarious liability is the manager's responsibility for the torts of his/her employees. Managers are liable for torts committed in the workplace even though they (the managers) were not present or aware that the tort was committed. The legal theory (*respondeat superior*) finds administrators responsible for the torts of their employees merely because they are administrators. In addition, administrators may be personally liable for having hired an incompetent employee or incompetent independent contractor.

Torts that are committed beyond the job description or the administrator's supervision are not covered under vicarious liability. The test of vicarious liability, or *respondeat superior,* is the administrator's right to control and direct the work of the employee. An administrator's status as a volunteer does not change his/her vicarious liability status. Intentional torts are not covered by vicarious liability unless the administrator has directed the employee to commit the intentional tort or has ratified the intentional tort after it was committed.

TYPES OF EMPLOYEES

Employer-employee categories are regular, at-will, contract, or membership in a labor union.

Regular Employee

Regular employee is the type of employment most often found in the work force. The regular employee works at the request of the employer; has income taxes, social security, and Medicare withheld from his/her income; and may be provided with insurance, pensions, and paid leaves. As mentioned earlier, the employer is liable for the torts of a regular employee, for providing a safe working environment, and for honoring the employee's legal rights.

At-Will

At-will employment occurs when an employer has a task to be done, seeks persons capable of doing the task, and offers a wage, followed by the parties' agreeing to the job. When one party no longer wishes to work with the other, the party merely informs the other of his/her wishes. The reason for either party's termination does not have to be given. Today, Florida, Georgia, and Louisiana are total at-will states. Bennett-Alexander and Hartman (2009) list the following as exceptions to the at-will categories: implied contracts, public policy, and good faith. Using information gathered from the Bureau of National Affairs Labor and Employment Law, they provide information on each of these exceptions by state (pp. 28, 29).

Contracts

There are two types of employment contracts: written agreements and implied contracts. Written agreements are used universally in certain businesses and industries. Universities tend to use written agreements; therefore, most collegiate athletic department agreements will be in written form. The details of written agreements (contracts) are outlined in the chapter on contracts. Implied contracts are agreements between parties usually based on the practice in the industry, verbal promises of long-term employment, and policies that would lead an applicant to feel secure in taking an offered position. Many states permit an implied-contract relationship through policies, handbooks, and promises.

Labor Unions

Labor unions (agencies that negotiate contracts with businesses) are private associations formed to represent groups of workers with common needs and a common desire to obtain the best wages possible for the entire group.

EMPLOYING, EVALUATING, AND TERMINATING EMPLOYEES

A business creates a system for employing each individual that begins with a need, followed by a job description, advertisements, candidate screening, and finally employment. There are several federal employment laws that prevent discrimination in hiring. Evaluation and, on occasion, termination of employees are influenced by the Fourteenth Amendment to the U.S. Constitution, the Due Process Clause.

Federal Employment Laws

Employers are subject to federal laws created to remedy discrimination on the basis of race, color, sex, age, religion, national origin, and handicap. The federal laws that deal with discrimination include the Equal Pay Act of 1963, the Executive Orders of the 1950s and 1960s, Title VII of the Civil Rights Act of 1964, the Age Discrimination in Employment Act of 1967, the Rehabilitation Act of 1973, and the Americans with Disabilities Act of 1990. The Equal Employment Opportunities Commission (EEOC) is the federal government agency responsible for administrating many of the discrimination acts. Affirmative action, a program designed to remedy past discriminatory practices in hiring minority groups, is used when discrimination has been found. It enables protected groups to receive special attention in employment until such time as their numbers are proportionate to the percentage of employees in the non-protected group. Employees may volunteer or be required to establish an affirmative action program.

Procedural Due Process

The Fourteenth Amendment of the U. S. Constitution states that "No state shall make or enforce any law which shall abridge the privileges or immunities of citizens of the United States; nor shall any state deprive any person of life, liberty, or property, without due process of law." State actions, not private actions, are covered under the Fourteenth Amendment. Procedural due process enables an individual who is about to lose a liberty or property right to present his/her side of the situation and to be assured of fair treatment. Analysis, under procedural due process, is the balancing of the interests of the state against the rights of the individual.

Procedural due process systems are to be tailored to meet the needs of the business or agency. Legal advice is to be obtained before finalizing a system. When an employer is about to remove a liberty or property right (job) from an employee, the employee must:

- know and understand the charge and complaint;

- have a right to a hearing and to be represented by counsel in the hearing;

- be able to prepare and respond to charges; and

- present witnesses and question adverse witnesses.

The system must be in writing and contained in employee handbooks or related documents. The appeal process is to contain the following steps:

- Written notice of charges including dates, times, and details.

- Time and date for hearing.

- Explanation of representation and how it will be used in the hearing.

- Ample opportunity to prepare for hearing.

- Hearing is to give each side an opportunity to present its case.

- The hearing is convened before an impartial panel.

- Effort is made to negotiate a viable settlement among the parties.

- Settlement is made at hearing, if appropriate.

- The decision and rationale for the decision is contained in a written report.

- Proceedings are recorded and available to the employee.

The employee may bring a lawsuit if not satisfied with the conduct of the hearing or if he/she believes that due process was compromised.

Employing

Search

The following suggestions are based on results in *Griggs v. Duke Power Company* (1971), *Equal Employment Opportunity Commission v. Atlas Paper Box Company* (1989), and *Ward Cove Packing Company v. Atonio* (1989). In preparation for an employee search, supervisors are to learn the labor laws and contracts that cover the job. They are expected to understand the agency or corporation's affirmative action program. The job description is the centerpiece of the employment process. It must contain an accurate and comprehensive description of the significant job tasks. Qualifications essential to success in carrying out the tasks of the job are to be stated. Experience and qualifications unrelated to the job are to be avoided. The job is to be advertised in publications read by potential candidates. If deadlines are used, they are published and enforced. The employer, in conjunction with the search committee, forecasts the worker pool for the newly created position. What will be the extent and magnitude of the pool? Will the pool contain a number of reasonable candidates for the position? Among those qualified, how many would be inclined to accept the job?

Screening

Initial screening of candidates is based on objective published criteria. Checklists that use job criteria are recommended for use in the process. Only those meeting the published criteria move into the second level of screening. Each level of screening increases the demands on the candidates. The screening instruments, size of interview pool, and use of recommendations in making decisions are determined prior to the start of the job search. With candidates' permission, each reference and former employer of the applicants is checked.

Interviewing

The interviewing process is designed to provide an in-depth assessment of the candidate's skills through a sufficiently civil process that enables the candidate to retain an interest in the position. In-service training may be provided to interviewers to avoid the possibility that an interviewer would ask a discriminatory question about such things as age, marital status, the likelihood that a spouse will move to the city, and provisions for childcare. Candidates should leave the interview understanding the employment relationship classification and, if it is a contract, the nature and contents of the contract. Interviewers are to submit common form-written evaluations for each candidate.

Documentation is the employer's key to the entire process. Each step within the process is outlined and defined prior to instituting the search. The job description is crafted with the needs of the job and requisite skills and credentials in mind. The job description is easy to explain and defend should it be challenged. Screening and interviewing checklists and reports are objective when possible, signed, and dated. They are gathered immediately after their use.

Many search committees inform candidates of their status throughout the review process; the only legal requirement is that eliminated candidates be informed of their status when the job has been filled. Employers are to create a plan, follow the plan, and carefully document each step in the process.

Evaluating

Employee evaluation is an assessment of the elements of the job description and day-to-day tasks of the position. It is to be made in a fair manner. *Griggs v. Duke Power Company* (1971) established the need for performance evaluation based on identified job requirements. If, for example, in-service training is highly valued in evaluation, evidence must exist that it is essential to successful job performance. Sound business management suggests that employees are to engage in an evaluation assessment dialogue prior to completing an evaluation. Results of an evaluation are to be available to the employee. Serious deficits in work habits and disagreements over the execution of job tasks are to be reviewed. A rehabilitation program to address work deficiencies is to exist and be used appropriately. Continuous monitoring of the success or failure of individuals in the program is to be maintained.

Terminating

The termination process is to be contained in the employee handbook and is to be carried out exactly as it has been described. Reasons for termination tend to be a comprehensive poor work record, documented by numerous evaluations over a substantially long period of time; violation of federal or state laws; or creation of a hazard in the work environment. The due process system is used in termination.

SUMMARY

Business organizations include sole proprietorships, partnerships, "C" and "S" corporations, and limited liability companies and partnerships. A sole proprietor assumes total liability and responsibility for the business, including all of his/her financial assets. Partnerships involve shared responsibility among partners. Corporations are legal entities where owners have only their investments in the corporation at risk. Subchapter "S" corporations have corporate liability status and individual tax status. Limited liability companies and partnerships have corporate liability status and partnership tax status. Regular employee, independent contractor, and leased employee are three potential employment relationships. Vicarious liability is the liability of administrators for the torts of their employees. Due process laws assist an employer in employing, evaluating, and terminating employees.

DISCUSSION QUESTIONS

1. You are starting your own business. Analyze the advantages and disadvantages of each of the following business organizations: sole proprietorship, subchapter S corporation, or limited liability company (LLC). Which one would you select and why?

2. What is the most popular business organization among professional team owners?

3. Contrast an independent contractor with a regular employee relationship.

4. What are the requirements for an internship under the Fair Labor Standards Act?

ACTIVITIES

1. Create a job description for a familiar position. In small groups, conduct interviews for the position.

2. A friend is starting a new business. Given the content of this chapter, what advice would you give your friend?

3. You are the owner of a leasing company that provides lifeguards for a local pool. Your contract states that each guard is to work Monday through

Saturday from 9 a.m. to 4:30 p.m. Two of the guards report that they have been asked to work until 7 p.m. nearly every night for the past month. What should you do? Is your status as an independent contractor threatened?

4. Prepare an evaluation form for a specific employee.

REFERENCES

Bennett-Alexander, D. R., & Hartman, L. P. (2009). *Employment law for business.* New York, NY: McGraw-Hill, Irwin.

Clement, A. (2004). Sport law: Product liability and employment relations. In B. L. Parkhouse (Ed.). *The management of sport* (4th ed.; pp. 164-177). St. Louis, MO: Mosby Year Book.

Equal Employment Opportunity Commission v. Atlas Paper Box Company, 868 F. 2d 1489 (1989).

Griggs v. Duke Power Company, 401 U.S. 424, 91 S. Ct. 849 (1971).

Internship Programs Under the Fair Labor Standard Act, Wage and Hour Division. (2010, April). Retrieved from http://www.wagehour.dol.gov

Uniform Partnership Act (1994), 614, Section 34, 300-499.

U.S. Department of Labor, Wage and Hour Division. (2010). *Handy reference to the Fair Labor Standards Act.* Washington, DC: WH Publications.

Ward Cove Packing Company v. Atonio, 104 L. Ed. 2d 733 (1989).

RECOMMENDED READING

Gutman, A. (2000). *EEOC and personnel practices.* Thousand Oaks, CA: Sage.

Noe, R. A., Hollenbeck, J. R., Gerharts, B., & Wright, P. M. (2008). *Human resource management* (6th ed.). New York, NY: McGraw-Hill, Irwin.

9

Labor Law and Antitrust

OBJECTIVES

Upon completing this chapter, you will:

1) have learned the history of labor law in the United States;

2) be familiar with the role of labor law in professional sport;

3) understand antitrust law and how it has been applied to sport;

4) be able to contrast the differences in the antitrust court decisions among a range of sports; and

5) understand contemporary antitrust court decisions involving the National Collegiate Athletic Association (NCAA), Electronic Arts (EA), and Collegiate Licensing Company (CLC).

INTRODUCTION

Black's Law Dictionary (2011) identifies antitrust as "the body of law designed to protect trade and commerce from unlawful restraints, monopolies, price-fixing and price discrimination" (p. 41). Although antitrust issues appear in both the private and public sectors of sport, most antitrust legislation is designed to provide control in the private sector or profit-making businesses. Article One of the U.S. Constitution, the Sherman Act of 1890, the Clayton Act of 1914, the Norris LaGuardia Act of 1932, and the National Labor Relations Act (a result of amendments to the Wagner Act of 1935) play a role in the understanding of antitrust. Three U.S. Supreme Court decisions have exempted professional baseball from all antitrust laws. Decisions in other professional and amateur sport have not received the same special treatment. In recent years, litigations surrounding collegiate sports and the governance of sport activities has increased.

LABOR LAWS

Article One of the United States Constitution

Article One, Section Eight (Number Three) of the U.S. Constitution states that Congress shall have the power "to regulate commerce with foreign Nations, and among the several States, and with the Indian Tribes." Section Eight (Number Eighteen) gives Congress the power "to make all laws which shall be necessary and proper for carrying into execution the foregoing powers, and all other Powers vested by this Constitution in the Government of the United States, or in any Department or Officer thereof."

Antitrust

Federal antitrust laws regulate interstate commerce in an effort to prevent the organization of monopolies. The laws cover goods, land, and services. Practices such as price fixing are in violation of these laws. When the courts are asked to examine a potential violation of antitrust law, the courts use a "rule of reason test" in which the illegal practice is balanced against the anti-competitive effect. When analyzing sport in the context of the following laws, sport is viewed as private and operated to make a profit.

Sherman Act of 1890

Section I of the Sherman Act states that every "contract, combination in the form of trust or otherwise, or conspiracy, in restraint of trade or commerce among the several States, or with foreign nations, is declared to be illegal. Every person who shall make any contract or engage in any combination or conspiracy hereby declared to be illegal shall be deemed guilty of a felony."

Section II adds that "every person who shall monopolize, or attempt to monopolize, or combine or conspire with any other person or persons, to monopolize any part of the trade or commerce among the several States, or with foreign nations, shall be deemed guilty of a felony."

Clayton Act of 1914

The Clayton Act is more precise than the Sherman Act and is thought to have further defined the Sherman Act. Sections Four and Six of the Clayton Act are significant to professional athletes, as they negotiate individual contract components and collective bargaining agreements. Section Four states that

> any person who shall be injured in his business or property by reason of anything forbidden in the antitrust laws may sue therefore in any district court of the United States in the district in which the defendant resides or is found or has an agent, without respect to the amount in controversy, and shall recover threefold the damages by him sustained, and the cost of the suit including a reasonable attorney's fee. The court may award under this section ... simple interest in actual damages for the period beginning on the date of service of such person's pleadings.

Section Six states that

> the labor of a human being is not a commodity or article of commerce. Nothing contained in the antitrust laws shall be construed to forbid the existence and operation of labor, agricultural or horticultural organizations, instituted for the purpose of mutual help, or to forbid or restrain

individual members of such organizations from lawfully carrying out the legitimate objects thereof; nor shall such organizations, or the members thereof, be held or construed to be illegal combinations or conspiracies in restraint of trade under the antitrust laws.

Norris-LaGuardia Act of 1932

The Public Policy provision of the Norris-LaGuardia Act of 1932 defined the liberty of contract and freedom of labor roles of the individual worker who was not part of a formal labor group. He/she gained the freedoms of association, self-organization, and representation granted to the groups in the earlier antitrust laws. The act provided a solid recognition for American labor. This recognition was fine-tuned in the National Labor Relations Act.

National Labor Relations Act

The National Labor Relations Act, a result of amendments to the Wagner Act of 1935, noted that "Employees shall have the right to self-organization, to form, join, or assist labor organizations, to bargain collectively through representatives of their own choosing, and to engage in other concerted activities for the purpose of collective bargaining or other mutual aid or protection, and shall also have the right to refrain from any or all of such activities except to the extent that such right may be affected by an agreement requiring membership in a labor organization as a condition of employment." An employer or a labor organization that restrains or coerces an employee in the exercise of the employee's rights commits an unfair labor practice. It is also an unfair labor practice for a labor organization to refuse to bargain collectively with an employer who is an official representative of their employees.

UNIQUE CHARACTERISTICS OF PROFESSIONAL SPORT

Sport is considered "big business." However, sport has a culture far different from the traditions associated with business and industry. The first distinction is in the definition of sport (the product). Sport competition is the product. For sport competition to be successful in the entertainment market, play must be exciting and lively with a close score throughout the event. The exciting, lively, and highly competitive (i.e., close score) encounter is most assured when a "level playing field" (or equal skills) has been established prior to competition. To create a level playing field, players must be allocated to competing teams on the basis of skill and talent so all teams in a competitive league have an equal start. Such items as drafts, trades, and salary caps are among the systems used to create this equality. Owners within a league work cooperatively to allocate players. Once all players have joined a team, each owner works diligently to win or beat the other league owners. This close working relationship coupled with a passionate desire to beat the very same teams is one of the hallmarks of professional league competition.

In business and industry, employees either join unions and accept collective bargaining agreements or individually negotiate their employment contracts. An employee in professional athletics automatically becomes a member of the players' union (the players' collective bargaining unit) and accepts the work, economic, and other benefits that have been negotiated by the union. Outstanding athletes then bargain individually, usually through an agent, for additional privileges. Thus, the second major difference between professional sports and business and industry is the role and use of labor unions and individually negotiated employment contracts.

Another difference between sport and business/industry is found in client interaction and satisfaction. In most businesses, an unhappy client or customer can search out another source for products or services. Often, the unhappy collegiate and professional sport client (spectator) cannot find another team to support. Gary Roberts (1991) noted that a legal problem in antitrust claims in sport is defining "the relevant market that the plaintiff claims has been monopolized. The market definition must include both a product and a geographic dimension—for example, professional football entertainment in the United States" (p. 138).

Career longevity is another difference between professional sport and business/ industry. Few employers expect a person's entire career to span an average of three to five years. Professional athletes have short timeframes for career success; this difference in length of careers prompts the professional athlete to want instant success and demand the gratification that accompanies such success. Employees in business and industry do not have to establish their value in the workplace in such a short time period. Because of the reality of the potential length of their careers, outstanding professional athletes want free agency status and the ability to test their skills in the free market as often as possible. They want these opportunities when they are playing at their best, not at the completion of three or five years of play. Also, they are concerned that career-threatening injuries may shorten their sport career. Each of these factors plays a role in the antitrust cases associated with professional athletes.

LITIGATION

Antitrust cases in sport include unique decisions awarded in professional baseball, football, basketball, hockey, collegiate sport, and sport organizations. The majority of the litigation in sport has been in professional "big business" team sports. Today, collegiate sport has become a party in antitrust cases, and individuals have used antitrust in defining player rights.

Professional Sport

Baseball

Three U.S. Supreme Court decisions (1992, 1953, and 1972) have exempted professional baseball from antitrust laws. The 1922 Supreme Court, under Justice Holmes, found in *Federal Baseball Club of Baltimore v. National League of Baseball Clubs* (1922) that professional baseball did not meet the Sherman Act "interstate commerce" clause, as its "business is giving exhibitions of baseball, which are purely state affairs" (208). The suit was brought over the "reserve clause" in relation to contracts signed by professional baseball players. As a result of this clause, a player was bound to an owner for his entire career unless the owner chose to trade him. This system, designed to create a level playing field (equal competition), prohibited a team from making an offer to a player who was under contract.

In the case of *Toolson v. New York Yankees* (1953), the plaintiff approached the Supreme Court believing that the court would find professional baseball part of "interstate commerce" due to the advent of television. Surely, national television broadcasts had turned professional baseball into "interstate commerce." Again, the issue was the "reserve clause" and that the contract clause violated the Sherman Act and Clayton Act. This time the Supreme Court said that baseball had operated successfully under the decision of *Federal Baseball Clubs of Baltimore v. National League of Baseball Clubs*, and as a result, it seemed appropriate to continue to exempt baseball from antitrust law.

Curt Flood, a player traded to another club without his knowledge, filed a cause of action (*Flood v. Kuhn*, 1972) under antitrust law. Again, the U.S. Supreme Court noted that baseball had operated successfully under the antitrust exemption and therefore the antitrust exemption should be maintained.

In 1995, the Major League Baseball Players Association (MLBPA), the collective bargaining representative for the players in the 28 clubs, reported the baseball owners' labor law violations to the National Labor Relations Board. The employment agreement expired at the end of 1993. The players went on strike in August of 1994. The action halted the season, resulted in the cancellation of the 1994 World Series, and continued through part of the 1995 season. The owners wanted a salary cap, the elimination of the salary arbitration system, and restricted free agency. The players' counterproposal was a tax system to "deter extravagant wage offers" (*Silverman v. Major League Baseball*, 1995, 252).

The National Labor Relations Board (Region 2) sought a preliminary injunction pending the outcome of their investigation. At issue were complaints "that the Owners had violated Section 8(a, 1) [to interfere with, restrain, or coerce employees in the exercise of guaranteed rights: wages, hours, and conditions of employment] and (5) [to refuse to bargain collectively with representatives of employees] of the Act by unilaterally eliminating, before an impasse had been reached, salary arbitration for certain reserve players, competitive bargaining for certain free agents, and the anti-collusion provision of their collective bargaining agreement" (*Silverman v. Major League Baseball*, 1995, 250).

The issues involved free agency and the "reserve clause." Under free agency, a player with six years or more of play could become a free agent. Once the player signed a new contract, the player had another five years before becoming a free agent. This agreement also limited the number of free agents that each club could sign in two top-performance categories. Reserve players, those with fewer than six years of play, were under the Uniform Players Contract. Each year they were offered a new contract with a salary adjustment. According to the Uniform Players Contract, "If the player refuses the offer, the owner is entitled to 'reserve' the player's services and the player is not permitted to play for other teams. An owner may only reserve a player once under this system" (*Silverman*, 1995, 251). After a three-year period, the athlete could request salary arbitration. The outcomes of the salary arbitration did not affect the player's reserve status.

In deliberation, the court in the *Silverman v. Major League Baseball* (1995) case noted that

> Collective bargaining in the context of professional sports presents issues different from most other contexts. On one hand, the talent of an individual athlete can provide him with extraordinary bargaining power, but on the other hand, a player may sell his talent only to a circumscribed group of owners, who have something akin to monopoly power in the sport at issue. These circumstances in professional sports have given rise to the development of the reserve/free agency system, which, perhaps not surprisingly, is quite different from other models of collective bargaining in less specialized and unique industries. (255–256)

The court issued an injunction directing Major League Baseball: "(1) to restore the terms and conditions of employment provided under the expired basic agreement which was effective January 1, 1990, including its free agency/reserve system with salary arbitration for eligible reserve players ... (2) immediately to rescind by written notice to all club members any actions taken ... and (3) to bargain in good faith without unilateral changes to the basic agreement with the Major League Baseball Players Association in compliance with 8(a, 1) and (5) of the National Labor Relations Act" (*Silverman v. Major League Baseball*, 1995, 261).

In 1998, Congress passed the Curt Flood Act. This legislation partially repealed baseball's exemption of antitrust. The act amended the Clayton Act by subjecting business practices, "directly relating to or affecting employment of major league baseball players ... to the antitrust laws to the same extent such ... practices ... would be subject to the antitrust law of ... persons in any other professional sports business affecting interstate commerce" (15 USC 27A [a]). The Curt Flood Act repealed baseball's antitrust exemption only as it affected labor issues between owners and players. It did not affect franchise ownership, expansion and relocation, existing broadcasting arrangements, the draft, and owner-commissioner agreements.

The case *Major League Baseball, et al. v. Crist* (2003) was a response to Major League Baseball's decision to eliminate two teams from the league (Florida Marlins and Tampa Bay Devil Rays). Crist, Florida's attorney general, began an investigation of Major League Baseball under Florida's Antitrust Act of 1980 to "determine whether there is, has been, or may be a violation of ... the [state or federal antitrust laws] ... by conduct, activities, or proposed action of the following nature: possible contracts, combinations, or conspiracies in restraint of trade, or monopolization, attempted monopolization, or combinations or conspiracies to monopolize trade or commerce, relating to the proposed contraction and/or relocation of the Tampa Bay Devil Rays and/or the Florida Marlins" (1180). The United States Court of Appeals for the Eleventh Circuit ruled that the federal exemption preempted state antitrust law and that the attorney general could not continue with the investigation. The decision provides a comprehensive analysis of antitrust law at the state and federal levels and how it is applied to baseball.

Football

Football players have long wondered why baseball was exempt from antitrust regulations and football was not exempt. Professional football was denied an antitrust exemption in *United States v. Shubert* (1955) and *Radovich v. National Football League* (1957). In 1974, football players decided to challenge the "Rozelle Rule" under antitrust law (*Mackey v. National Football League,* 1976). The "Rozelle Rule" required a team signing a veteran free agent to compensate the team losing the player with cash or a draft choice. The district court found that the "Rozelle Rule" violated the Sherman Act; the Eighth Circuit affirmed the decision. As a result, the "Rozelle Rule" was replaced by the "Right of First Refusal," a system found to be less offensive to the players. A right of first refusal is a contract right that belongs to the current contract holder, in this case, an NFL team, to match the offer made to a specific player by another team in or outside of the league, within a designated period of time. If the offer is not made in the time period, the player goes to the new team; if the offer is made, the player stays with the current team.

Powell, the plaintiff in *Powell v. National Football League* (1988, 1989, and 1991), brought a case on behalf of a number of members of the National Football League Players Association (NFLPA) against the National Football League (NFL) for violation of the Clayton and Sherman Acts. The dispute was "over the rights of veteran free agents to play for the NFL clubs of their choosing. For more than a decade, the movement of veteran free agents has been subject to the Right of First Refusal/Compensation System" (*Powell, et al. v. National Football League, et al.,* 1988, 813).

The parties returned to the District Court of Minnesota requesting a preliminary injunction. The court denied the injunction, stating that such a grant would be in conflict with the purpose (to bargain in good faith) of the Norris-LaGuardia Act. The first decision of the Minnesota District Court was appealed to the United States Court of Appeals, Eighth Circuit. The Eighth Circuit reversed and remanded the decision and held that "the antitrust laws are inapplicable under the circumstances of the case as the non-statutory labor exemption extends beyond impasse" (*Powell, et al. v. National Football League,* 1989, 1304). Powell returned to the same court and requested an opportunity to consolidate with the *McNeil* case (*McNeil v. National Football League,* 1992) which is analyzed below. The request was denied.

In the *McNeil* case, eight NFL players whose contracts had expired brought a cause of action under the Sherman Act against all the NFL team owners. This was not an NFLPA action as presented in *Powell;* it covered only the named players. The complaint was over the wage scale and a plan created by the owners that they called "Plan B." The players' goal was to prevent the enforcement of the first refusal compensation plan. Plan B allowed each team to retain limited rights to 37 players each season. Players classified as unprotected would become unrestricted free agents and would be free to sign with any NFL club. Owners retained a right of first refusal for all protected players. If a protected player signed with a new team, the new team was expected to provide a draft choice to the player's original team. The jury found components of the wage plan in violation of the Sherman Act. Only those players that were found to have sustained injury were awarded money damages.

Finally, as a result of the *McNeil* case, today's existing system was created. It allows teams to have exclusive control over players for their first three years. The players have limited rights of first refusal for years four and five, and unrestricted free agency after five years. As soon as the decision was final, ten players immediately requested and were granted a temporary restraining order to prevent the enforcement of the first refusal compensation (*Jackson, et al. v. National Football League*, 1992).

Two weeks after the *McNeil* decision, Reggie White and five other named plaintiffs representing all professional, college, and other persons who had played or wanted to play professional football from 1987 to the completion of the case, brought a class action suit against the National Football League over "the right of first refusal rules of Plan B, the college draft, the NFL Player Contract, and the preseason pay rule" (*White v. NFL*, 1993[1], 1394). The settlement agreement provided for the NFLPA to be the exclusive bargaining agent for the players:

> (a) the terms of the Stipulation and Settlement Agreement fundamentally modify the NFL's rules, policies, and practices regarding veteran player movement and employment. The settlement also fundamentally modifies, by agreement, the college draft, the NFL Player Contract, and various other terms and conditions of NFL player employment.

> (b) the revised player mobility and employment rules represent a successful effort by NFL players to eliminate Plan B, and to bring about substantial modifications in the principles relating to veteran player transfer. (*White v. NFL*, 1993[2], 1464)

The plaintiff notified class members of the proposed settlement. A hearing was held in which many players objected to the details of the settlement. The district court overruled the objections. Shortly thereafter, the NFL and the NFLPA entered into a new collective bargaining agreement that included the terms of the settlement. Those who objected to the settlement filed a claim with the United States Court of Appeals for the Eighth Circuit to open the settlement. The court affirmed the approval of the settlement of the district court.

The parties extended the collective bargaining agreements with amendments in 1996 and again in 2006 for the contract through 2012. In May of 2008, the NFL asked to be relieved from the current agreement for financial reasons. At the same time, the NFL recognized that in order to achieve their interests, a lockout might be necessary. The players wanted to avoid a lockout.

The media rights became the issue. The broadcast contracts provided about half of the NFL's total revenue. The exiting broadcast contracts did not require the media to pay rights fees during a lockout. So the NFL decided to extend broadcast rights with any of the media agencies willing to renegotiate. This would mean that the players could not use the revenue loss from the media as a bargaining tool in future negotiations. Under the new DirecTV contract, the "NFL could receive substantially more from DirecTV in 2011 if it locks out the players than if it does not" (*White, et al. v. National Football League,* 2011, 945). Other deals were negotiated with CBS and Fox, NBC, ESPN, and Comcast and Verizon. In June of 2010, the players sued the NFL for violating the SSA agreement by extending and renegotiating the broadcast contracts without trying to get the greatest revenue. As a result of a special master's report, the court awarded the players $6.9 million in damages for the NBC violation and found that the players had not met the burden of demonstrating damages for other media deals. The players objected.

The United States District Court for the District of Minnesota considered four factors in determining whether an injunction should be issued: "(1) the threat of irreparable harm to the movant in the absence of relief, (2) the balance between that harm and the harm that the relief may cause the non-moving party, (3) the likelihood of the movant's ultimate success on the merits, (4) the public interest. Money damages were not discussed. For that reason the court determined that additional briefing and a hearing be held before the final order was issued" (*White, et al. v. National Football League,* 2011, 954). On March 12, 2011, the players filed a complaint that the lockout threatened by the NFL would violate antitrust laws, state contracts, and tort law. Again they asked for an injunction.

> On March 12, the League imposed a lockout of the players. At that point, the League notified players under contract that, among other things, they were not permitted to enter team facilities except in connection with a non-team event or a charitable event, they would not receive compensation or health insurance benefits from their teams, and they were not permitted to play, practice, work out, attend meetings, or consult with team medical or training staff at team facilities. The League also filed an amended unfair labor practice charge with the National Labor Relations Board on March 11, alleging that the NFLPA's disclaimer was a "sham" and that the combination of a disclaimer by the union and subsequent antitrust litigation was a "ploy and an unlawful subversion of the collective bargaining process." The League had filed a previous charge in February 2011, alleging that the union failed to confer in good faith during negotiations over a new collective bargaining agreement. (*Brady, et al., v. National Football League, et al.,* 2011[3], 788)

The court of appeals for the Eighth Circuit in *Brady* did not agree with the district court's view in *White,* that the "balance of the equities tilts heavily in favor of the Players" (793). They looked at the four factors listed above and on May 16, 2011 granted a stay pending the final disposition of the expedited appeal. The *Brady, et al. v. NFL* case was dismissed after the lockout on August 26, 2011, by the United States District Judge Susan Richad Nelson.

The issue in *American Needle, Inc. v. National Football League* (2008, 2010) was whether the NFL was a single entity or a group of separate teams. The day of the filing of the suit, the NFL had 32 separately owned and operated football teams. They played a series of games throughout the season with the Super Bowl as the finale. NFL defined "the product that teams produced jointly—NFL football—requires coordination and integration between the teams" (*American Needle, Inc. v. National Football League,* 2008, 737). In the early 1960s, the individual teams pooled their intellectual property rights and the NFL granted licenses to a number of different vendors, including American Needle, to create products. In 2000, the NFL requested bids from vendors with the decision to select an exclusive licensee. The contract, for ten years, went to Reebok; none of the licensees were renewed. American Needle, one of the former vendors, sued under antitrust, a "contract, combination, … or conspiracy in restraint of trade" (738). American Needle claimed that the NFL's requirement to pool individual team trademarks under one license vendor was a conspiracy. They felt that each team should hire their own vendors.

The NFL claimed single entity; American Needle responded that they did not have enough information to know if the NFL was a single entity. Discovery became detailed, with American Needle requesting documents the NFL claimed had nothing to do with the single entity status. Finally, the court determined that the NFL was a single entity; American Needle's claims failed as a matter of law. The court of appeals affirmed the district court's decision. The United States Supreme Court reversed and remanded. The Supreme Court made the decision under the "rule of reason" test. Was there a contract, combination, or conspiracy among the individual teams? Was there concerted action? The Court found that "The NFL teams do not possess either the unitary decision making quality or the single aggregation of economic power characteristic of independent actions. Each … is a substantial, independently owned, independently managed business whose general corporate actions are guided or determined by separate corporate consciousness, and whose objectives are not common" (*American Needle, Inc. v. National Football League,* 2010, 2205). Thus, the court reversed the earlier court's decision and remanded the case for further study.

Basketball

The National Basketball Association (NBA) negotiated a contract in 1988 that expired in 1994 (*NBA, et al. v. Williams, et al.,* 1995). In the 1994 contract negotiations, the players

> demanded the elimination of three provisions in the 1988 Collective Bargaining Agreement (CBA); the "College Draft," the "Right of First Refusal," and the "Revenue Sharing/Salary Cap System":
>
> *The College Draft is the process by which exclusive rights to negotiate with eligible college players are apportioned among the NBA Teams.…
>
> *The Right of First Refusal permits a team to match any offer made to one of its current players by another team and thus to retain the player's services.…

*The Revenue Sharing/Salary Cap System establishes an overall wage framework that provides that the: (i) total player salaries and benefits paid by all NBA Teams will be no less than a specified percentage of revenues; and (ii) the total salary paid to players by each team is subject to both a maximum and a required minimum.

*The Right of First Refusal and the present version of the College Draft have been incorporated in all the CBA's signed by the parties since 1976; the Revenue Sharing/Salary Cap provision has been included in every CBA since 1983. (*NBA, et al. v Williams, et al.,* 1995, 685)

In July of 1994, Judge Duffy of the Southern District of New York granted the NBA its request for relief and dismissed the case. The players appealed. The United States Court of Appeals for the Second Circuit affirmed. The court held "that the antitrust laws do not prohibit employers from bargaining jointly with a union, from implementing their joint proposals in the absence of a CBA, or from using economic force to obtain agreement to those proposals" (693).

Hockey

In 1977, McCourt signed a three-year National Hockey League (NHL) Standard Player Contract to play hockey for the NHL's franchise located in Detroit. In an effort to gain a new player, the Detroit Red Wings gave McCourt to the Los Angeles Kings. Instead of going to Los Angeles, McCourt sued the NHL, Los Angeles Kings, National Hockey League Players Association, and Detroit Red Wings (*McCourt v. California Sports, Inc., et al.,* 1979). He alleged that the reserve system violated the Sherman Act. McCourt received a preliminary injunction restraining defendants from enforcing the arbitration award and his reassignment. The NHL appealed. The United States Court of Appeals, Sixth Circuit, vacated the injunction and remanded the case. The court held that the non-statutory labor exemption applied since the reserve system was incorporated into the collective bargaining agreement as a result of a good faith bargain.

The value of a brand has increased measurably in the last ten years. The NHL decided to grow hockey by improving the strength of the League brand. They planned to achieve the entertainment successes experienced by baseball and football. To attain such visibility, they considered enticing the individual NHL Clubs to assign their trademarks to the League so that the League could be marketed on a collective basis. In 1994, member clubs granted the League exclusive rights to use or license trademarks for advertising, and for the sale and distribution of products and services. The clubs also "agreed that the right to develop and exploit the internet as a marketing tool resided in the League" (*Madison Square Garden, L.P. v. National Hockey League, et al.,* 2007, 5).

In 2000, the clubs decided to change the Internet approach to a hybrid model. The League's and the clubs' websites would be part of an integrated network, with certain elements available on the clubs' websites and others available on NHL.com (*Madison Square Garden, L.P. v. National Hockey League,* 2007, 5). The commissioner's Internet plan restricted a portion of each team's website for NHL content and reserved 35% of each club's website for NHL-controlled advertising. The rules also required that all merchandise sales were to be made through the League Store.

The NHL is an unincorporated association of thirty member clubs organized as a joint venture. They share a common constitution and bylaws. The League Commission has the power to interpret the constitution, bylaws, League rules, and resolutions. Member clubs are separately owned, and have separate assets, stadium rights, employees, and intellectual property rights in team logos and designs. In 2005, the League again examined the media revenues and decided centralization was necessary. A committee commissioned to review the situation recommended consolidation of team sites to a common technology platform with a single content manager. The consolidation was expected to save approximately $2 million.

In February of 2007, the League and Rangers met to discuss differences, one of them the Internet regulation. They failed to reach agreement on any of the issues. Thus, the Rangers decided to set up an "Internet Store" to sell Ranger merchandise, use virtual advertising and signage in Ranger home game broadcasts, and stream broadcasts of Ranger games on the Internet. All were illegal according to League rules (*Madison Square Garden, L.P., et al. v. National Hockey League, et al.*, 2007, 10). Deputy Commissioner Daly sent them a letter instructing them to stop or be fined $100,000 a day for the violation. The Rangers remained in violation for two days and $200,000. Both groups met to resolve the differences. Negotiations broke down, and the League said they would begin fines the first day of the season if the Rangers did not agree to a common Internet site. The Rangers went to court for an injunction against the League. The Rangers alleged that the League had "become an 'illegal cartel' in its attempts to prevent office competition between and among NHL member clubs" (14). The Rangers' motion for a preliminary injunction was denied. They had failed to demonstrate a likelihood of success on the merits. They appealed. The Court of Appeals for the Second Circuit affirmed the district court's decision.

Collegiate Sports

The National Collegiate Athletic Association's acquisition of women's collegiate sports was a model hostile takeover of a business or agency where the plaintiff's only chance for survival was antitrust law. This decision is discussed in detail in Chapter 5, Fourteenth Amendment and Title IX (*AIAW v. NCAA*, 1983, 1984; Hult, 1980; Uhlir, 1982). The decisions freed the NCAA to become "big business" athletics similar to professional team sports. It was the day that higher education traded the academic sport model for a semi-professional system. Since that time, NCAA has been plagued with litigation.

In January of 1991, the National Collegiate Athletic Association (NCAA) adopted a bylaw (11.02.3) that restricted the earnings of the fourth member of a Division One (D-1) basketball staff and various other D-1 coaches. The earnings were restricted to $12,000 for the year and $4,000 for the summer. It was known that some of these coaches had made as much as $60,000 to $70,000 prior to the change. The cap was an effort to reduce the costs in D-1 competition. A number of restricted-earnings coaches filed suits against the NCAA. Eventually, the cases were consolidated within *Law, et al. v. NCAA* (1996). The plaintiffs sued, alleging price fixing in violation of the Sherman Act and claiming that the NCAA had conspired to limit the maximum compensation it would pay to one category of coaches. The United States District Court for the District of Kansas found that the NCAA's restricted-earnings rule represented price fixing and violated antitrust laws. The court stated that "Because the Restricted Earnings Coach Rule is a restraint of trade as prohibited by the Sherman Act, the NCAA bears a heavy burden in this case to establish that the restraint enhances competition or, in other words, promotes a legitimate, pro-competitive goal. On this record, the Court finds that the NCAA has not met this weighty burden and that plaintiffs are entitled to judgment as a matter of law on the issue of liability" (*Law, et al. v. NCAA,* 1995, 1410).

Electronic Arts, the creator and marketer of sport video games, was sued for antitrust violations by the athletes whose likenesses have been used in games (*Keller, et al. v. Electronic Arts, Inc., National Collegiate Athletic Association, and Collegiate Licensing Company,* 2010; *O'Bannon, et al. v. National Collegiate Athletic Association, Collegiate Licensing Company, et al.,* 2009, 2010; *In re Student-Athlete Name & Likeness Licensing Litigation,* 2011). Among Electronic Arts games are Madden NFL 10, Madden NFL 11, NCAA Football 10, and NCAA Football 11. The athletes have sued and continue to sue Electronic Arts under "The Right of Publicity" as described in Chapter 10, Intellectual Property.

Their antitrust claim is that in signing the forms required to play sports under NCAA rules, they had to agree to release their rights to their personal image, likeness, and/or name for use by NCAA on merchandise and licensees. When the athletes signed the release they were not informed that the release was forever, not just for the four years of NCAA play. Specifically, the defendants, the National Collegiate Athletic Association (NCAA), and the Collegiate Licensing Company (CLC) have "engaged in anticompetitive conduct in two ways. First, they … conspired to fix the prices they received for the use and sale of their images, likenesses and/or names at zero dollars…. Second, … defendants engaged in a group boycott/refusal to deal conspiracy that required all current student athletes to sign forms … to relinquish all rights in perpetuity for use of their images, likenesses, and/or names and to deny Antitrust Class Members compensation in the form of royalties for the continued use of their images, likenesses, and/or names for profit" (*In re: NCAA Student-Athlete Name and Likeness Litigation,* 2011[2], 10). The athletes' legal complaints are in violation of the Sherman Act for unreasonable restraint of trade, group boycott, refusal to deal, unjust enrichment, and an accounting.

Early complaints were filed by Keller and O'Bannon. Both cases were filed as representing themselves and all other affected athletes. Sam Keller was a starting quarterback for Arizona State University and the University of Nebraska football teams. Among the charges in his complaint was that Electronic Arts was using his likeness without consent; misconduct on the part of the NCAA and Collegiate Licensing Company (CLC) for violating one of the NCAA's bylaws; civil conspiracy; and breach of contract. A purpose in filling the claim was to request the permission of the court for a class action suit (*Keller, et al. v. Electronic Arts, Inc., NCAA, and CLC,* 2010). In 2009, O'Bannon, a Nevada resident who had played basketball for UCLA, submitted a similar claim against the NCAA and CLC to the United States District Court for the Northern District of California. NCAA, in response to the suit, requested a change of venue to Southern Indiana. The court denied the request (*O'Bannon, et al. v. NCAA and CLC,* 2009). O'Bannon made the following claims, first under the Sherman Act and later under common law:

Violation of Section I of the Sherman Act:

A. Existence of a contract, combination or conspiracy. Contract was proved through NCAA's requirement that athletes sign Form 08-3a which gives away their personal rights. Arrangements between NCAA, CLC, and Electronic Arts created a second contract. Thus, O'Bannon satisfied prong one of the Sherman Act.

B. Unreasonable restraint of trade (Rule of Reason). Conduct constituted price-fixing and a group boycott. The complaint is that NCAA has fixed the price of former athletes' image at zero and has created a boycott of former student-athletes in the collegiate licensing market.

C. Under the Statute of limitations, his plea for a continuing violation was accepted.

D. Standing must be accomplished when "(1) he or she suffers a concrete, particularized injury; (2) there is a causal connection between the injury and the conduct complained of; and (3) the injury will likely be redressed by a favorable decision." (*O'Bannon, et al. v. NCAA, CLC, et al.* 2009, 16)

    Standing was established; and he succeeded under the common law claim of unjust enrichment (*O'Bannon, et al. v. NCAA, et al., 2009,* 22).

The court order as of January 15, 2010, was for the Keller and O'Bannon actions to file a consolidated amended complaint and to attend a case management conference. The athletes joined together and the case name became *In re: Student-Athlete Name and Likeness Litigation.* There were seventeen named plaintiffs in the action. In February of 2011, the action for a change in venue denied earlier was denied again. In May of 2011 litigation, Electronic Art's motion to dismiss the Sherman Act claims was granted; NCAA and CLC motions to dismiss similar claims were denied. On July 28, 2011, EA's motion for dismissal of common law claims was denied. No further actions are in print as of this publication.

Sport Organizations

Antitrust claims have played a role in disputes over eligibility rules and re-organization of sport competitions. Maurice Clarett, an outstanding Ohio State University football player, decided to join the National Football League (NFL). Clarett, a sophomore, was denied the opportunity due to an NFL rule limiting eligibility to players three seasons following high school play. Clarett sued under antitrust. He based his claim on what he perceived as an unreasonable restraint of trade. The plaintiff noted that "Antitrust law will not tolerate a contract which unreasonably forbids anyone to practice his calling" (*Clarett v. National Football League*, 2004, 382). The District Court for the Southern District of New York granted Clarett's motion for summary judgment and denied the NFL's motion. "Because the Rule violates the antitrust law, it cannot preclude Clarett's eligibility for the 2004 NFL draft. Accordingly, it is hereby ORDERED that Clarett is eligible to participate in the 2004 NFL draft" (*Clarett v. National Football League*, 2004, 410–411).

The Association of Tennis Professionals (ATP) sponsors the worldwide tennis circuit. A re-organization of the tour moved some events and players to top tier play while others were downgraded. The Hamburg, Germany, tournament was moved from first tier to second tier, prompting this lawsuit (*Deutscher Tennis Bund, et al. v. APT Tour, Inc., et al.*, 2010). The suit alleged that the plan, called "Brave New World," violated Sections 1 and 2 of the Sherman Act and that the ATP Directors had breached duties owned to the Federation (824). Also, individual players had complaints concerning the number and types of tournaments they would be required to play. The jury returned a verdict for ATP, stating that "the Federation failed to prove ATP entered into a contract, combination, or conspiracy with any separate entity under Section 1 of the Sherman Act, and did not establish a relevant product market under Section 2 of the Sherman Act" (824). The Federation appealed the verdict. ATP alleged it was a single entity or a single enterprise. The United States Court of Appeals for the Third Circuit affirmed the jury verdict for defendants on the Sherman Act claims and found for defendants on the breach of duties.

SUMMARY

Antitrust laws promote competition by regulating against monopolies. Article One of the United States Constitution, the Sherman Act, the Clayton Act, the Norris-LaGuardia Act, and the National Labor Relations Act play a role in protecting organizations from antitrust. Sport is particularly sensitive to antitrust legislation due to efforts on the part of professional sport owners to create a "level playing field." Baseball has achieved a status beyond antitrust; players have not been as successful in using antitrust as a theory against owners in other sports as they have been in baseball. The collegiate antitrust litigation involving image and likeness is somewhat unique and bears observation in the future.

DISCUSSION QUESTIONS

1. Could the method for selecting the teams for the Bowl Championships be challenged under antitrust law?

2. What do you anticipate as the next antitrust complaint in collegiate sports?

ACTIVITIES

1. Locate the case, *In re: Student-Athlete Name and Likeness Litigation,* and outline the activity in the case since July 28, 2011, the last reported decision in the text. What do you think of the decision? Identify the final decisions for Electronic Arts, Collegiate Licensing Company, and the National Collegiate Athletic Association. These decisions are expected to have a substantial impact on each of the parties.

2. Contrast the antitrust issues found in the professional sport decisions with those found in the collegiate sport decisions.

3. Who should control trademarks? Leagues or individual teams?

4. Locate the *AIAW v. NCAA* decision and contrast the theory of student-athlete with theory of "big business sport."

REFERENCES

AIAW v. NCAA, 558 F. Supp. 487 (1983); 735 F. 2d 577 (1984).

American Needle, Inc. v. National Football League, 538 F. 3d 736 (2008); 130 S. Ct. 2201 (2010); 391 Fed. Appx. 546 (2010).

Black's Law Dictionary. (2011). St. Paul, MN: Thomson Reuters.

Brady, et al. v. National Football League, et al., 779 F. Supp. 1043; 638 F. 3d 1004, 2011; 640 F. 3d 785 (2011).

Clarett v. National Football League, 306 F. Supp. 2d 379 (2004 [1]); 369 F. 3d 124 (2004 [2]).

Clayton Act of 1914, 15 USC 15, (4) and (6).

Curt Flood Act, 15 USCA 27a(a).

Deutscher Tennis Bund, German Tennis Federation, et al. v. ATP Tours, Inc., et al., 610 F. 3d 820 (2010).

Federal Baseball Club of Baltimore v. National League of Baseball Clubs, 259 U.S. 200 (1922).

Flood v. Kuhn, 316 F. Supp. 271 (1970); 443 F. 2d 264 (1971); 407 U.S. 258 (1972).

Hult, J. S. (1980). The philosophical conflicts in men's and women's collegiate athletics. *Quest, 32*(1), 77–94.

In re: NCAA Student-Athlete Name and Likeness Litigation, 763 F. Supp. 2d 1379 2011 (1) ; 2011 U.S. Dist. LEXIS 46841 (2); 2011 U.S. Dist. LEXIS 82682 (3).

Jackson, et al. v. National Football League, 602 F 2d 226 (1992).

Keller, et al. v. Electronic Arts, Inc., National Collegiate Athletic Association, and Collegiate Licensing Company, 2010 U.S. Dist. LEXIS 10719.

Law, et al. v. NCAA, 902 F. Supp. 1394 (1995); 167 F. R. D. 464 (1996).

Mackey v. National Football League, 543 F. 2d 606 (1976); 434 U.S. 801 (1977).

Madison Square Garden, L.P. v. National Hockey Leagues, et al., 2007 U.S. Dist. LEXIS 81446; 270 Fed. Appx. 56 (2008); 2008 U.S. Dist. LEXIS 80475.

Major League Baseball v. Crist, 331 F. 3d 1177 (2003).

McCourt v. California Sports, Inc., et al., 600 F. 2d 1193 (1979).

McNeil v. National Football League, 764 F. Supp. 1356 (1991); 790 F. Supp. 871 (1992).

NBA, et al. v. Williams, et al., 45 F. 3d 684 (1995).

National Labor Relations Act, 29 USC 157.

Norris LaGuardia Act of 1932, 29 USC 1101–1115.

O'Bannon, et al. v. National Collegiate Athletic Association, Collegiate Licensing Company, et al., 2009 U.S. Dist. LEXIS 122205; 2010 U.S. Dist. LEXIS 19170.

Powell, et al. v. National Football League, et al., 678 F. Supp. 777 (1988); 690 F. Supp. 812 (1998); 930 F. 2d 1293 (1989); 764 F. Supp. 1351 (1991).

Radovich v. National Football League, 352 U.S. 445 (1957).

Roberts, G. (1991). Professional sports and the antitrust laws. In P. D. Staudohar & J. A. Mangan (Eds.), *The business of professional sport* (pp. 135–151). Chicago, IL: University of Illinois Press.

Sherman Act of 1890, 15 USC Section 1 & 2.

Silverman v. Major League Baseball, 880 F. Supp. 246 (1995); 67 F. 3d 1054 (1995).

Toolson v. New York Yankees, 346 U.S. 356 (1953).

Uhlir, A. (1982). The wolf is our shepherd: Shall we not fear? *Phi Delta Kappa, 64*(3), 172.

United States v. Shubert, 348 U.S. 222 (1955).

White, et al. v. National Football League, et al., 585 F. 3d 1129 (2009); 766 F. Supp. 2d 941 (2011).

White, et al. v. National Football League, et al., 822 F. Supp. 1389 (1993) (1); 836 F. Supp. 1458 (1993) (2); 836 F. Supp. 1508 (1993) (3); 41 F. 3d 402 (1994); 899 F. Supp. 410 (1995); 972 F. Supp. 1230 (1997); 88 F. Supp. 2d 993 (2000); 92 F. Supp. 2d 918 (2000); 149 F. Supp. 858 (2001).

RECOMMENDED READING

Block, B. M., & Ridings, M. D. (2011). Antitrust conspiracies in franchise systems after American Needle. 30 *Franchise L. J.* 216.

Carrabis, A. B. (2010). Strange bedfellows: How the NCAA and EA sports may have violated antitrust and right of publicity laws to make a profit at the exploitation of intercollegiate amateurism. 15 *Barry L. R.* 17.

Grow, N. (2011). Antitrust & the Bowl Championship Series. 2 *Harv. J. Sports & Ent. L.* 53.

10

Intellectual Property

OBJECTIVES

Upon completing this chapter, you will:

1) understand the differences between copyright, trademark, and patent law, and how each influences sport;

2) recognize the rights of the copyright owner, including fair use;

3) appreciate the value of registering and licensing creative works;

4) understand the system the court uses in analyzing the violation of a trademark for confusion, dilution, trade dress, cancellation, or abandonment;

5) be aware that trademark infringement may be civil or criminal; and

6) know the value of intellectual property to the economics of sport.

INTRODUCTION

Chapter 9 discussed the importance of competition in the marketplace and the protection provided entrepreneurs by the United States government. The free enterprise economy of the United States is based on competition. Intellectual property laws such as copyright, trademark, right of publicity, and patent law protect those engaging in marketplace competition and reward the creators of such materials for the fruits of their labor with ownership rights. These rights are treated by the law as personal property; they can be contracted to others through traditional agreements. Copyrights and trademarks can be licensed, sold, loaned, or given to others. Patents receive the same treatment with some restrictions. Intellectual property laws include federal, state, and common law—the results of court decisions. In recent years, criminal laws have been added to the civil law enforcement.

COPYRIGHT

Copyright is a system for protecting the "original works of authorship fixed in any tangible medium" (Copyright Act, 17 USC 102). Required elements of copyright are that the work is original and that it is fixed in a tangible medium, such as in print, motion pictures, or sculpture. Works of authorship include:

- literary works;

- musical works, including any accompanying words;

- dramatic works, including any accompanying music;

- pantomimes and choreographic works;

- pictorial, graphic, and sculptural works;

- motion pictures and other audiovisual works;

- sound recordings; and

- architectural works. (17 USC 102)

With the fixation requirement for copyright protection, it is important to recognize that copyright protection for an original work of authorship does not extend to an "idea, procedure, process, system, method of operation, concept, principle, or discovery, regardless of the form in which it is described, explained, illustrated, or embodied in such work" (17 USC 102). Copyright can be obtained for compilations and derivative works; however, the copyright covers only the materials attributed to the new author. The original materials continue to belong to the first author (17 USC 103).

While the Copyright Act of 1790 covered books and maps, technological changes necessitated an expansion of copyright protection to include electronics, films, computer programs, and choreography. In 1971, the law was extended to sound recordings. The Sonny Bono Copyright Term Extension Fairness in Music Licensing Act of 1998 extended copyright protection to the life of the author and 70 years beyond the life of the author. Works made for hire or commissioned by an employer are protected for 95 years following publication or for 120 years after their creation (17 USC 302). The Sensenbrenner Amendment to the law provides an exemption that permits music to be played, without royalty, in restaurants and malls.

The area of choreography is fully covered under the statute but not always recognized by the public. For example, when a broadcast of a "football game covered by four television cameras, with a director guiding the activities of the four cameramen and choosing which of their electronic images are sent out to the public and in what order, there is little doubt that what that cameramen and the director are doing constitutes authorship" (Copyright Law Revision, H.R. Rep. No. 94–1476, 1976). However, courts have recognized that the underlying sporting event itself is not copyrightable since there is no authorship of the spontaneous event (*NBA v. Motorola,* 1997). Golf courses and unique sport venues usually involve architectural plans and drawings. When these fix plans are unique or custom designed, copyright protection is warranted.

Prior to 1976, all copyrighted materials had to contain a copyright notice such as the following: ©2010 Susan Jones. The 1989 Berne Convention, an international agreement, required participating nations to give copyright protection without formalities. This makes notice optional in the United States. To encourage the registration of copyrights in the United States the statute notes that the "certificate of registration is prima facie evidence that the copyright is valid" (Copyright Act, 17 USC 410).

Rights of Copyright Owners

The owner of a copyright has the exclusive right to do and to authorize any of the following:

- to reproduce the copyrighted work in copies or phonorecords;

- to prepare derivative works based upon the copyrighted work;

- to distribute copies or phonorecords of the copyrighted work to the public for sale or other transfer of ownership, or by rental, lease, or lending;

- in the case of literary, musical, dramatic, and choreographic works, pantomimes, and motion pictures and other audiovisual works, to perform the copyrighted work publicly;

- in the case of literary, musical, dramatic, and choreographic works, pantomimes, and pictorial, graphic, or sculptural works, including the individual images of a motion picture or other audiovisual work, to display the copyrighted work publicly; and

- in the case of sound recordings, to perform the copyrighted work publicly by means of a digital audio transmission. (17 USC 106)

The owner of a computer program may make a copy as an essential step in the utilization of the machine or for archival purposes. The owner of the computer program may not make a copy for another person (17 USC 117). Ownership of copyright passes at death as personal property.

Rights of Copyright Consumers—Fair Use

The fair use doctrine enables the public, under specific circumstances, to make use of a copyrighted work without infringing on the rights of the owner. Fair use is often associated with educational settings, and it has been applied from classroom materials to performances since 2002. For example, written materials, plays, and choreography may be used, without permission, by an "instructor in the course of face-to-face teaching activities of a nonprofit educational institution, in a classroom or similar place devoted to instruction" (17 USC 110). Also, copyrighted work may be reproduced "for purposes such as criticism, comment, news reporting, teaching (including multiple copies for classroom use), scholarship, or research" (17 USC 107).

Infringement

In determining liability for infringement, courts look at:

1) the purpose and character of the use, including whether such use is of a commercial nature or is for nonprofit educational purposes;

2) the nature of the copyrighted work;

3) the amount and the substantiality of the portion used in relation to the copyrighted work as a whole; and

4) the effect of the use upon the potential market for or value of the copyrighted work. (17 USC 107)

Adapting a work into a different form is prohibited. Adapting a book into a play without permission, for example, is infringement. Remedies for infringement are injunctive relief (e.g., stopping the infringer's use of the copyrighted materials), monetary or compensatory damages, destruction of infringing articles, and criminal penalties. Monetary or compensatory damages are assessed to make the injured party whole. The copyright owner may elect to receive statutory damages rather than compensatory damages. Statutory damages, determined by the court, will not be less than $30,000.00 or more than $750,000.00 (17 USC 504).

Work for Hire

Section 101 of the Copyright Act defines a "work for hire" as:

1) a work prepared by an employee within the scope of his or her employment; or

2) a work specially ordered or commissioned for use as a contribution to a collective work ... if the parties expressly agree in a written document, signed by them, that the work will be considered a work for hire. (17 USC 101)

Work made under an independent contractor agreement is not considered work for hire unless it has been identified as a "work for hire" within the agreement.

Licensing

The owner of a copyright may license others to use or make copies of the copyrighted materials. These licenses are to be legal, written contracts. A license should state the protected rights of the owner and of the person receiving the license. Topics such as date of agreement, form in which the materials will appear, and other details are to be included. Failure to carry out the license as agreed constitutes breach of contract and infringement of copyright.

COPYRIGHT CASES

Definition

Copyright, by definition, is the right of an owner to a registered, original, and fixed document. *Curtis v. Benson et al.* (1997) and *Bouchat v. Baltimore Ravens Limited Partnership, et al.* (2008) are examples of court decisions addressing the definition of copyright. Curtis, the original architect for the Superdome, sued the owner of the building and recent building architects for reproducing and using his original drawings, without permission, for future work. Defendants claimed that when Curtis gave his registered architectural plans to Tulane University Architectural Archives, including the 1967 Superdome original drawing and the 1987 drawings for the renovation/modification of the Dome, all plans became part of the public domain. In 1997, the issues before the court were:

1) whether plaintiff's state law claims are preempted by the federal Copyright Act;

2) whether plaintiff's claim for statutory damages and attorney's fees pursuant to the Federal Copyright Act should be dismissed as a matter of law; and

3) whether Tulane University must be joined in these proceedings as a necessary or indispensable party. (*Curtis v. Benson, et al.,* 1997, 2)

The Court dismissed the plaintiff's state law claims and struck the request for statutory damages and attorney fees. This case identifies the need for an understanding of ownership of architectural drawings and other copyrighted materials in drafting building contracts.

The *Bouchat v. Baltimore Ravens, et al.* (2008) case has an interesting historical background. When the Cleveland Browns moved to Baltimore in 1995, they were forced to leave their logo and brand in Cleveland. Upon settling in Baltimore, the team began to explore a new team name and brands (i.e., team logos) that might accompany the new name. Bouchat, a security guard and amateur artist, took a real interest in the team and began to draw various logos for the names the team was exploring, including a wing shield for the name "Ravens." A few months later, when the team elected that name, Bouchat sent his shield drawing to the Maryland Stadium Authority, asking the authority to pass the drawing on to the Ravens' president. If the president decided to use the shield, Bouchat wanted a letter of recognition and a signed helmet. Bouchat received no response. "Through a series of misunderstandings, Bouchat's Shield Drawing was sent to the Stadium Authority Chairman's law office, forwarded to the Ravens' temporary headquarters, forwarded to the NFL in New York, and then to the commercial artists working on the Ravens project. There is no reason to believe that the Ravens or NFL intentionally caused the Shield Drawing to be provided to the artists. Nevertheless, the Shield Drawing was provided to the artists who used Bouchat's drawing as the basis for the 'Flying B Logo'" (*Bouchat v. Baltimore Ravens et al.,* 2008, 693).

The Ravens' new logo, the "Flying B," created by the National Football League Properties (NFLP), looked a great deal, if not exactly, like Bouchat's submission. The Ravens were unaware that the NFLP had taken the work from a third party. Bouchat sued the Ravens and the NFLP for infringing his copyright on the shield drawing and a number of other drawings. He asked for ten million dollars (*Bouchat v. Baltimore Ravens Football Club, Inc.,* 2003). The court bifurcated the case, trying the liability issue first and then the damages. A jury found for Bouchat because his shield drawing had been copied. The Copyright Act (17 USC 504) entitled him to actual damages and any profits that were not taken into account in computing the actual damages. The jury had difficulty in arriving at the appropriate damage award and ended by not making an award.

Bouchat appealed. He stated that he should at least get the statutory damage allocated in the law. Again, Bouchat was not clear about the actual losses he sustained from the infringement of his copyright, so the court denied monetary damages. Thus, the district court affirmed the trial court's decision. In 2007, Bouchat brought suit against all licenses of the NFLP. The United States Court of Appeals, Fourth Circuit, confirmed the district court's decision that statutory damages were not to be awarded because the artist had "failed to register his copyright before the infringement began" (*Bouchat v. Bon-Ton Department Stores, Inc. et al.,* 2007, 315).

Rights of Copyright Owners—Fair Use

The use of a registered copyright by another, without permission, was the issue in *Ticketmaster, LLC v. RMG Technologies, Inc. et al.* (2007) and The *Authors Guild, et al. v. GOOGLE, Inc.,* (2009). Ticketmaster filed for a preliminary injunction against RMG, alleging infringement for creating and selling an automated device that was able to access the Ticketmaster website to "snipe" tickets, a practice whereby scalpers use the software to inundate Ticketmaster's website with automated requests, enabling the scalpers to purchase large quantities of tickets before the general public. They cited copyright claims and infringement, claims under the Digital Millennium Copyright Act, breach of contract, computer fraud and abuse, and irreparable harm. The United States Court for the Central District of California, Western Division, granted Ticketmaster's request for an injunction and stopped RMG from using the automated device, gaining access to the Ticketmaster website, copying portions of the website in excess of the licenses granted by Ticketmaster, purchasing tickets from the website for commercial use, and otherwise accessing or using the website beyond its regular terms of use.

Fair use enables the public to use materials under copyright, particularly library holdings and music files, for research and education without a formal agreement. Google is an example of the work of an agency claiming fair use. In *The Authors Guild v. GOOGLE, Inc.* (2009), Google made arrangements with the libraries of Harvard, Oxford, Stanford, Michigan, and the New York Public Library to scan their volumes without author permission and put the holdings online, making them available to the public. The Authors Guild represented the publishers and individual authors of the publications. Google has been working with the parties involved, under court direction, to establish a system for providing royalty payments to known publishers, and establishing a Books Rights Registry to manage and distribute the royalty payments.

Licenses and Secondary Transmissions

Mob Music Publishing, et al. v. Zanzibar on the Waterfront, LLC, et al. (2010) was an action for copyright infringement against Zanzibar for giving "unauthorized public performances of six musical compositions" at their waterfront establishment (199). Mob Music Publishing represented a group of musicians who, as members of the American Society of Composers, Authors, and Publishers (ASCAP), have nonexclusive rights to license their copyrighted music. Zanzibar had a license to play ASCAP's music but lost the right when they failed to pay the agreed-upon fee. Zanzibar continued to play ASCP music and refuse to pay the fee. The establishment was checked a number of times by ASCAP personnel to determine what music were being played. ASCAP identified six musical compositions mentioned in the complaint. The plaintiff filed an action for statutory damages in the amount of $10,000 for each cause of action, an injunction to stop the playing of ASCAP music, and payment of reasonable fees.

The plaintiff had valid copyrights to each of the musical compositions at issue. The defendants also argued and lost First Amendment fair use defense claims. The court found the defendants liable for infringing behavior at $40,000 in statutory damages. The defendants were enjoined and restrained from performing any and all ASCAP music without proper authorization.

Two sport situations in which broadcast rights were questioned were *J&J Sports Productions, Inc. v. Live Oak Country Post No. 6119 Veterans of Foreign Wars, et al.* (2009) and *Innovative Sports Marketing, Inc. v. Medeles, et al.* (2008). In *J&J Sports*, the owner of an exclusive license for closed-circuit television fights filed a complaint against a lounge that intercepted the program without authorization. The court denied summary judgment "because there existed an issue of fact as to whether or not the lounge acted willfully" (1).

In *Innovative Sports Marketing*, the defendants also intercepted a soccer match on closed circuit TV. Here, however, the defendants failed to appear for a court hearing; thus, the plaintiff succeeded (*Innovative Sports Marketing, Inc. v. Medeles, et al.,* 2008).

TRADEMARKS

Trademarks are governed by the Trademark Act of 1946, more commonly known as the Lanham Act (2010), and the United States Code. Three distinct categories exist under the umbrella term trademark: trademark, service mark, and collective mark. They are distinguished by what they represent.

Trademark – "Any word, name, symbol, or design or any combination thereof, adopted and used by a manufacturer or merchant to identify his goods, and distinguish them from those manufactured or sold by others" (Lanham Act, 15 USC 1052)
Ex: Nike (trademark for sport clothing and equipment)

Service Mark – "A mark used in the sale of advertising of service to identify the services of one person and distinguish them from the services of others" (15 USC 1053)
Ex: International Management Group (IMG)

Collective Mark – Either a trademark or a service mark or both used by the "members of a cooperative, an association, or other collective group or organization and includes marks used to indicate membership in a union, an association, or other organization" (15 USC 1054)
Ex: The North American Society for Sport Management (NASSM)

A party wishing to obtain a trademark must file a formal application with the Patent and Trademark Office. The application is to include the dates of the first use of the mark and the first use of the mark in commerce, goods, or services. It should also include a drawing of the mark or an explanation of the service, an attestation that the mark is original, and areas in which the mark will be used (Lanham Act, 1051–1054). A certificate of registration is returned to the owner and is published in the Official

Gazette of the Patent and Trademark Office (15 USC 1051). The certificate is valid and prima facie evidence of the mark's existence (15 USC 1057). Registration is for ten years (15 USC 1058), and re-registration should occur prior to the end of the ten-year period. A registered mark may be assigned to another; however, the assignment must be in writing (15 USC 1060), be recorded with the U.S. Patent and Trademark Office, and be published in the Official Gazette, the United States Patent and Trademark Office's official journal (15 USC 1060).

A registration may be refused by the Patent and Trademark Office for the following reasons:

   a)   consists of or comprises immoral, deceptive, or scandalous matter, or matter which may disparage or falsely suggests a connection with persons, living or dead, institutions, beliefs, or national symbols, or brings them into contempt, or disrepute; …

   b)   consists of or comprises the flag or coat of arms or other insignia of the United States, or of any State or municipality, or of any foreign nation, or any simulation thereof;

   c)   consists of or comprises a name, portrait, or signature identifying a particular living individual, except by written consent; or

   d)   consists of or comprises a mark which so resembles a mark registered in the Patent and Trademark Office. (15 USC 1052)

Trademark owners are cautioned to monitor the Official Gazette for new applications for marks that could damage or infringe the owners' registered marks. If such a registration appears in the Gazette, the owner should file an opposition to the registration of the proposed mark in the Patent and Trademark Office. A hearing will be held by the Trademark Trials and Appeals Board and a decision will be made by the board. The decision can be appealed to a federal court. If the mark is successfully opposed the applicant is denied registration. A registered mark may be challenged in court because it was obtained fraudulently, was abandoned (i.e., not used for a significant period of time), misrepresented goods or services, or violated antitrust law (15 USC 1115). Courts will analyze the mark for the elements of confusion, dilution, trade dress, cancellation, or abandonment.

Confusion

Confusion is usually the result of either false designation of origin or false description of a product or program. The law states that

   1)   any person who, on or in connection with any goods or services, or any container for goods, uses in commerce any word, term, name, symbol, or device, or any combination thereof or false designation of origin, false or misleading description of fact, or false or misleading representation of fact which

a)   is likely to cause confusion, or to cause mistake, or to deceive as to the affiliation, connection, or association of such person with another person, or as to origin, sponsorship, or approval of his or her goods, services, or commercial activities by another person, or

b)   in commercial advertising or promotion, misrepresents the nature, characteristics, qualities, or geographic origin of his or her or another person's goods, services, or commercial activities shall be liable in a civil action by any person who believes that he or she is likely to be damaged by such act. (15 USC 1125)

Dilution

Dilution is a claim brought by owners of famous marks who believe that another party's use of a similar mark will diminish or weaken the association that consumers have between their marks and their products or services. The claim is based on the likelihood that the public will become confused over common elements of two different marks. The major factor in the court's decision is whether the public will be harmed as a result of the confusion. Owners of marks used by others in parody have requested injunctions or sued for infringement; often, these sales involve altered forms of trademarks on T-shirts, caps, towels, and similar merchandise. Defenses to a dilution complaint are that the mark is confusingly similar but not the same, or that the element of distinctiveness cannot be satisfied.

To state a claim for dilution, the party must show:

1)   that the plaintiff owns a famous mark that is distinctive;

2)   that the defendant has commenced using a mark in commerce that allegedly is diluting the famous mark;

3)   that a similarity between the defendant's mark and the famous mark gives rise to an association between the marks; and

4)   that the association is likely to impair the distinctiveness of the famous mark or likely to harm the reputation of the famous mark in the context of blurring, distinctiveness refers to the ability of the famous mark uniquely to identify a single source and thus maintain the selling power. (15 USC 1125)

Congress passed the Federal Trademark Dilution Act (FTDA) of 1995, creating a federal cause of action for dilution. In 2006, dilution was further defined by the concepts of blurring and tarnishment (15 USC 1125). "Blurring takes place when a single term activates multiple, non-confusing associations in a consumer's mind ... [and] involves relatively extended activation of two different meanings for a mark" (Tushnet, 2008, p. 519). Tarnishment differs from blurring in that the person immediately recognizes the difference between the two objects or associations.

Trade Dress

Trade dress is the overall appearance of a product, including the color, shape, size, logo, and other characteristics. The décor of vendors, ball parks, fitness chains, restaurants, stores, and other places of business may be trade dress. For example, the consistent exterior and interior of building designs may be protected under trade dress. While trademark law has not always been specific on trade dress, the case *Abercrombie & Fitch Company v. Hunting World Incorporated* (1976) identified the components of trade dress as generic, descriptive, suggestive, arbitrary, or fanciful (8). Generic marks are common descriptive names of objects. The mark is or becomes generic when it is the common name of the object. For example, the word "Kleenex" is routinely used in the English language to refer to a tissue. However, the manufacturers of Kleenex prevent the mark from becoming generic by running advertisements to reinforce in consumers' minds that they are the leading brand of this type of consumer product. Thus, this is a distinctive mark and is considered a strong mark. Other types of distinctive marks include suggestive, arbitrary, and fanciful marks. A suggestive mark "requires imagination, thought, and perception to reach a conclusion as to the nature of the goods" (*Abercrombie & Fitch Company v. Hunting World Incorporated*, 1976, 8). For example, Greyhound bus lines suggest speed. A fanciful mark is not a real word in the English language, but is invented to be used as a mark, such as Kodak or Clorox. An arbitrary mark applies a common word in an unfamiliar way. Puma is an arbitrary mark used to identify one source of athletic gear.

Descriptive marks, on the other hand, are considered weak marks because they lack secondary meaning. Since the mark is descriptive, it does not cause mental recognition in the buyer's mind about the source of the product. A mark is descriptive if it describes the product's features, qualities, or ingredients in ordinary language or describes the use to which the product is put. For example, onion rings describe the product, rather than identify the source of the product, whereas Ball Park Franks identify a unique source and brand of hot dogs rather than the general product category.

Cancellation

A registered mark can be canceled:

- by petition by the owner of a similar mark within five years of the registration of the mark;
- if the registered mark becomes a generic name for goods or services;
- if the mark has been abandoned; or
- if the mark was obtained fraudulently.

"The primary significance of the registered mark to the relevant public rather than purchaser motivation shall be the test for determining whether the registered mark has become the generic name of the goods and services on or in connection with which it has been used" (Lanham Act, 15 USC 1064). When a party has sustained a five-year period during which the mark has not been challenged, he/she may file to make the mark incontestable (15 USC 1065).

Relief can be injunctive (i.e., stopping the action), or compensatory. Compensatory relief may include recovery of defendant's profits, damage sustained by plaintiff, cost of court and appeal processes, and destruction of infringing articles. All court decisions become part of the Patent and Trademark Office records.

Abandonment
A mark is abandoned if its use has been discontinued with intent not to resume its use in regular trade. Nonuse for three years is prima facie evidence of abandonment (15 USC 1127).

Infringement
To recover for infringement of a registered mark under Section 32(1) of the Lanham Act,

> a plaintiff must establish first, that its mark is valid and second, that the defendant's use of the mark is likely to cause confusion. A defendant is then liable for infringement if he uses (1) any reproduction, counterfeit, copy, or colorable imitation of the mark; (2) without the registrant's consent; (3) in commerce; (4) in connection with the sale, offering for sale, distribution, or advertising of any goods; (5) where such use is likely to cause confusion or to cause mistake or to deceive (15 USC 1114 [1, a]) ... Section 43(a) of the Lanham Act provides a civil cause of action for infringement of unregistered marks. In order for an unregistered mark to be protectable under section 43(a), the mark must be capable of distinguishing the plaintiff's services from those of others. (15 USC 1125[a])

Validity and likelihood of confusion are the two criteria examined closely for service mark infringement.

Criminal Acts in Trademark
Trademark counterfeiting or pirating of memorabilia, apparel, and equipment are serious crimes affecting the sport industry. In an effort to curb these multimillion-dollar losses in sales tax revenue, the Federal Bureau of Investigation (FBI), the Internal Revenue Service (IRS), and the Department of Homeland Security have joined forces to curb, or at least control, the situation. The U.S. Border Patrol is also working with these organizations. "The Coalition to Advance the Protection of Sports Logos (CAPS), an alliance formed by the Collegiate Licensing Company (CLC), Major League Baseball Properties, NBA Properties, NFL Properties, and NHL Enterprises, works in conjunction with local law enforcement agencies to seize counterfeit property" (Grady, Clement, & Woishnis, 2009).

The Lanham Act allows manufacturers, sellers, and producers of goods and services to prevent a competitor from:

1) using any counterfeit, copy, or imitation of their trademarks (that has been registered with the U.S. Patent and Trademark Office), in connection with the sale of any goods or services in a way that is likely to cause confusion, mistake, or deception, (15 USC 1114) or

2) using in commercial advertising any word, term, name, symbol, or device, or any false or misleading designation of origin, or false or misleading description or representation of fact, which: (a) is likely to cause confusion, mistake, or deception as to affiliation, connection, or association, or as to origin, sponsorship, or approval, of his or her goods, services, or commercial activities by another person or (b) misrepresents the nature, characteristics, qualities, or geographic origin of his or her or another person's goals, services, or commercial activities. (15 USC 1125)

Potential penalties include an injunction to stop the use of the mark, destruction of articles containing the mark, and money damages. Treble damages are fines of three times the cost of the damage. Statutory damage under the Lanham Act are also available as an alternative to seeking defendant's profits or plaintiff's actual losses resulting from infringement in the amount of not less than $1,000 or more than $200,000 per counterfeit mark per type of goods or services sold (15 USC 1116–1118, 2010).

The Trademark Counterfeiting Act of 1984 provides that "whoever intentionally traffics or attempts to traffic in goods or services and knowingly uses a counterfeit mark on or in connection with such goods or services shall, if an individual, be fined or imprisoned" (18 USC 2320 [a], 2010). A violation of the federal counterfeiting statute requires that the following elements be established:

1) the defendant trafficked or attempted to traffic in goods and services;

2) that such trafficking, or the attempt to traffic was intentional;

3) that the defendant used a "counterfeit mark" on or in connection with such goods or services; and

4) that the defendant "knew" that the counterfeit mark was so used. (18 USC 2320 [a], 2010)

TRADEMARK CASES

The following trademark cases will be addressed under the categories of confusion, dilution, trade dress, cancellation, and abandonment.

Confusion

The word "Olympic" and the interlocking rings associated with the Olympics have been the subject of litigation since 1982. In the *United States Olympic Committee, et al. v. Intelicense Corp. S.A.* (1984), exclusive ownership of the word "Olympic" was given to the United States Olympic Committee (USOC). The decision, along with the Amateur Sports Act of 1978, a federal statute, gives exclusive ownership of the word and rings to the USOC.

An example of litigation was the *United State Olympic Committee, et al. v. Xclusive Leisure & Hospitality, Ltd., et al.* (2009). The United States Olympic Committee (USOC), the International Olympic Committee (IOC), and the 2008 Beijing Olympic Games Organizing Committee sued beijingticketing.com for name confusion in their use of USOC and IOC marks protected under the Lanham Act (Lanham Act, 15 USC 1114) and the Amateur Sports Act (2010). The defendants had created a website using USOC and IOC logos to sell illegal tickets for the 2008 games. Unbeknownst to the illegal website owners was the fact that (a) many of the Beijing Official Olympic tickets, including the opening and closing ceremonies, contained microchips that identified the owner and that (b) ownership could only be transferred once through a complex process. Those who purchased tickets from the illegal site never received tickets. The lawsuit was the Beijing Organizing Committee's preferred method of stopping the illegal website from conducting further operations which may have been directing traffic away from the official ticket website. The United States Court for the Northern District of California found a likelihood of confusion and granted an injunction to close the website. The plaintiffs were also permitted to protect their marks and to seek damages, as well as to pursue possible criminal action.

The term "March Madness" has been the subject of ongoing litigation for nearly ten years. In a series of decisions beginning in 2001, the March Madness Athletic Association (MMAA), the National Collegiate Athletic Association (NCAA), and the Illinois High School Athletic Association (IHAA) sued Netfire, d/b/a Sport Marketing International (SMI), and Matthew Jones. In 2000, the Illinois High School Athletic Association sued Netfire for trademark infringement, dilution, and unfair competition. Later, the March Madness Athletic Association replaced the high school group in that suit and "amended its complaint to add a claim for cybersquatting, or using a domain name in order to profit dishonestly from the reputation of someone else's trademark" (*March Madness Athletic Ass'n, LLC. v. Netfire, Inc.,* 2005, 542). Netfire responded with claims for fraud, tortuous interference with contract and business relations, and conversion and civil conspiracy against IHSA and NCAA. The district court granted IHSA and NCAA summary judgment on SMI's counterclaims and sent the remaining claims to trial. In 2003, the U.S. Court of Appeals for the Fifth Circuit found for MMAA on infringement and cybersquatting and against MMAA on civil conspiracy (543). The court also found that the phrase "March Madness" was a protectable trademark, not a generic term. In addition, the court found that there was a likelihood of confusion between the protected trademark and the website. Factors examined in determining the likelihood of confusion were:

1) The type of mark allegedly infringed

2) The similarity between the two marks

3) The similarity of the products or services

4) The identity of the retail outlets and purchasers

5) The identity of the advertising media used

6) The defendant's intent

7) Any evidence of actual confusion. (*March Madness Athletic Ass'n, LLC,. v. Netfire, Inc.,* 2005, 49)

Ownership of the domain name was transferred from SMI to MMAA. In 2005, the parties appealed the 2003 decisions again to the Fifth Circuit believing that they had new information regarding false information. The court confirmed their earlier decision.

In 2008, Intersport, a corporation, was permitted by the Circuit Court of Cook County, Illinois, to retain the license to the trademark "March Madness" to advertise, promote, and sell videos of sports programming. The corporation had been distributing content to wireless communication devices and had used the mark "March Madness" since 1986. NCAA and March Madness Athletic Association appealed the decision to the Illinois Court, First District, Third Division. The court affirmed the lower court's decision, noting that the selling of videos was within the broad range of the license agreement (*Intersport, Inc. v. National Collegiate Athletic Association and March Madness Athletic Association, LLC,* 2008).

Even though ESPN did not have a registered mark, it sued Quicksilver, a manufacturer of clothing products for surfers, for the stylized X which each party claimed was its well-recognized trademark (*ESPN, Inc. v. Quicksilver, Inc.,* 2008). Quicksilver had begun using the "X" symbol on its products in 1986 and had a valid and protectable trademark that had been used in commerce. ESPN created the X Games, a sport competition featuring sports like skateboarding, snowboarding, and surfing. ESPN had a pending application for the X mark and sought to cancel Quicksilver's valid mark. The Court found for Quicksilver; ESPN's motion to dismiss Quicksilver's mark was denied. The case confirms that a registered mark usually takes precedence over an application for a mark.

On August 20, 2010, The Ohio State University (OSU) filed a motion for a temporary restraining order and preliminary injunction against Keith Antonio Thomas and GDS Marketing, LLC for trademark infringement. GDS had infringed eight of OSU's trademarks registered between 1981 and 1997 and a series of common-law trademarks, including the colors scarlet and gray, the website, and the block O (*The Ohio State University v. Keith Antonio Thomas, et al.,* 2010). OSU's licensing program was over 30 years old and had generated royalties of $35 million over the past five years. The defendants published two electronic magazines, "Buckeye Gameday" and "Ohio State Buckeye E-Book," freely using any and all of OSU's registered and common-law trademarks. The court found that OSU owned the marks, that the marks had been used in commerce, and that a likelihood of confusion existed. OSU was granted a temporary restraining order and a preliminary injunction; the defendants were required to stop their infringement.

A thirteen-year trademark battle existed between the University of South Carolina and the University of Southern California over the interlocking "SC" logo used by athletic teams at both schools. The University of Southern California owned the registered mark. The University of South Carolina petitioned the U.S. Trademark Trial and Appeals Board to cancel Southern California's registration of the mark, arguing that "SC" represented their state, South Carolina, and had been used prior to Southern California's use. The Board refused to register South Carolina's logo and also refused to cancel Southern California's trademark. The certiorari petition to the United States Supreme Court was denied (*University of South Carolina v. University of Southern California*, 2010).

Dilution

A recent decision that involved both confusion and dilution was *Dallas Cowboys Football Club, LTD., et al. v. America's Team Properties, Inc.* (2009). America's Team Properties (ATP), incorporated in Minnesota in 1998, took the assignment of the U.S. trademark, "America's Team" to be used in selling T-shirts and other apparel. The previous owner had obtained the mark in 1990; ATP purchased the mark for $100.00. In 1999, the owner of ATP ran an advertisement in *USA Today* in an effort to auction the mark to the highest bidder with a minimum bid of $500,000. ATP called the Dallas Cowboys to notify the team that the registration was for sale.

The Dallas Cowboys responded by filing suit alleging common-law rights against ATP for trademark infringement. They stated that the mark "America's Team" was protected and that they possessed priority over America's Team Properties. ATP filed a counterclaim against the Dallas Cowboys seeking a declaratory judgment that the registration was valid and sought cancellation of the mark on the basis that it had not been used. Two questions were raised at trial; would the common marks be confused by consumers (the likelihood of confusion) and, if both were retained, could the value of the mark be weakened (dilution)? The court concluded that a likelihood of confusion would exist as the marks were exactly the same; however, nearly all of the remaining factors favored the plaintiffs.

Trademark dilution was identified, by the court, "as the weakening of the ability of a mark to clearly and unmistakably distinguish the source of a product" (*Dallas Cowboys Football Club, Ltd. v. America's Team Properties, Inc.*, 2009, 642). In blurring, the court considered similarity, distinctiveness, and exclusive use of the mark. Tarnishment occurs when the mark represents poor-quality products or some other event such as an inferior website. When one of two marks is weak, and confusion exists, people will think of both products as weak. The Dallas Cowboys sensed both blurring and tarnishment as a result of the same mark and requested that the court cancel the ATP mark. The Court cancelled America's Team Properties' mark. An immediate injunction was ordered as was the removal of all products from the defendant's website.

In another case, 24 Hour Fitness, USA, Inc. sued 24/7 Tribeca Fitness, LLC, alleging trademark dilution under false designation of origin and unfair competition. Distinctiveness was measured by the following five categories: 1) generic; 2) descriptive; 3) suggestive; 4) arbitrary; or 5) fanciful, as discussed above in the *Abercrombie & Fitch*

Company v. Hunting World Incorporated (1976) case. As the names were found not to be similar, the court dismissed 24 Hour Fitness's claims of infringement against the name and mark. Judgment was entered in favor of 24/7; the likelihood of confusion was insufficient (*24 Hour Fitness USA, Inc., v. 24/7 Tribeca Fitness LLC, et al.,* 2000).

In 2000, the Heisman Trophy Trust entered into a settlement following Smack Apparel's sale of a shopping bag with a picture of a potential Heisman winner suspected of shoplifting superimposed on a picture of the Heisman Trophy. In the agreement, Smack Apparel stated that they would "cease and permanently reframe from manufacturing, displaying, selling, or offering for sale any clothing or merchandise bearing the Heisman marks" (*The Heisman Trophy Trust v. Smack Apparel Company,* 2009, 324). In 2008, Smack Apparel again produced thirteen Heisman Trophy-related T-shirts without permission, thus prompting a suit. The lawsuit alleged breach of contract regarding the breach of the 2000 settlement, trademark infringement, and dilution. The request was for a preliminary injunction. The court found a likelihood of confusion and granted the injunction.

In the case of *University of Kansas and Kansas Athletics, Inc. v. Larry Sinks, et al.* (2008), the University of Kansas and Kansas Athletics owned the registered marks "Kansas," "KU Jay Hawks," "Allen Field," "The Play," and several Jay Hawk designs for the university's name, nickname, and design. KU did not own a trademark for the crimson and blue colors. However, these colors had been used for over 100 years. KU licensed its trademarks to businesses and to apparel companies. The licensing was managed by Collegiate Licensing Company (CLC), a popular sport licensing firm that serves several high-profile collegiate athletic departments. Larry Sinks, owner of Midwest Graphics, a licensee of KU, sold Midwest Graphics and purchased Victory Sportswear. Victory Sportswear opened Joe-College under Sinks's management. Sinks approached KU for a license and was denied. The Joe-College store was only a few blocks from the University in Lawrence, Kansas. Joe-College sold inexpensive T-shirts and shorts that contained KU registered and non-registered marks and used KU colors with references to sex and alcohol. Signs were posted throughout the store (essentially acting as a disclaimer) alerting customers to the fact that these products were not licensed. Although Joe-College was not licensed by the university, the company submitted a federal trademark registration for Kivisto Field upon hearing of the name of the new university field.

In May of 2006, the director of athletics for the University of Kansas requested that Joe-College cease production of all KU apparel. He then sued Sinks, et al., d/b/a Joe-College for federal and state trademark infringement (*University of Kansas, et al. v. Larry Sinks, et al.,* 2008). One of the Kansas claims was similarity of marks; similarity was tested on sight, sound, and meaning. Would the marks be confusing to the public? Did the defendant intend to benefit from the reputation of the university? The court found many of the shirts to be similar and evidence provided actual confusion. The claims were confusion, unfair competition, and dilution. Under unfair competition KU established that most of their marks were registered and that those not registered had been used for an extended period of time.

In considering the trademark dilution claims, evidence was provided that KU's marks were widely recognized, and that the defendants had used their marks commercially without authorization. Also, the court found that the defendants' use of KU's marks, particularly those involving violent and abusive messages, had created a negative image for the institution. The court found that the marks "KU," "Kansas," and "Jay Hawks" were incontestable as the university had continuously used each mark for five or more consecutive years after the date of registration (Lanham Act, 15 USC 1065). The court granted summary judgment in part to KU Athletics and the University of Kansas. In 2009, after more litigation, attorney fees and expenses in the amount of $667,507.42 were eventually granted to the plaintiff.

Trade Dress

Golf courses may place service marks on their names and on distinguishing aspects of the course or on a particular hole on the course. *Pebble Beach Co. v. Tour 18 I, Ltd.* (1996) was an action for service mark and trade dress infringement, unfair competition, and false advertising. Confusion and dilution played an important role in the case. The action was brought by the owners of a number of famous golf courses against the developer of an 18-hole course in Humble, Texas. The Texas golf course consisted of replica holes from these famous courses. The developer for Tour 18 freely used the marks of Pebble Beach, Pinehurst, and Harbour Town. In response to the suit, Tour 18 asserted counterclaims under Texas law for unfair competition and interfering with an existing business. The developer claimed that the suit was a frivolous attempt to put Tour 18 out of business.

Pebble Beach and Pinehurst provided evidence of federal service mark registration for their marks; Sea Pines did not own a federal service mark for Harbour Town or the lighthouse at Harbour Town. Its exerted claim for protection was the common-law service mark under Section 43(a) of the Lanham Act. Tour 18 unsuccessfully argued a number of issues, among them the fact that Sea Pines no longer owned the lighthouse and had therefore abandoned the mark. Sea Pines continued to hold the mark after the sale of the lighthouse and had license agreements with the new owners to enable the new owners to use the mark in agreed-upon ways.

Under the likelihood of confusion analysis, the court stated that "while golfers at Tour 18 may not be confused as to the course since they will know they are playing a replica constructed by Tour 18 and not the real Pebble Beach Hole 14, they may still be confused into believing Pebble Beach sponsored or approved Tour 18's use of their service marks and golf hole designs" (*Pebble Beach Co. v. Tour 18 I, Ltd,* 1998, 1542). The court found that the plaintiffs had shown the validity of their respective marks, "Pebble Beach," "Pinehurst," "Harbour Town" and the lighthouse in Harbour Town; that the defendants, without the plaintiffs' consent, copied a colorable imitation of plaintiffs' registered marks; and that Tour 18's use of plaintiffs' marks was likely to cause confusion as to affiliation, sponsorship, and/or permission. Accordingly, the court found for the plaintiffs.

Trade dress was "the shapes of plaintiffs' golf holes, the length and width of the holes, the placement and shape of sand and water hazards, the size and shape of the greens, the slope and elevation of the holes, and the golf holes' surrounding vegetation" (1555). Also, the evidence indicated "that there is an unlimited number of alternative designs to plaintiffs' golf hole configurations. Additionally, while plaintiffs' design is particularly beautiful and challenging, there is no evidence to indicate that the designs are superior to the many available alternatives. Consequently, there is no need for Tour 18 to copy plaintiffs' golf hole designs to achieve the functions of a golf hole" (1556).

The issue under dilution was whether the uses of the mark would cause injury to the business reputation or dilute the distinctiveness of the owner's mark. The court found that only the 18th hole at Harbour Town and the lighthouse had the "strong, distinctive, source-identifying characteristics required for protection under the antidilution statute" (1567). Thus, the court found for Sea Pines in dilution.

The court "found Tour 18 liable for the following: service mark infringement, trade dress infringement, and unfair competition in violation of the Lanham Act" (1571). The plaintiffs were given permanent injunctive relief, preventing Tour 18's use of a replica of the Harbour Town Lighthouse, Harbour Town Golf Link Hole 18, Harbour Town Golf Links, Pebble Beach Golf Links, Pinehurst, or Pinehurst No. 2. Corrective action was also necessary to eliminate confusion between Harbour Town Hole 18 and the lighthouse and Tour 18's rendition. The defendants were required to place a bold disclaimer of any affiliation with the original golf holes in all of their advertisements. The court of appeals affirmed the lower court's decision in finding a likelihood of confusion from Tour 18's use of Pebble Beach and other marks (*Pebble Beach Co. v. Tour 18 I, Ltd.,* 1998).

In 2005, golf litigation turned to a golf video game (*Incredible Technologies, Inc. v. Virtual Technologies, Inc. d/b/a Global VR,* 2005). The golf game, *Golden Tee,* was a game played by many in bars. Incredible Technologies, Inc. was not happy when *PGA Tour Golf,* created by Virtual Technologies, became a competing game. Incredible Technologies sued Virtual Technologies for an injunction under trade dress. The request was denied and the decision was appealed. The court stated that "IT's expressions on its control panel are not dictated by creativity, but rather are simple explanations of the trackball system; at best, they are entitled to protection only from virtually identical copying; the video displays contain many common aspects of the game of golf and IT's trade dress is functional" (1010–1011). The court of appeals affirmed the earlier court's decision and found for Virtual Technologies.

Color schemes, such as a university's team colors, are entitled to protection as trade dress as a result of the decision in *Board of Supervisors of Louisiana State University, et al. v. Smack Apparel Co., et al.* (2006). In 2006, Smack Apparel, a manufacturer of humorous and occasionally irreverent T-shirts, was found by the U.S. Court of the Eastern District of Louisiana to have intentionally infringed on the marks owned by the Collegiate Licensing Company and those of The Ohio State University, Louisiana State University, University of Oklahoma, and University of Southern California. In 2008, the Fifth Circuit affirmed the Eastern District's decision, concluding that "the record established secondary meaning in the marks. Next, it found that plaintiffs possessed strong marks in their use of color schemes and other identifying indicia on college sports-themed merchandise" (*Board of Supervisors of Louisiana State University, et al. v. Smack Apparel, et al.,* 2009, 465). The Eastern District of Louisiana Court awarded the plaintiffs $38,912.37 for attorney fees and $7,312.73 for costs.

Cancellation

A mark can be canceled if it becomes common or generic, is offensive, or is successfully challenged by another party. It is considered to be abandoned if not used for a long period of time. In 1992, Susan Harjo petitioned the Trademark Trial and Appeals Board (TTAB) to cancel six Washington Redskin trademarks containing the word "redskin(s)" on the grounds that the word was offensive, scandalous, and disparaging to Native Americans. In 1999, the TTAB ruled in favor of Harjo and the Native Americans. Pro-Football brought suit to review the board's decision (*Pro-Football, Inc. v. Harjo, et al.,* 2000). Pro-Football argued that "the trademarks do not disparage Native Americans ... [and] do not bring Native Americans into contempt or disrepute ... [and] that the Native Americans' cancellation petition was barred by the doctrine of laches" (5–6). The claim, under laches, was the only issue discussed in the court proceedings. Laches bars relief to those who wait to file a claim. In this case, the view was that the agency holding the mark for twenty-five years had continuously invested time and money into the brand, and that if one wishes to contest a mark, it should be done in a timely manner.

To counter Pro-Football's laches defense and to obtain a judgment on the pleadings, Harjo asserted that "because a laches argument requires a showing of economic prejudice, they are entitled to broad discovery of Pro-Football's financial records" (*Pro-Football, Inc. v. Harjo, et al.,* 2002, 80). Pro-Football claimed the records were confidential. The court ruled on the documents and depositions that were obtained and agreed to continue litigation.

In 2003, after a lengthy trial, the United States Court for the District of Columbia reversed the TTAB's finding that disparagement was not supported by substantial evidence. The court found for the Washington Redskins. In 2005, the Native Americans appealed the District Court's decision to grant Pro-Football summary judgment. The United States Court of Appeals, District of Columbia Circuit found that the District Court applied the wrong standard in evaluating laches and returned the case to the District Court. In 2008, the parties returned to the court. Summary judgment was granted to Pro-Football, Inc. and was denied to Harjo. The court concluded that the owners established the opposing party's lack of diligence, with no excuses, in delaying contestation of the mark. The owners of the Washington Redskins were able to establish economic prejudice showing heavy investments in marketing and developing the brand. Cancellation of the marks was stopped.

RIGHT OF PUBLICITY

The term "right of publicity" was coined in *Haelan Laboratories, Inc. v. Topps Chewing Gum, Inc.* (1953). The right evolved principally for entertainers, celebrities, and public figures who were facing either misappropriation of name, First Amendment invasion of privacy violations, or both. Misappropriation is "the unauthorized, improper, or unlawful use of ... property for a purpose other than that for which it is intended" (*Black's Law Dictionary*, 2009). McCarthy defines the right of publicity as the "right of everyone to control the commercial use of his or her identity" (McCarthy, 2000, p. 3:1).

In 1960, Prosser organized the right of privacy into four distinct torts: "(1) unreasonable intrusion upon another's seclusion; (2) public disclosure of private facts; (3) false light invasion of privacy; and (4) appropriation of another's name or likeness" (ABA Section of Intellectual Property Law, 2004).

RIGHT OF PUBLICITY CASES

The use of athletes' identity in fantasy sports games became an issue in professional sports in *CBC Distribution and Marketing, Inc. v. Major League Baseball Advanced Media L.P., et al.* (2005) and *CBS Interactive, Inc. v. National Football League Players Association, Inc., et al.* (2009) and later in collegiate sports in *Keller, et al. v. Electronic Arts, Inc., NCAA, and Collegiate Licensing Company* (2010). The media arm of Major League Baseball and the NFL Players Association (NFLPA) alleged that CBC Distribution and Marketing, a fantasy game company, had violated their license agreement by operating a fantasy game using players' identities without permission or a license. CBC provided not only the games, but also up-to-date information on players, most of which was available in newspapers. CBC entered into a license agreement with the NFLPA in 1995. The 2002 License Agreement, among other items, stated "that upon termination CBC would have no right ... to use in any way the Rights, the Trademarks, or any Promotional Material relating to the Licensed Products and that upon expiration or termination of the License Agreement, CBC shall refrain from further use of the Rights and/or the Trademarks or any further reference to them, either directly or indirectly" (*CBC Distribution and Marketing, Inc.*, 2005, 8).

"Between 2001 and January 2004 Advanced Media offered the fantasy baseball game on MLB.com without obtaining a license and without obtaining permission from the Players Association" (*CBC Distribution and Marketing, Inc.*, 2006, 1081). When CBC anticipated a lawsuit, they filed a complaint against Advanced Media for declaratory judgment, stating that CBC had exclusive ownership of player statistics associated with players' names, and for injunctive relief that Advanced Media be enjoined from interfering with CBC businesses. Advanced Media and the NFLPA countered with contract violations based on the 2002 License Agreement and that CBC violated players' rights of publicity based on CBC's exploiting the identity of players, including their names, nicknames, likenesses, signatures, jersey numbers, pictures, player records, and biographical data. The contract issues were resolved.

The 8th Circuit found a violation of the right of publicity in that the players' identities had been used for commercial profit. However, they concluded that the right of publicity was secondary to CBC's First Amendment right to use the players' names and statistics. Names and statistics are facts and thus cannot be copyrighted, but under the First Amendment, names and statistics are available to the public and are therefore part of the public domain. Thus, CBC succeeded because the First Amendment was viewed as more important than the players' right of publicity. A petition for a Writ of Certiorari (an order to review the case) was denied (*Major League Baseball Advanced Media, L.P., et al. v. CBC Distribution and Marketing, Inc.*, 2008).

Another case examining the same issue was *CBS Interactive, Inc. v. National Football League Players' Association* (2009). CBS Interactive was a leading provider of fantasy football. Prior to the 2008/2009 season, the NFL had a license agreement with CBS Interactive to use the names, likenesses, pictures, photographs, voices, etc. of the individual players who had entered into the Group Licensing Agreement. In 2008, the NFL's licensing division, Players Inc., asked CBS Interactive to pay a licensing fee to the players. CBS refused, citing the decision in *CBC Distribution and Marketing*, discussed above. Players, Inc. "informed CBS Interactive that the Eighth Circuit's decision in the fantasy game litigation was wrongly decided and that if CBS Interactive failed to pay the licensing fees, Players, Inc. would file a law suit" (9). CBS Interactive's motion for partial summary judgment was granted, essentially permitting use of the players' names and stats without a license.

In *Keller, et al. v. Electronic Arts, Inc., NCAA, and Collegiate Licensing Company* (2010), the same issue was litigated at the collegiate level. Sam Keller, a former star quarterback for Arizona State, filed a class action suit on behalf of collegiate football and basketball players. The claims were on the alleged use of players' identities, without permission, in NCAA football, basketball, and March Madness video games. Even though players' names were not used, sufficient information was provided for the average sports fan to easily identify the players. The plaintiff's first claim was that the NCAA violated the Indiana Right of Publicity Law, a right to his likeness or image. The court did not support his position and the claim was dismissed.

The claim against Electronic Arts was analyzed using several different balancing tests, which are, in effect, defenses, to reconcile the competing interests of the athletes' rights of publicity and the First Amendment rights of Electronic Arts. The court first used the "transformative use" balancing test. Transformative use examines whether the likeness was original or the likeness had been transformed so that it no longer represented the celebrity. Electronic Arts (EA) stated that the video game had used transformative elements in depicting the athletes. In denying EA's transformative use defense, the court noted, "These cases show that this Court's focus must be on the depiction of plaintiff in 'NCAA Football' not the game's other elements" (*Keller, et al. v. Electronic Arts, Inc., et al.*, 2010, 18). Under public interest, California law states that "no cause of action will lie for the publication of matters in the public interest, which rests on the right of the public to know and the freedom of the press to tell it." The defense argued that the names and statistics were public interest and were not part of the right of publicity. The court found that EA had used more than the mere names and the statistics; it had used athletes' physical characteristics and had moved far beyond what the court had considered in the *Major League Baseball Advanced Media, L.P., et al.* case. EA lost using the public interest test. Next, the court considered if the public affairs exemption was applicable. The public affairs exemption is provided in California civil law to avoid First Amendment concerns in the use of a person's name when the issue is a matter of public interest. The court found that, "although NCAA Football is based on subject matter considered public affairs, EA is not entitled to the statutory defense because its use of Plaintiff's image and likeness extends beyond reporting information about him" (24). *Keller, et al. v. Electronic Arts, Inc., et al.* is pending and has been consolidated with other cases raising similar claims by current and former student athletes, as *In re: NCAA Student-Athlete Name and Likeness Litigation* (2010).

The "Tony Twist" sequence of court decisions provides an interesting analysis of the interplay between an athlete's right to his/her name and image, and the public's First Amendment rights. Anthony R. Twist was "regarded as one of the most violent 'enforcers' in hockey and attained a national reputation for violence on the ice hockey rink" (*Doe, a/d/a Tony Twist v. TCI Cablevision, et al.,* 2002, 3). Todd McFarlane, a comic book writer, created a comic book series called *Spawn* that featured a superhuman creature of the same name. Later, he introduced a character, Tony Twist, as an antagonist to Spawn.

Anthony Twist became aware of the comic book character, and he subsequently filed suit against McFarlane and others for damages and an injunction for defamation and misappropriation of name. McFarlane countered that neither the contents nor description in the Spawn book identified the plaintiff. The trial court, using the First Amendment, dismissed the defamation claim and found that the misappropriation of name claim did not apply. The misappropriation claim was sent to the jury. The jury awarded Twist $24.5 million. The judge overruled the jury verdict, stating that there was insufficient evidence of intent (*Doe v. TCI Cablevision, et. al.,* 2002, 2). In 2003, the Missouri court identified, for the first time, the difference between the use of a person's name and identity for expression versus for commercial purposes. Under the First Amendment, protection exists for expression but does not exist for commercial use (Grady, McKelvey, & Clement, 2005). The Supreme Court of Missouri ordered a new trial. McFarlane's Petition for Certiorari to the United States Supreme Court was denied. In 2007, the case was settled for a reported $5 million.

PATENT LAW

Like copyright and trademark law, patent law evolved from Article I of the United States Constitution. It grants Congress the power to "promote the progress of science and useful arts, by securing for a limited time to authors and inventors the exclusive right to their respective writings and discoveries" (U.S. Const., Article I, Section 8, Clause 8). The Patent Act of 1952 states that a patent is obtained by "whoever invents or discovers any new and useful process, machine, manufacture, or composition of matter, or any new and useful improvement of the above" (Patent Act, 35 USC 101). A person is entitled to a patent unless:

a) the invention was known or used by others in this country … or

b) the invention was patented or described in a printed publication in this or a foreign country … or

c) he has abandoned the invention or …

d) he did not himself invent the subject matter sought to be patented. (35 USC 102)

Also, "a patent may not be obtained though the invention is not identically disclosed or described as set forth in section 102 …, if the differences between the subject matter sought to be patented and the prior art are such that the subject matter as a whole would have been obvious at the time the invention was made to a person having ordinary skill in the art to which said subject matter pertains" (35 USC 103). A patent is infringed when someone "without authority makes, uses, offers to sell, or sells any patented invention, within the United States or imports into the United States any patented invention during the term of the patent" (35 USC 271). Damages for infringing on a patent are to be adequate to compensate for the infringement or a reasonable royalty. A court may increase the damage award to three times the damage assessed (35 USC 284).

Patent applications need to demonstrate that the invention or discovery is novel and non-obvious. The application is expected to describe the object of the patent in detail. Patent law does not cover laws of nature, physical phenomena, or abstract ideas (*Diamond v. Kiehr,* 1981; Patent Act, 35 USC 101). According to Harkins (2008), a patent gives the owner a monopoly on the registered object. Currently, the life of a patent begins on the date of issue and ends twenty years from the date of application (Patent Act, 35 USC 154).

The majority of patents received in sport throughout the years have been for equipment. For example, the reader can trace the evolution of golf club and tennis racket patents as the selection of materials and the precision of mechanics changed the trajectory of the golf club swing and the sweet spot of the tennis strings. The reader who checks the patent registrar for sport equipment will be impressed with the volume of awards for sport in any one year.

PATENT LAW CASES

Everything Baseball v. Wilson Sporting Goods Company, et al. (2009) and *Aqua-Lung America, Inc. v. American Underwater Products, Inc.* (2009) are sport examples of patent infringement. Everything Baseball sued Wilson Sporting Goods Company and others, alleging that Wilson was infringing their patent No. 6,161,226, a baseball chest protector. Wilson and others, including Rawlings and Riddell, moved for summary judgment; the patent was invalid as anticipated by three prior art references. The three prior art references were: No. 5,530,966, issued to Joseph West; a chest protector, manufactured and sold by Douglas under the West patent; and the "hang tag" attached to a chest protector, manufactured and sold by Wilson under the West patent. All three chest protectors were compared and found to be different from Everything Baseball's chest protector. As a result, the defendant's motion for summary judgment was denied.

Aqua-Lung America, Inc. v. American Underwater Products, Inc. (2009) concerned the design of a scuba tank valve that was intended to link the first stage (tank-end) regulator to the scuba tank. At issue were three patents: the 674 Patent, a device called the pressure responsive element (PRE); the 958 Patent, discussing a device called a "retractable valve member;" and the 609 Patent referring to the PRE as a "retractable filter cover." Oceanic contended that Aqua-Lung's Kronos, Legend, and Titan families of regulators each included valves employing an "automatic closure device" that infringed on Oceanic's patents. Aqua-Lung's complaint sought a declaratory judgment that their valve does not infringe the three patents in suit. Aqua-Lung also sought a declaratory judgment of invalidity as to all three Oceanic patents.

Patent infringement analysis involves two steps: 1) claim construction; and 2) application of the properly construed claims to the accused device or method. The court completed the first step, a question of law, with the claim construction order. Next, the court determined if there had been patent infringement, it would have been a question of fact. To prove infringement, a patent holder must show that the accused device or method meets each claim limitation, either literally or under the doctrine of equivalents. The court granted Aqua-Lung's motion for summary judgment on its non-infringement claim with respect to the 958 and 609 Patents and denied Oceanic's motion for summary judgment or infringement of these patents. Aqua-Lung's motion for summary judgment or invalidity also was denied with respect to all three patents.

Process Sport Patents

Technology has had a profound impact on patent law and is directly responsible for many of the recent changes in the law. The 1998 decision in *State Street Bank and Trust Co. v. Signature Financial Group, Inc.,* however, identified a new avenue for patent registration in the sport industry. Signature Financial Group, Inc. was the assignee of a patent called the Data Processing System for Hub and Spoke Financial Services Configuration. It was a

> data processing system (the system) for implementing an investment structure which was developed for use in Signature's business as an administrator and economic agent for mutual funds.... The system ... facilitates a structure whereby mutual funds (Spokes) pooled their assets in an investment portfolio (Hub) organized as a partnership. The investment configuration provided the administrator of a mutual fund with the advantages of a partnership. (*State Street Bank and Trust Co. v. Signature Financial Group, Inc.,* 1998, 1370)

The term process was defined as "a process, art or method, and includes a new use of a known process, machine, manufacture, composition of matter, or material" (Patent Act, 35 USC 100). The question was whether HUB and SPOKE could receive a patent; the court said no, it was an idea, not a process. The court of appeals reversed, holding "that the transformation of data, representing discrete dollar amounts, by a machine through a series of mathematical calculations into a final share price ... produces a useful, concrete and tangible result" (1373). The petition to the United States Supreme Court was denied.

While the public championed the decision of the court of appeals as an invitation to the software industry to patent achievements, the sport industry saw it as a means to secure rights to strategy and skill innovations. Following the decision, a number of authors suggested that sport strategies and movements could receive not only copyright and trademarks, but protection under patent law as well. Robert Kunstadt (1996), a partner in a law firm representing the National Basketball Association (NBA) and the United States Olympic Committee (USOC), led this bold initiative for broader intellectual property protection of sport moves with his article titled "Are Sport Moves Next in IP Law?" Other authors, including Griffith (1998), Kukkonen (1998), Smith (1999), Das (2000), and Maurer (2001), provided influential approaches to the potential for placing patents on sport skill sequences and strategies. Bambauer (2005) described ways patents might be acquired in professional sport and sport training programs.

Clement and Hartman (2000) built a case for patent and/or copyright for the open/closed system of classifying human movement devised by Poulton (1957) and refined by Knapp (1963) and Robb (1972). "Closed movements are planned sequences of movement repeated in the same manner every time. They are predetermined routines. Open movements are movements executed in response to the movement of others. They are used to react to the movements of others. Performers in open movement know many different movements and strategies; they do not, however, know the actual movement that they will execute in any event until the opponents begin to make their plays. Gymnastics, figure skating, and archery represent closed movements; basketball, fencing, and tennis favor open movements" (Clement & Hartman, 1994, p. 21). All closed movements and original routines of such movements that are new and unique are easily fixed and thus readily suitable for copyright; some may also meet the requirements of a patent. Open movements will be more difficult to copyright or patent; however, newly created strategies should qualify.

Griffith (1998) argued for the value of patents for sport skills and techniques as a matter of economics, suggesting that as sport skills and strategies increased in monetary value while technology was making it easier to copy creative accomplishments, athletes should take steps to secure their innovations. It is not difficult for an enthusiastic synchronized swimmer to film the performance of a recent Olympic championship routine, play the stunts and sequences frame by frame, and eventually replicate the performance. Das (2000) and Maurer (2001) placed an emphasis on guiding young performers toward seeking a patent for their original creations (inventions and discoveries) and a copyright for their routines. Das provides an in-depth analysis of sport plays (strategies) as viable subjects for both patent and copyright, while Maurer concentrates on the economics of sport patents.

Among the more recent writers on the patenting of sport skills and sequences are Bambauer (2005), Magliocca (2009), McJohn (2009), and McFarlane and Litts (2010). Bambauer suggests how patents would work in professional sport and sports training. He cites the Arena Football League, U.S. Patent, No. 4,911,443, issued in 1990, as an example of such a patent. His work also recommends that patent agencies may wish to distinguish between "methods used in competition and methods used to prepare for it" (p. 422, p. 423). Magliocca (2009) advances the idea that the concept in sport of a level playing field prohibits the patenting of sport skills. His thesis is that no one should hold a monopoly on a key aspect of sport; it violates the idea of competition. This approach to process patents seems to conflict with all patents held by companies on various sport equipment. McJohn (2009) and McFarlane and Litts (2010) provide detailed discussions of recent court decisions in patent law.

There are a number of issues that have been discussed recently that may have an impact on the future of patents as they relate to sport. Patent law is expected to change considerably in the next few years. With passage of the Leahy-Smith America Invents Act in 2011, the U.S. patent system in 2013 will switch from a "first to invent" to a "first to file" system, bringing the U.S. in line with other countries who predominantly use "first to file." The new law will also eliminate inference proceedings and develop post-grant opposition in patent disputes.

SUMMARY

Intellectual property is the body of laws that a) protect the creative aspects of the sport industry and b) reward investment by sport properties, organizations, and manufacturers that develop a recognizable brand in their products or services. The law also protects the commercial aspects of a celebrity athlete's persona, but not facts or statistics that are already in the public domain. With innovations in technology, the ability to create digital images of star athletes will raise new concerns about how to sufficiently protect these athletes' brands. Intellectual property rights are property rights that can be licensed, sold, or transferred to others. Infringement of copyright, trademark, and patent by competitors is often the focus of litigation involving this rapidly evolving area of law.

DISCUSSION QUESTIONS

1. Explain the identification, evaluation, and control system used in risk management.

2. What are the major differences between risk management and disaster management and recovery?

3. What is the difference between a release signed by a minor and a release signed by the minor' parents?

ACTIVITIES

1. Obtain a copy of one court decision found in the chapter from each of the areas: copyright, trademark, right of publicity, and patent (use LexisNexis). Brief each case using the information found in the research chapter. At the completion of the analysis prepare a brief summary in your own words.

2. Outline the difference between statutory damages and compensatory damage.

3. Using LexisNexis, obtain a patent or trademark registration for a sport. Be ready to discuss your findings in class.

REFERENCES

24 Hour Fitness USA, Inc. v. 24/7 Tribeca Fitness, LLC, et al., 447 F. Supp. 2d 266 (2006); 247 Fed. Appx. 232 (2007).

Abercrombie & Fitch Company v. Hunting World Incorporated. 537 F. 2d 4 (1976).

Amateur Sports Act. 36 USCS 220506(a). (2010).

American Bar Association, Section of Intellectual Property Law. (2004). Report to the House of Delegates. Retrieved from http://www.abnet.org

Aqua-Lung America, Inc. v. American Underwater Products, Inc. (2009).

Bambauer, K. (2005). Legal responses to the challenges of sport patents. 18 *Hav. J. Law & Tec.* 401.

Black's Law Dictionary. (2009). St. Paul, MN: West Publishing.

Board of Supervisors for Louisiana State University, et al. v. Smack Apparel Co., et al., 438 F. Supp. 2d 653 (2006); 574 F. Supp. 2d 601 (2008); 550 F. 3d 465 (2009); 2009 U.S. Dist. LEXIS 27652.

Bouchat v. Baltimore Ravens Limited Partnership, et al., 215 F. Supp. 611 (2002); 346 F. 3d 514 (2003); Cert to S. Ct. denied, 124 S. Ct. 2171 (2004); 587 F. Supp. 2d 686 (2008).

Bouchat v. Von Ton Department Stories, Inc., et al. 506 F. 3d 315 (2007).

CBC Distribution and Marketing, Inc. v. Major League Baseball Advanced Media, L.P., et al., 2005 U.S. Dist. LEXIS 24900; 443 F. Supp. 2d 1077 (2006); 505 F. 3d 818 (2007); 128 S. Ct. 2872, cert denied (2008).

CBS Interactive, Inc. v. National Football League Players Association, Inc., et al., 2009 U.S. Dist. LEXIS 36800.

Clement, A. (2000). Contemporary copyright and patent law and sport. 10 *J. Legal Aspects of Sport* 143.

Clement, A., & Hartman, B. G. (1994). *The teaching of physical skills.* Dubuque, IA: William C. Brown & Benchmark.

Copyright Act of 1976, 17 USC 101–1332 (2010).

Copyright Law Revision, House Report, No. 94–1476 (1976).

Curtis v. Benson, The New Orleans Saints Limited Partnerships, et al., 1997 U.S. Dist. LEXIS 5030; 959 F. Supp. 348 (1997).

Dallas Cowboys Football Club, LTD, et al. v. America's Team Properties, Inc., 616 F. Supp. 2d 622 (2009).

Das, P. K. (2000). Offensive protection: The potential application of intellectual property to scripted sports plays. 75 *Ind. L.J.* 1073.

Diamond v. Kiehr, 450 U.S. 175; 101 S. Ct. 1048 (1981).

Digital Millennium Copyright Act, 17 USC 512, 1201–1205, 1301–1332, 28 USC 401 (1998).

Doe, a/d/a Tony Twist v. TCI Cablevision, et al., 2002 Mo. App. LEXIS 1577; 110 S. W. 3d 363 (2003); cert denied 124 S. Ct. 1058 (2004).

ESPN, Inc., v. Quicksilver, Inc., 586 F. Supp. 2d 219 (2008).

Everything Baseball v. Wilson Sporting Goods Company, et al., 611 F. Supp. 2d 832 (2009).

Federal Trademark Dilution Act of 1995 (FTDFA). 15 USC 1125.

Grady, J., Clement, A., & Woishnis, J. (2009). Trademark counterfeiting of sport merchandise and criminal law. In J. W. Lee & J. C. Lee (Eds.). *Sport and criminal behavior* (pp. 151–167). Durham, NC: Carolina Academic Press.

Grady, J., McKelvey, S., & Clement, A. (2005). A new "Twist" for "The Home Run Guys"? An analysis of the right of publicity versus parody. 15 *J. Legal Aspects of Sport* 267.

Griffith, W. T. (1998). Beyond the perfect score: Protecting routine-oriented athletic performance with copyright law. 30 *Conn. L. Rev.* 675.

Haelan Laboratories, Inc. v. Topps Chewing Gum, Inc., 202 F. 2d 866 (1953).

Harkins, C. A. (2008). Throwing Judge Bryson's curveball: A pro patent view of process claims as patent-eligible subject matter. 7 *J. Marshall Rev. Intell. Prop. L.* 701.

Hawaii-Pacific Apparel Group, Inc. v. Cleveland Browns Football Company, LLC, et al., 418 F. Supp. 2d 501 (2006).

Incredible Technologies, Inc. v. Virtual Technologies, Inc. d/b/a Global VR, 400 F. 3d 1007 (2005).

Innovative Sports Marketing, Inc. v. Medeles, et al., 2008 U.S. Dist. LEXIS 31409.

Intersport, Inc. v. National Collegiate Athletic Association and March Madness Athletic Association, LLC, 885 N. E. 2d 532 (2008).

J&J Sports Productions, Inc. v. Live Oak County Post No. 6119 Veterans of Foreign Wars, et al., 2009 U.S. Dist. Lexis 84947.

Jesien, K. (2007). Don't sweat it: Copyright protection for yoga. 5 *Cardozo Pub. L. Pol'y & Ethics J.* 623.

Keller, et al. v. Electronic Arts, Inc., National Collegiate Athletic Association, and Collegiate Licensing Company, 2010 U.S. Dist. LEXIS 10719; consolidated as In re: NCAA Student-Athlete Name & Likeness Licensing Litigation, 2010 U.S. Dist. LEXIS 139724.

Knapp, B. (1963). *Skills in sport, the attainment of proficiency.* London: Routledge & K. Paul.

Kukkonen, C. A. (1998). Be a good sport and refrain from using my patented putt: Intellectual property protection for sports related movements. 80 *J. Pat. & Trademark Off. Soc'y* 808.

Kunstadt, R. M., Kieff, F. S., & Kramer, R. G. (1996, May 20). Are sport moves next in IP law? *National Law Journal,* p. C2.

Lanham Act, 15 USC 1051–1141 (2010).

Leahy-Smith America Invents Act, Public law 112-29 (2011).

Magliocca, G. N. (2009). Patenting the curve ball: Business methods and industry norms. 2009 *B. Y. U. L. Rev.* 875.

Major League Baseball Advanced Media, L.P., et al. v. CBC Distribution and Marketing, et al., 128 S. Ct. 2872 (2008).

March Madness Athletic Association, LLC v. Netfire, Inc., et al., 2001 U.S. Dist. LEXIS 21078; 310 F. Supp. 2d 786 (2003); 120 Fed. Appx. 540 (2005).

Maurer, E. S. (2001). An economic justification for a broad interpretation of patentable subject matter. 95 *Nw. U. L. Rev.* 1057.

McCarthy, J. T. (2001). *The right of publicity and privacy.* Deerfield, IL: Clark Boardman Callaghan.

McFarlane, R. A., & Litts, R. G. (2010). Business methods and patentable subject matter following In Re Bilski: Is "anything under the sun made by man" really patentable? 26 *Santa Clara Computer and High Tech. L. J.* 35.

McJohn, S. (2009). Scary patents. 7 *Nw. J. Tech. & Intell. Prop.* 343.

Mob Music Publishing, et al. v. Zanzibar on the Waterfront, LLC, et al., 698 F. Supp. 2d 197 (2010).

NBA v. Motorola, 105 F. 3d 841 (2nd Cir. 1997).

Patent Act, 35 USC 1–376 (1952).

Pebble Beach Company, Resorts of Pinehurst, Inc., and Sea Pines Company, Inc. v. Tour 18 1, LTD., 942 F. Supp. 1513 (1996); 155 F. 3d 526 (1998).

Poulton, E. C. (1957). On prediction of skilled movements. *Psychological Bulletin, 54*(6), 467–478.

Pro-Football, Inc. v. Harjo, et al., 2000 U.S. Dist. LEXIS 19792; 191 F. Supp. 2d 77 (2002); 284 F. Supp. 2d 96 (2003); 415 F. 3d 44 (2005); 2006 U.S. Dist. LEXIS 51086; 567 F. Supp. 2d 46 (2008); 565 F. 3d 880 (2009); cert to Supreme Court denied 130 S. Ct. 63 (2009).

Prosser, W. L. (1960). Privacy. 48 *Calif. L. Rev.* 383.

Robb, M. D. (1972). *The dynamics of motor-skill acquisition.* Englewood Cliffs, NJ: Prentice Hall.

Satellite Home Viewer Act, 1988 (SHWA), 17 USC 119 (2010).

Smith, J. A. (1999). It's your move—no it's not! The application of patent law to sport moves. 70 *U. Colo. L. Rev.* 1051.

State Street Bank & Trust Co. v. Signature Financial Group, Inc., 149 F. 3d 1368 (1998). Petition for writ of certiorari to the U.S. Supreme Court denied, 119 S. Ct. 851 (1999).

The Authors Guild, et al. v. GOOGLE, Inc., 05 Civ. 8136 (DC), 2009 U.S. Dist. LEXIS 116175.

The Heisman Trophy Trust v. Smack Apparel Company, 595 F. Supp. 2d 320 (2009); 637 F. Supp. 146 (2009); 379 Fed. Appx. 12 (2010).

The Ohio State University v. Keith Antonio Thomas, et al., 2010 U.S. Dist. LEXIS 96478.

Ticketmaster, LLC v. RMG Technologies, Inc., et al., 507 F. Supp. 2d 1096 (2007).

Trademark Act of 1946, 15 USC 1051–1141 (2010).

Tushnet, R. (2008). Gone in sixty milliseconds: Trademark law and cognitive science. 86 *Tex. L. Rev.* 507.

United States Olympic Committee and the International Olympic Committee v. Xclusive Leisure & Hospitality, Ltd; Beijingticketing.com, et al., 2009 U.S. Dist. LEXIS 12698.

United States Olympic Committee v. Intelicense Corp. S. A., 737 F. 2d 263 (1984); Cert Denied, Intelicense Corp. S. A. v. United States Olympic Comm., 105 S. Ct. 387 (1984).

University of Kansas and Kansas Athletics, Inc. v. Larry Sinks, Clark Orth, and Victory Sportswear, LLC, 565 F. Supp. 2d 1216 (2008); 2008 U.S. Dist. LEXIS 23763; 2009 U.S. Dist. LEXIS 89783; 644 F. Supp. 2d 1287 (2009).

University of South Carolina v. University of Southern California, 367 Fed. Appox. 129 (2010) cert. to the United States Supreme Court denied, 131 S. Ct. 387 (2010).

RECOMMENDED READING

Dennie, C. (2009). Tebow drops back to pass: Videogames have crossed the line but does the right of publicity protect a student-athlete's likeness when balanced against the First Amendment? 62 *Ark. L. Rev.* 645.

Kaburakis, A., Pierce, D. A., Fleming, O. M., Clavio, G. E., Lawrence, H. J., & Dziuba, D. A. (2009). NCAA student-athletes' rights of publicity, EA sports, and the video-game industry. 27 *Ent. & Sports Law* 14.

Kerner, J. (2009). "It's third and eight!" The third circuit adopts an eight factor test for likelihood of confusion in false endorsement claims in Facenda v. NFL films. 32 *Hastings Comm. & Ent. L. J.* 111.

Kline, J. (2009). Black and blue: An examination of trade marketing university color schemes. 16 *Sports Law J.* 47.

McKelvey, S., Fairley, S., & Groza, M. D. (2010). Caught in the web? The communication of trademark rights and licensing policy on university official athletic websites. 20 *J. Legal Aspects of Sport* 1.

Riccard, K. E. (2009). Product placement or pure entertainment: Critiquing a copyright-preemption proposal. 59 *Am. U. L. Rev.* 427.

Schull, M. C. (2011). Biting the hand that feeds: How trademark protection might threaten school spirit. 21 *Marq. Sports L. Rev.* 641.

Siegel, B. (2009). Colorful trends in collegiate trademark protection. 26 *Ent. & Sports Law.* 19.

11

Risk, Disaster, and Recovery Management

OBJECTIVES

Upon completing this chapter, you will:

1) know the difference between risk management and disaster management;

2) be able to prepare a recovery plan;

3) recognize that a release is a contract;

4) be conversant with the identification, evaluation, and control system in risk management; and

5) know where to look for up-to-date materials on disaster and recovery management.

INTRODUCTION

The goal in risk management is to avoid those dangers that one can envision. Disaster management, in contrast, is a plan for experiencing or facing hazardous situations and living through them. Disaster management includes recovery management—a system of rehabilitation of people, property, and businesses damaged or destroyed by a disaster.

Risk management is the identification, evaluation, and control of loss to property, clients, employees, and the public. A risk management program requires a systematic examination of the environment, with the identification of potential for exposure to loss and legal liability in all facets of the organization. The purpose of risk management is to make the sport and physical activity environment as safe as possible for participants and spectators, and the business as efficient as possible using accepted business practices. Many people view risk management solely as a means of reducing legal liability; however, a safe, honest, and efficient environment will not only reduce legal liability but will enhance the positive reputation of the business. Disaster management involves the identification of threats and vulnerabilities to natural and manmade hazards. Once the threats and vulnerabilities are identified, they are evaluated, and plans are prepared to meet, control, and survive the hazards that may occur. In recovery, the object is to return people, property, and businesses to the level at which they were before the incident. While risk management is driven by the desire to reduce accidents and possible litigation, disaster and recovery management are driven by the need for the survival of people, property, and businesses.

Persons who hold the positions of safety coordinators and committee members are to have an understanding of safety in the business of the agency. Further, staff handbooks are to contain policies and procedures relevant to safety, risk, and disaster management. An understanding of the components of a lawsuit are important to these areas (see Introduction).

RISK MANAGEMENT

Risk and disaster management must be comprehensive. This means that the entire league, team, management company, agency, business, school, or corporation participates in all components of the plan. Even if an agency refuses to plan for risks or disasters, professionals should create their own plans and programs. Insurance companies have been known to demand that ongoing risk management systems be present before providing coverage to a business or other agency; other companies have reduced rates when such programs are instituted.

This text has provided numerous illustrations of liability in sport and physical activity. Each of the major topics presented included an overview of the applicable law. Hypothetical examples and real cases illustrated most of the legal theories. This information, coupled with the student's practical experiences, is to be used to devise risk, disaster, and recovery management programs.

The risk management system consists of the identification, evaluation, and control of risks. The following risk management system was created for the first edition of this text (Clement, 1988).

Identification

The first step of risk management is to identify all areas of potential exposure to risk. Exposure means any and every event that could cause an agency to become vulnerable to a particular risk. The following is a list of elements that might be used in creating a risk management audit. This list is not meant to be comprehensive, nor has it been tailored to a specific agency or service. However, an effort has been made to demonstrate the vast array of topics a professional might consider in devising an audit. The elements include: local, state, and federal codes and regulations; professional organizations and other industry standards; policies and procedures; facilities; equipment; personnel; supervision; instruction; participant education; fiscal issues; and contracts.

Local, State, and Federal Regulations

Local, state, and federal laws, codes, and regulations that affect sport and physical activity and/or the agency under study are identified. The laws are published as health, safety, bathing, buildings, waste disposal, water pollution, medical emergency, weather, fire, crime, swimming pools, electrical, heating, refrigeration, air conditioning, industrial hygiene, and others. Agencies of importance include the Occupational Safety and Health Administration (OSHA), the Environmental Protection Agency (EPA), and the Department of Agriculture. Building codes are important. Waterslide regulations, for example, are found in amusement parks. Other examples are elevator codes and agriculture regulations. The agency's status—"for profit" or "not for profit"—will, on occasion, affect its standing under a law.

All laws, codes, and regulations are to be posted, made available to employees, and reviewed with each worker whose job is impacted. They must also be retained on file, brought up to date yearly, and strictly enforced. For example, fire safety regulations, including alarms, extinguishers, and sprinkler systems, are to be in order and must meet local codes. Enforceable provisions for electrical failure are to be made. Systems for evacuation for tornadoes, hurricanes, and severe storms are to be planned and posted, and staff must be prepared to carry them out. Employees must be educated about the differences between codes, laws, regulations, and guidelines. They should know that laws, codes, and regulations must be followed, whereas guidelines are followed on a volunteer basis. Failure to follow a *code* can result in civil punishment; failure to follow a *guideline* will not result in civil punishment. A court can, however, ask why the professional ignored a guideline. Agencies choosing to ignore popular guidelines should document their knowledge of the guideline and the reason(s) for rejecting it.

Professional Organizations and Industry Standards

Managers need to know professional certificates and guidelines that affect their businesses. They are to be aware of professional organizations related to each aspect of their agencies. The literature and services of such organizations are to be evaluated and a commitment made to track the offerings of selected organizations. Records of job competencies, verifications of employee certificates and test results, and attendance at safety meetings are to be on file. Staff credentials are checked in initial employment and periodically throughout job tenure. Criminal and other background checks are conducted, and drug testing is required when appropriate. Industry standards are known and maintained. Should a professional or an agency choose to differ from industry standards, reasons for the differences are documented. Often, professionals adhere to standards that are higher than industry standards—such quality is to be encouraged.

Policies and Procedures Common to the Industry

Policies for employees, participants, facility management, and conduct of activities exist in writing and are readily available, widely known, and enforced. Employee handbooks contain all policies and procedures—including behavior, appearance, attendance, and alcohol/drug use. Policies for participants also address alcohol and drug use. Due process systems (described in Chapter 4, U.S. Constitutional Amendments) exist and are explained to employees and participants.

Facilities

The facility is to be given major attention in any sport or physical activity risk management program. This is because it has been a primary subject of litigation. The following standards should be met:

1) A record of all property, including its condition and (if possible) value, exists and is readily available in the event of a fire, tornado, riot, attack by terrorists or vandals, or other loss. These lists are a requisite for insurance collection.

2) A detailed system for checking facilities exists and is used routinely. Hazards and cleanliness are but two of the topics. Frequency of inspection and name of the inspector are identified for each part of the audit. The facility audit process is reviewed bi-yearly by the same administrators who examine the results of injuries and emergency maintenance.

3) Facilities meet all code requirements, including lighting. Emergency lights for electrical failure easily lead people to exterior exits. Ground fault circuit interrupters are found in wet areas and locker rooms.

4) Verifications of building compliance with codes are on file.

5) The general condition of a facility is compared with appropriate guidelines (i.e., the American Council of Sports Medicine [ACSM], the National Intramural-Recreational Sport Association [NIRSA], etc.).

6) Protocols for repair, follow-up, and the closing of a facility in need of repair exist, and are used. These protocols are reviewed at least bi-yearly.

7) Parking lots, entrances, exterior traffic patterns, and internal structures meet the Americans with Disabilities Act (ADA) requirements.

8) Facility designs that create hazards are identified and remedied.

9) Exit and entrance signs are lit and visible to all. Entrances are secure and participants' safety is of the utmost importance.

10) A system for opening and closing the building each day is in writing, is followed, and is monitored by management.

11) Where appropriate, the facility is monitored hourly by a person with current CPR and first aid credentials.

Equipment

Equipment risk management demands that the purchaser be able to communicate with the seller. Furthermore, it requires that the purchaser comprehends the warranties and the proper uses of the equipment. Maintenance appears to be a primary cause for equipment to become part of the pattern in litigation. The following are equipment-related requirements that need to be included in any risk management plan:

1) A master list of equipment exists.

2) The equipment—permanently mounted or free standing—is cleaned and inspected routinely. Signed inspection documents are retained.

3) Any requests for equipment repair are in writing. When necessary, equipment is taken out of service if it cannot be repaired immediately.

4) The equipment is maintained as specified by manufacturers. All equipment with warranties that dictate specific repair and service are honored. Equipment is repaired and cleaned according to accepted industry practices.

5) All of the manufacturers' warnings and instructions are posted in a conspicuous place on equipment or on walls near equipment so participants can see them. The statements by manufacturers and retailers about the use of equipment are honored.

6) The staff is trained in the use of new equipment. New employees receive training before beginning work.

7) The equipment meets the standard established by the sport.

8) The statutes of the state, with reference to equipment, are known and followed.

9) All rescue equipment meets acceptable standards and is clean and ready to use.

10) Safety equipment is provided or required of participants; when participants do not have appropriate safety equipment, they do not participate. Safety equipment fits properly to assure the safety for which it was designed.

Personnel

Audit components for personnel are organized into three categories:

- employing, evaluating, and terminating;
- employee education; and
- staff training.

Employing, Evaluating, and Terminating

1) Written procedures for advertising jobs and soliciting candidates are designed, used, and recorded.

2) Job descriptions—including tasks, appropriate experience, and credentials to carry out the tasks—exist for each position. Job descriptions explicitly identify safety responsibilities. These descriptions are used for evaluation and termination. Employees are given copies of their job description.

3) Employee records contain:

   a) minimum and advanced qualifications for each employee with reference to responsibilities;

   b) contracts, references, and observations; and

   c) evaluation, performance, and attendance.

4) Employers verify that

a) agencies licensing or certifying employees adhere to acceptable professional standards;

b) employees know and adhere to the duty of care recommended by their profession, licensure, and certifications; and

c) professionals know and apply the latest research, when appropriate.

5) Employee evaluation, retention, and termination policies exist and are used, and records are kept. Evaluations support quality, and a due process system is available and used.

6) Termination procedures include:

a) warnings of inadequate or poor-quality work, and evidence that these flaws are in tasks contained in the employee's job description;

b) opportunity for rehabilitation and change; and

c) termination, after a continued pattern of incompetence, following rehabilitation.

Employee Education

1) The employees know and understand their job descriptions.

2) The staff members understand legal liability in the tort, civil rights, and business components of this text and how each relates to their job descriptions and routine tasks.

3) The members of the staff understand the risk management system and the role they play in the system.

4) The employees know of injuries inherent in sport and physical activity and recognize the characteristics of participants who might be vulnerable to injuries.

5) The staff members understand the standard of care inherent in their jobs and how the standards would be evaluated by peers and a court of law.

6) Professionals who are engaged in the supervision or coaching of competitive athletes know they could be held for an intentional tort as a result of teaching the violation of a game rule.

7) The staff is capable of performing all safety techniques requisite to the job.

8) There are employee and participant handbooks, and these documents contain detailed information on emergency and injury protocol. Employees are asked to sign a statement that they have read and understood the information, and that they will comply with the policies and procedures contained in the manual.

9) Employees and participants know the drug and alcohol rules and agree to abide by them.

10) A system for release of employee and client documents has been devised and is used. It identifies when, why, and to whom each category of document can or should be released. Employee privacy rights are secured.

11) The staff knows about the company's/facility's insurance coverage.

12) The work environment is safe for employees and they are encouraged to report unsafe conditions.

Staff Training

1) Staff training is formal, occurs during work hours, and is mandatory.

2) Orientations are provided for new personnel.

3) Evidence of the content and attendance at all meetings involving safety education and skill training are retained and available for inspection.

Supervision

The majority of the lawsuits in physical activity specifically state that there was no supervision or that the supervision was inadequate. Whether supervision should exist in a particular activity becomes part of the standard of care. When the standard demands supervision, the supervision must be adequate.

1) Rules are prepared, reviewed, and reformulated at least yearly.

2) Rules are posted.

3) Signage meets codes and is easy to read and understand.

4) A detailed written description of the supervision process exists. It identifies the role of each employee and is contained in each employee's job description.

5) A system for crowd control exists and is rehearsed periodically.

6) Actions have been taken to eliminate horseplay.

7) Advertised standards are maintained.

8) A code of behavior exists and is in writing.

9) Penalties are established to punish participants who behave in an unsafe manner. The penalties are sufficient to deter participants from continuing unsafe behavior.

10) Control in the activity environment is maintained at all times.

Instruction and Coaching

Faulty instruction has been found in physical activity and coaching litigation. The following suggestions should be considered in the creation of risk management plans involving instruction and coaching:

1) Instructional content is used by those prepared to use the content. Licenses, certificates, and college degrees are often required to interpret educational content. An understanding of the application of physiology and biomechanics

is essential to the successful interpretation of instructional materials in sport, physical activity, and the coaching of athletics.

2) Instructional content is selected with knowledge of the client's capabilities in mind. An instructor is able to explain the physical demands placed on the performer.

3) Planning is documented. Courses of study, curricular programs, lesson plans, learning sequences, routines, and other planning materials that could be presented to a court of law, if requested, are preserved.

4) Records document the client's major learning benchmarks. Records document the learner's readiness for advanced risk-taking skills.

5) When possible, computer printouts or schedules of a participant's progress are retained.

6) The following elements are considered in program planning:
   a) Performers are matched when body contact is involved.
   b) Appropriate safety equipment is used.
   c) Athletes are properly hydrated at all times.

7) The methodologies employed for instruction meet the test of peer scrutiny.

8) Official games are played according to recognized rules and officials are used. Officials are responsible only for officiating.

Participant Education

Participants are to be informed of the risks of activities, particularly those involved in competitive sport. Warnings are to be provided to persons engaging in high-risk activities. Much of this risk management information is provided in a form often referred to as a waiver, warning, release, etc. The statement can be a legal document that results in a contract or merely an information sheet. Under contract law, an adult can, in many states, contract for almost anything—including contracting away his/her rights. By signing a statement and fully understanding the ramifications of the risks described, adults can contract away their rights to be reimbursed for any injury. A minor cannot contract away the minor's rights. Parents signing a statement for their child to engage in an activity cannot contract away the child's rights. They can, however, contract away their rights as a parent. Items such as statements and waivers are often used merely to alert parents to the risks involved in physical activity and to make it known that their offspring are engaged in a hazardous undertaking.

In negligence situations, the courts have tended to uphold a waiver when the party signing the contract was an adult and fully understood what he/she was releasing. Under no circumstances have the courts upheld a statement absolving an agency or a person from an intentional tort.

Information statements provide an ideal method of alerting participants to the potential of catastrophic injury as well as to the serious risks involved in various physical activities. The statements should be clear, easy to understand, specific to the activity, and they should describe the situation in detail. The documents should clearly outline the participant's responsibility for his/her own safety and for the safety of other participants. A note should be made that rules will be enforced and that participants are to adhere to rules or be denied entrance to the activity or event. The information statements should not only deal with the possibility of injury but should also include the personal safety required of the participant and a description of how the participant will be treated in an accident setting. These statements are to be read, understood, and agreed to by the signer of the document. Contracts and information statements are to be reviewed by legal counsel to be sure they accomplish the objectives desired and are in conformity with state law and recent court decisions.

Fiscal Issues

As mentioned earlier, the best business practices need to be used at all times in sport and physical activity in both for-profit and non-profit organizations. The following items provide a model to use in thinking through the risks one's agency might encounter:

1) In programs in which gate receipts or the staging of major events are essential to revenue generation, the risk of a riot, terrorist attack, or other hazard has been assessed.

2) When possible, contracts spread liability among vendors and users. All contracts are drafted by legal counsel who will be expected to defend the contracts.

3) Leases and/or contracts are required for groups using facilities.

4) State and local statutes and regulations with respect to fiscal and contract obligations are followed.

5) When transferring risks to others by contract, the transferee knows what he/she is signing. If a part-time employee is asked to sign an independent contractor agreement, the employee knows what is involved in being an independent contractor.

6) Avoid signing hold-harmless or indemnification agreements with manufacturers or retailers of athletic equipment. A hold-harmless agreement is a contractual arrangement whereby one party assumes the liability inherent in a situation, thereby relieving the other party of responsibility. Indemnification is securing another against loss or damage. Professionals need to be sure they have not assumed—by contract—the liability for a product. Should such a contract have been signed, the agency or person signing is liable for injury, loss, or damage incurred by anyone as a result of using the equipment. All contracts are to be reviewed by legal counsel before they are signed.

7) Medical examinations are recommended and, when appropriate, required. These records are examined by the staff and are used in program and participation decisions. Written medical clearance is required for injured athletes returning to play.

Evaluation

Risks are identified. Each is evaluated for probability, severity, and magnitude to determine the amount of risk that exists. The continuums shown in Figure 11.1 are used to make judgments about the potential risks.

A risk may have a high probability of occurring, but should it occur only a few people will suffer minor discomfort. A risk may have a low probability of occurring, but should it occur there is a good chance someone will die. An activity scoring high on any one of the characteristics is to be given serious thought. Even minor discomforts for large populations of people can result in a public relations disaster. A single death can be devastating to an agency.

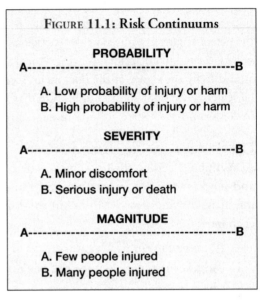

FIGURE 11.1: Risk Continuums

PROBABILITY

A--B

A. Low probability of injury or harm
B. High probability of injury or harm

SEVERITY

A--B

A. Minor discomfort
B. Serious injury or death

MAGNITUDE

A--B

A. Few people injured
B. Many people injured

Control

Control is the third essential component in successful risk management programs. Liability can be controlled by:

1) accepting the risk and assuming the responsibility;

2) retaining the activity and transferring the risk through contracts or insurance;

3) altering the activity to reduce the risk; or

4) eliminating the activity.

Accepting the Risk and Assuming the Responsibility

When a decision is made to retain the risk or maintain a program vulnerable to litigation or negative public image, a defense strategy is devised. The two most important components of the defense strategy are (1) a comprehensive safety or compliance check so the agency and other interested parties realize that every effort had been made to take all precautions with reference to the risk, and (2) an assessment of the cost of maintaining the risk or vulnerable program.

Transferring the Risk Through Insurance or Contract

When the decision is made to maintain an area that appears vulnerable to risks, risks can be transferred by insurance or contract. Insurance is obtained when the purchaser believes that there is a chance injury could occur and as a result, he/she is willing to pay insurance premiums to cover an injury and the need to defend, should litigation occur. The purchase of insurance is one means of transferring the risk of loss that might occur should a participant be injured. A number of different kinds of insurance are available. They include a regular policy with an insurance carrier, a regular policy with a high deductible, self- insurance, and a risk management pool.

Self-insurance involves a group of similarly situated professionals who put an identified sum of money in escrow in case one of them should sustain a catastrophic incident. The money is invested but easy to obtain. Should an incident occur, the money is paid to the investor involved; should none of the investors draw on the money, the money becomes an asset of the investors. Self-insurance—or small group pooling of monies for insurance—is particularly valuable when none of the parties has had a major incident in 10 or 15 years and when regular insurance rates are established by mixing high-incident-rate groups with accident-free populations.

Regular insurance policies with large deductibles combine the options of self-insurance and regular insurance. Individuals or agencies self-insure for minor losses and carry regular insurance for major disasters. Significant reduction in premiums usually accompanies these policies. A risk management insurance pool is the grouping of many like agencies in a common pool under an insurance carrier. As this is a new trend, many agencies requiring similar insurance against common potential losses are forming groups and going to insurance brokers to obtain coverage. These groups usually keep statistics on their injury rates. In addition, employers are contracting their risks to employees through independent contractor arrangements. They hire personnel to conduct risk activities that are independent from the agency with which they are working. The independent contractor carries insurance and is liable for incidents that occur under his/her direction.

Changing the Activity to Reduce Potential Injury

An alternate program may meet the goals of the program considered vulnerable. When such a substitute is available, the prudent manager will accept the alternate program. Sometimes, merely changing components of the activity can result in a substantially safer activity. Improving injury recordkeeping, instituting safety procedures, changing or improving supervision, or training employees can reduce the injury rate.

DISASTER MANAGEMENT

Risk management is avoidance; disaster management is facing, surviving, and returning to normal following a disaster. Disaster management requires comprehensive knowledge of the effect of previous disasters in similar facilities and situations. Planning for a disaster is anticipating an event that is difficult to imagine. Hurricanes and winter storms will often have one or more days of warning, allowing people to prepare. Tornados, gas leaks, fire, and lightning strikes give limited or no warning and must therefore be anticipated at all times. Preparation for a disaster involves many different problems ranging from biological weapons to floods and rockslides. It includes identifying, preparing for, facing and surviving the event, as well as recovery after the event.

Identification

The first step is to identify the threats and vulnerabilities in an environment (and its surroundings) to natural and man-made hazards and disasters. With the use of information from one or more of the agencies listed below, identify natural and man-made hazards and disasters for your agency.

1) Examples of natural disasters are hurricanes, wind and snow storms, floods, tornadoes, rockslides, lightning strikes, earthquakes, and fires.

2) Examples of man-made disasters are violent attacks against individuals and groups of people; contagious and non-contagious biological agents (including smallpox and anthrax); and chemical, radiological (dirty bombs), and nuclear agents.

3) Natural and man-made disasters often result in gas leaks, fire, washed-out roads, contaminated water, damage to electrical circuits, chemical spills, dead animals, etc.

4) Location within the United States influences the potential for certain natural disasters. Population density, media coverage, psychological impact, ease of success, and financial destruction drive man-made hazards.

Preparation

Preparation for a disaster—whether it is weather-related, geologic, or man-made—prompts different plans. One or more persons become safety and security coordinators; adequate staff and time are available for them to engage in the preparation. In an anticipated incident, staff remains in operation headquarters and is ready to face the incident. In light of the fact that many incidents cannot be anticipated, those in charge of safety and security are to provide back-up persons to do their jobs if they will not be available for a period of time. Safety and security professionals and first responders need to know their roles as business owners in collaboration with: law enforcement, fire service, emergency medical, hazardous materials, and public works. Following are some of the many questions that will be addressed in planning:

1) What will be the size of the population affected by the disaster?

2) How long will an evacuation site be used? A storm may be over in a day or two; a man-made attack may consume a week.

3) Will evacuees have a place to return to?

4) Will evacuees remain in place following the event?

5) Will sport facilities become evacuation centers?

6) Will a particular facility be used for emergency care and rescue? If so, how will it be prepared and who will provide adequate food, water, first aid supplies, sleep arrangements, and hygiene facilities?

   a) How often will the facilities be cleaned?

b) How many people can any one facility accommodate? If everyone within a fifty-mile radius needs evacuation, will the facility selected be adequate?

c) Should people be warned to seek shelter early? Is it possible or necessary to turn away people immediately before an event?

d) In the event of damage to an emergency facility, will movement to another facility be possible? How will the move be handled?

7) How will medical and emergency personnel coordinate activities to avoid overloading of a particular care facility?

The following are tips to aid personnel in preparation for the event:

1) Design a mail handling procedure to avoid contaminated deliveries.

2) Back up all Internet properties and store them off the premises; if possible, store one close and one far away from the home or business.

3) Be sure all locks, alarms, surveillance, and lighting are up to standards.

4) Limit access points and control those that exist.

5) Maintain a high standard for basic housekeeping. Avoid items that could be used to store hazardous materials.

6) Screen employees carefully.

7) Encourage high standards for disaster management security.

8) Discover organizations or individual members that are targets for man-made attacks.

9) Discover organizations or persons in your neighborhood that could cause an incident.

10) Identify sensitive data that might be attractive to terrorists.

11) Assess whether an incident in your surroundings would attract greater media attention than would an incident in another setting.

12) Develop scenarios and rehearse situations with a focus on safety, health, and survival.

13) Work closely with local authorities. When possible, conduct training and rehearse with these agencies. Be sure the agencies are aware of your planning.

14) Convince people to become physically fit in an effort to withstand injury, to flee rapidly if needed, and to become certified in first aid and emergency care. An alert and fit public will make the difference in the survival of the masses.

15) The most sophisticated communication devices are to be in the hands of professionals and used to locate the injured. A system of alerts and anticipated priorities in decision-making is practiced by all who have such technology.

16) The role of medical personnel, first responders, grief counselors, and volunteers is well understood. Communication supervisors are prepared to guide these people to the locations where they are most needed.

17) Always include media in rehearsals of incidents.

18) Have prepared a communication plan with the media that emphasizes the importance of their role and support to respond accurately to local and national audiences.

There are many agencies available to assist a person in creating the most up-to-date plan for meeting both personal and business needs and responsibilities for every kind of disaster imaginable. Monitor selected agencies for up-to-date information as plans are revised and rehearsed. Be aware of the work of the National Institute of Standards and Technology on Public Safety and Security. Some of the books that have analyzed 9/11 and Katrina may provide suggestions for increasing safety in your personal and business environments. The following are suggestions for locating materials on the Internet for use in planning.

The Department of Homeland Security's National Incident Management System (NIMS), originally devised by the Federal Emergency Management Agency (FEMA), is a good model for use in planning. NIMS

> provides a systematic, proactive approach to guide departments and agencies at all levels of government, nongovernmental organizations, and the private sector to work seamlessly to prevent, protect against, respond to, recover from, and mitigate the effects of incidents, regardless of cause, size, location, or complexity, in order to reduce the loss of life and property and harm to the environment. NIMS works hand in hand with the National Responses Framework (NRF). NIMS provides the template for the management of incidents, while the NRF provides the structure and mechanisms for nation-level policy for incident management. (NIMS Resource Center)

Their preparedness is for natural hazards, technological hazards and terrorism, and recovery from disaster. Their recovery system for individuals is particularly outstanding and a must for planning.

The International Association of Assembly Managers, Inc. (IAAM), through the Academy for Venue Safety and Security, provides comprehensive risk and disaster management programs, and training opportunities for persons managing and employed in sport facilities and arenas. Structures, personnel, spectators, and services are addressed in IAAM packages for facilities. IAAM works closely with Homeland Security, Health and Human Services, and numerous state and federal agencies.

The National Counter Terrorism Security Office provides many publications on specific topics that will aid the protection of sport interests. Their publication for Stadia and Arenas was published in 2006.

The Centers for Disease Control and Prevention (CDC) and the U.S. Department of Health and Human Services Office of the Assistant Secretary for Preparedness and Response have taken over the role of the agency for health care research and quality and will provide information on bioterrorism and public health emergencies.

The University of Southern Mississippi National Center for Spectator Sports Safety and Security (NCS4) provides detailed information for evacuation of spectator sport sites. Their materials, training, and advice include identifying vulnerability and threats, creation and implementation of protective systems, emergency response and recovery, evacuation capabilities, role of ushers as first responders, and evacuation drills.

The Centre for the Protection of National Infrastructure is a United Kingdom approach to the securing of facilities and the infrastructure that supports public buildings including stadiums and arenas. They conduct vulnerability and protection research; provide information on threats, incidents, and mitigation; and work closely with security programs in the United States, Canada, Australia, New Zealand, and Europe.

Meet, Control, and Survive an Incident

Immediately following the incident, all persons assess the human situation: deaths, life-threatening injuries, and illnesses. One or more command centers are established for agencies and persons designated to respond as efficiently as possible given the known circumstances of the incident.

1) If possible, designated first responders and those who remain healthy should quickly identify the survival territory. People may work in pairs or some other combinations. The nature of the disaster dictates the size of a group. An open area may allow persons to work alone or in pairs, while it may take a number of people to remove building parts in order to free the injured.

2) First aid supplies and other equipment are to have been positioned at strategic locations prior to the event. If such positioning is inefficient, healthy persons, not first responders, will move equipment to the best sites and keep first responders supplied according to their needs.

3) Hopefully, medical personnel will be available to make priority decisions on rescue. Some persons will be pronounced dead at the scene; many will have non-life-threatening injuries, and those with life-threatening injuries and illnesses will require immediate evaluation and care.

4) Within an hour of the incident, first responders and medical professionals will find heart problems and severe psychological stress among survivors, especially among those with non-life-threatening conditions.

5) If the incident is a chemical, radiological (dirty bomb), nuclear, or biological event or if one or more of these threats was part of other attacks, first responders must be able to recognize the symptoms of each, timing of recognition, and most appropriate assistance. Homeland Security continuously updates

information on the threats on its website. The website needs to be checked periodically, or a communication line should be established with a source to provide such information as soon as it becomes available. All of these incidents require a quick response.

6) Low-lying clouds and haze, without fog, and strange odors may signal chemical conditions.

7) Unexplained illnesses within the following days or weeks may be related to the incident.

Recovery Management

Recovery is returning people, property, and businesses to what they were prior to the event. The needs of people, then property, and finally businesses are to be addressed. Considerable preplanning must exist for recovery to be systematic and efficient.

People

1) Nearest medical facilities are ready for those with physical injuries and diseases.

2) Systems are in place to treat physical and psychological problems faced by people over the anticipated period of time the facility will be in use. In some situations, people able to return to their homes may need to continue to use the facilities for these services.

3) Ultimately, physical and psychological services may be provided and continued for the first responders, those engaged in search and rescue, and those who clean up the mess.

4) Information must be provided to those who experience biologic, fire, or other physical properties that may create long-term health risks. Efforts are to be made to restore persons suffering from long term illnesses created by the disaster.

5) Information about returning to homes, if that is possible, is to be provided. When will utilities be restored? What will be the process for evaluating home security?

6) The NIMS system provides a detailed analysis of home precautions, including such information as properly pumping out a water-filled basement and ridding the home of unwanted wild animals.

Structures

1) Can the owner or renter return to his/her home or will new quarters need to be obtained? And for how long?

2) Can the owner or renter return to the property to secure whatever remains? Will they be guided by police and security personnel or can they return on their own? This assumes that community forces are prepared for looters.

3) Total architectural and building revision plans, and total interior descriptions are to be secured in an off-business or home location that is perceived to be safe from fire, weather, and hazardous activity. Should hazards become more significant, all documents need to be secured in at least two very different locations.

4) Will structures be cared for by personal insurance or is the damage such that FEMA and other help will be essential?

Businesses

1) Business buildings and facilities are to be checked much as a home would be examined.

2) Financial records for the past three to five years are to be stored off location. The owner of the business should be able to accurately evaluate the damage to the business and be ready to make claims to insurance companies.

3) Insurance policies, tax returns, employee information, and other pertinent information should have been stored prior to the incident.

4) Plans for running the business in the interim are necessary and to be implemented within a few days of the disaster. For businesses with multiple U.S. and international offices, transfer of business responsibilities should be made as businesses close before the disaster, immediately after the disaster occurs, or otherwise as soon as possible.

5) Businesses should be sensitive to the needs of employees.

EMERGENCY PLANS

The results of litigation suggest that when liability can be found for managers of physical activity for foreseeable injuries, an emergency action plan is demanded. *Kleinknecht v. Gettysburg* (1991, 1992) was the case that brought the need for an emergency plan to the public. Since that time, health spas in at least three states have been found liable for failure to provide adequate emergency care. Emergency action plans must accommodate severe injuries, apparent drowning, heart attacks, fires, power failures, fights, robberies, vandalism, chemical discharges, bomb threats, severe weather, and other problems. Injuries that require emergency services at the scene of the accident and those that require medical service at a later date are evaluated. The emergency action system consists of research, planning, learning the system, rehearsal, and follow-up.

Research

1) Become aware of the types of injuries that might occur.

2) Simulate emergency care for each of the injuries.

3) Create an injury surveillance system. The surveillance system can classify emergency incidents as cuts and bruises, injuries that might be serious, and serious injuries. Serious injuries are those for which emergency care is required.

4) Where appropriate, medical clearance—including health histories and examinations—are analyzed in light of the incidents.

5) Litigation in the institution and in similar institutions is examined. Legal counsel and insurance representatives are invited to review injury-reporting procedures.

Planning

1) Create an emergency action plan. Put the plan in writing.

2) The plan includes three phases of response:
    a) Identification of injured person.
    b) Further identification of injury and initiation of first aid; decision to seek external emergency support is made.
    c) External emergency support is obtained.

3) Phase one, immediate and temporary care, is handled by competently trained personnel in CPR, first aid, and when appropriate, water rescue. For example, under American Red Cross standards, the staff is to be prepared in infant and adult CPR, community first aid, and prevention of communicable diseases.

4) Phase two is the recognition of an injury requiring emergency medical assistance.

5) The emergency plan is executed by telephone. The telephone has the emergency number or the usual 911 on the phone or on a card next to the phone. When the phone is on a wall or desk, this message is posted immediately above the phone and in a position that will make it easy to read. The following information is available:
    a) Appropriate number (i.e., 911) to summon emergency medical care. If numbers differ for fire and chemical exposure, list them.
    b) Exact name and address of facility.
    c) Location of door where vehicle will be met.
    d) Number of the telephone in use.
    e) Approximate time needed for emergency unit to reach facility.

6) The following instructions are to be used when making a call:
    a) Dial 911.

b) Remain calm.

c) Give your name and title.

d) State the emergency medical care sought, the exact address of the facility, and the location of the facility relative to highways and obvious structures. This information must be clear and concise.

e) The injury is (give general description). Note whether the victim is conscious or unconscious. Be able to provide the approximate age of the victim.

f) You are calling from (give number).

g) Who will meet emergency medical or fire staff?

h) Do not hang up until the operator hangs up.

Learning the System

1) Identify each employee's role in the emergency action plan.

2) Simulate various situations and identify how each will be handled.

3) First aid kits, rescue equipment, and other emergency equipment and supplies are adequate and appropriately packed for use. The equipment is checked daily and carefully repacked after each use.

4) The staff knows how to use all equipment.

5) The system is created with input from emergency medical and fire departments.

Rehearse

1) The plan is rehearsed with the staff and with the emergency medical and fire department. The approximate times required to reach the facility are determined by each of these agencies. These times will be compared to times used in an actual event to see if personnel were able to make decisions and obtain assistance in a reasonable amount of time.

2) The rehearsals are to be held periodically and whenever new staff is employed.

3) The records of all practices are retained.

Follow-up

1) Identify follow-up procedures for seriously injured persons.

2) Have on record the persons who should be contacted if a staff member or a participant sustains a serious injury.

3) Be sure that staff members are aware of workers' compensation and company insurance.

4) Parents of minors are to be notified and informed.

5) A means of working with the media exists. Often the members of the media come in response to the 911 call.

6) The entire system is known by all, rehearsed often, and periodically monitored for flaws.

ACCIDENT REPORTS

Accident reports become the first description of the incident and are often the most accurate description. Accident reports must be objective and accurate. Rescuers should freeze the incident in their minds, creating a snapshot of the incident in order to visualize it from start to finish. To be successful in this venture, one must practice freezing routine situations and being able to recall all aspects of an incident. Was anything observed prior to the incident? Commit the image to paper as soon as possible. Often, this cannot happen until the emergency care vehicle door has been closed and the professional can return to his/her office.

1) Provide immediate and temporary care.

2) Attend to the needs of the victim. Do not make a statement.

3) If possible, contact management at once. Management needs to be contacted immediately after contacting the external emergency medical personnel.

4) Accident reports must be readily available.

5) Complete the accident report as soon as practical following the incident.

6) If possible, obtain a statement from the victim; copy that statement exactly as the victim made the statement, using quotation marks, etc.

7) Obtain the names and locations of at least three witnesses to the incident. If possible, obtain statements from these people immediately after taking care of the victim.

8) Note all emergency care on the accident report. Attend to the needs of the victim.

9) Retained attorney should be familiar with the accident report form and believe it provides the best protection. Avoid after-the-fact descriptions of the incident.

10) Contact insurance carrier. Know when your insurance carrier will want a full-scale investigation.

11) Copies of completed accident reports are to be given to administrators within one hour of the incident.

12) Staff is to be debriefed as soon as possible following the incident.

13) Decisions about closing the facility or continuing the facility in use—given certain incidents—are a part of the emergency action plan. Arrangements are made to relieve staff directly involved in the incident and the rescue.

SUMMARY

Risk management is a comprehensive system of identification, evaluation, and control of risks. The identification system consists of the examination of local, state, and federal regulations; professional organizations and industry standards; policies and procedures; facilities; equipment; personnel; supervision; instruction; participant education; fiscal issues; and contracts. Each of these risks is evaluated in light of its probability, severity, and magnitude. A system of control includes avoiding or eliminating the activity; accepting the risk and assuming responsibility; changing the activity to reduce the risk; or transferring the risk through contract or insurance.

In disaster management, threats and vulnerabilities to natural and manmade hazards become the concerns. Often, it is impossible to avoid the risks so efforts are made to experience the incident as safely as possible and to engage in rescue and survival. Once the incident has occurred and rescue is complete, rebuilding lives, houses, physical structures, businesses, and industry becomes the goal.

ACTIVITIES

1. Prepare a disaster checklist for an open air sport facility that may experience a chemical or biological hazardous attack.

2. You have been invited to give a thirty-minute presentation to the ushers in a high school football stadium on how to handle crowd control in a lightning situation. What would you say?

3. Prepare a risk management plan for a basketball facility.

REFERENCES

Clement, A. (1988). *Law in sport and physical activity.* Carmel, IN: Benchmark.

Kleinknecht v. Gettysburg College, 989 F. 2d 1360 (1991).

RECOMMENDED READING

American College of Sports Medicine. (2009). *Health/fitness facility standards and guidelines.* Champaign, IL: Human Kinetics.

Baker, T. A., Connaughton, D., & Zhang, J. J. (2007). Perceived risk of terrorism and related risk management practices of NCAA Division 1A football stadium managers. 17 *J. Legal Aspects of Sport* 27.

Berlonghi, A. (1990). *The special event risk management manual.* Mansfield, OH: Bookmaster.

Berlonghi, A. (1996). *Special event security management, loss prevention, and emergency services.* Mansfield, OH: Bookmaster.

Hall, S., Cooper, W., Marciani, L. & McGee, J. (2011). *Security management for sports and special events.* Champaign, IL: Human Kinetics.

LaFree, G., & Dugan, L. (2009). Research on terrorism and countering terrorism. 38 *Crime & Just.* 413.

Nicholson, W. C. (2010). Obtaining competent legal advice: Challenges for emergency managers and attorneys. 46 *Cal. W. L. Rev.* 343.

Sawyer, T. H. (2009). *Facilities planning and design for health, physical activity, recreation, and sport* (12th ed.). Urbana, IL: Sagamore.

Taddeo, L. (2009). The best way to prepare for a catastrophe: Head to the place where they engineer it. *Popular Science, 277*(3), 48–51, 74–75.

Glossary

administrative law. Rules, regulations, and directives created by Acts of Congress.

affirmative action. Action designed to eliminate discrimination.

AIAW. Association for Intercollegiate Athletics for Women.

amicus curiae. A brief, on a special topic, presented to the court.

answer. The defendant's first written response to the complaint.

appeal. An application to a higher court to change or modify the judgment of a lower court.

appellant. The party that takes an appeal from one court to another.

appellee. The party against whom an appeal is taken; often called a respondent.

arbitration. A binding third-party resolution.

assault. Apprehension or belief that a person will experience imminent contact. A threat; no contact occurred.

assumption of risk. The victim knew of the potential risk of the activity and voluntarily assumed the risk.

attractive nuisance. The land attracts a minor or young child.

battery. Intentional, harmful, or offensive touching or striking.

breach of contract. Failure, without legal excuse, to perform the obligations and terms of a contract.

case law. The results of a court decision; often referred to as judge-made law or common law.

cause of action. A legal right of redress against another, including the right to sue and the right to recover in a court of law.

certiorari. A writ issued by a superior court (i.e., the United States Supreme Court) directing a lower court to send up records and proceedings in a case.

collective bargaining agreement (CBA). An agreement between an employer and a labor union; governs wages, hours, fringe benefits, and other essential working arrangements.

comparative fault. The relative degree of negligence on the part of the plaintiff and defendant, with damages awarded on a basis proportionate to each person's carelessness.

compensatory damages. Money awarded equivalent to the actual value of damage or injury.

complaint. The initial pleading in a civil action filed by the plaintiff.

consent. Failure to object to the act. *See also* ***express consent*** and ***implied consent.***

contract. An agreement that includes an offer, acceptance, and consideration.

contributory negligence. The victim contributed to his/her own injuries.

defamation. Holding up a person to ridicule or contempt; harming a person's reputation.

defendant. The party against whom the lawsuit is brought.

demurrer. A pleading of the defendant admitting to the plaintiff's allegation of facts but asserting that the plaintiff's claim fails to state a cause of action.

deposition. A written record of verbal testimony in the form of questions and answers made before a public officer for use in a lawsuit.

disability. A physical or mental impairment that limits one or more of the major life activities, a record of such, or being regarded as having such an impairment.

discovery. The process by which opposing parties obtain information in preparation for trial.

dismissal. An order or judgment disposing of an action or suit without trial of the issues involved.

disparate impact. A legal theory that requires an institution to show percentages of people given specific opportunities to be the same as their respective groups.

disparate treatment. Practices that appear neutral in the treatment of different groups but fall more harshly on one group than another.

due process. A legal proceeding for the enforcement of private rights; includes notice and a hearing.

duty. A legal obligation.

Establishment Clause (of freedom of religion). Separates church and state.

express consent. A signed agreement that meets the standard of a contract and relieves the provider of the activity of negligence.

fair use. Certain privileges for the use of copyright materials.

false imprisonment. Intentional confinement or restraint without consent or justified cause.

fiduciary. A person with a duty to act primarily for another's benefit; for example, a person who manages someone's money.

foreseeability. The ability to anticipate an incident.

Fourth Amendment to the United States Constitution. The right of people to be secure in their persons, houses, papers, and effects.

Free Exercise Clause (of freedom of religion). Grants the right to practice one's religion.

freedom of the press. Freedom to publish and disseminate information..

freedom of speech. The freedom to speak, remain silent, advocate, and communicate ideas.

good Samaritan law. Immunity is given to those who provide emergency care.

hostile environment. An adverse or unfriendly situation.

IAAF. International Amateur Athletic Federation.

immunity. Freedom from suit.

implied consent. A person who understands the risk of the activity consents to the risk by participating in the activity.

indemnify. To compensate a person for a loss or to reimburse a person for expenses incurred.

independent contractor. A businessperson who agrees to a specific project for a set price. The owner of the contract is responsible for his/her employees.

injunction. A court order requiring a person to act or refrain from acting in a certain manner.

injunctive relief. An order from the court to stop a person from committing an action in which he/she is currently engaging.

intentional tort. A deliberate act that results in harm. There is intent to commit the act and not always an intent to injure.

invitee. A person invited onto the land of another, usually for an economic benefit.

judgment notwithstanding the verdict (JNOV). A judgment entered by the court for legal reasons that are contrary to the verdict rendered by the jury.

jurisdiction. The authority of the court to hear and decide a lawsuit.

law in sport. The range of legal concepts found in day-to-day decisions in the sport industry.

LexisNexis Academic Universe. An electronic research system used to retrieve legal literature, including court decisions.

liability. A legal responsibility, duty, or obligation.

licensee. A person who is on the land of another for no economic benefit.

mediation. An informal dispute resolution process in which a neutral third person helps the parties reach an agreement.

motion. An application to the court or judge to direct an act in favor of the applicant; for example, a request for a directed verdict, a new trial, etc.

negligence. Conduct falling below the standard of care required of a reasonable and prudent person in the protection of others.

offer. A promise to do or to refrain from doing something.

open and obvious. An owner of land is not liable to a trespasser when the danger is obvious.

plaintiff. Person who brings an action.

pleading. Formal paper filed in a court action, including the plaintiff's complaint and the defendant's answer. It shows what is alleged by the plaintiff as well as what is admitted or denied by the defendant.

precedent. A decision considered as an example or authority for an identical or similar case arising under a similar question of law.

premise liability. Liability of the owner of property.

prima facie case. A case in which the evidence is so strong that the adverse party can overthrow the evidence only by sufficient rebutting evidence.

primary source. An original work.

product liability. The liability of the manufacturer, retailer, and seller of a dangerous or defective product.

professional relationship standard of care. The duty that exists when a body of knowledge exists and is the recognized level of performance expected.

punitive damages. Financial damages assessed to punish a party for wrongdoing. The amount assessed is based on the assets of the party causing the damage.

qualitative research. Use of non-statistical techniques to describe phenomena.

quantitative research. Research using statistics to describe phenomena.

reasonable person standard of care. What an average person would do in the situation.

release. An agreement to release someone from liability. To be effective it must meet the requirements of a contract.

remand. Action of an appellate court sending a case back to a trial court for further action.

respondeat superior. A legal rule that holds an employer liable for the negligent acts of employees.

right of publicity. The right of one to control his/her name and likeness and to prevent its use by others for commercial benefit.

secondary source. An article or book reporting the results of primary source materials.

self-defense. Enables a person under attack to defend himself/herself.

special relationship standard of care. The duty of care owed by parents and schools to children and youths.

sport law. Basic law and court decisions unique to sport.

standards of care. The attention and caution that the average person would exercise in a situation. The three standards of care are reasonable person, special relationship, and professional.

stare decisis. A court doctrine recognizing the value and use of prior court decisions in future court cases in the same jurisdiction. For example, decisions of the Supreme Court are binding on the entire United States.

statutes of limitations. Statutes of the federal and state governments setting a maximum time period for the filing of lawsuits.

summary judgment. A decision of a court on the merits of a lawsuit when the pleadings and other documents reveal that there is no genuine issue of material facts, and the party who sought the judgment is entitled to it as a matter of law.

TAC. The Athletic Congress.

Title IX. A federal statute that extends the principles articulated under the Fourteenth Amendment to public and private schools that rely upon federal or state funds.

trespasser. A person on the land of another without the owner's permission.

vacated. Set aside, canceled, or rescinded; as with a court order or judgment.

vicarious liability. Substituted or indirect responsibility for another's actions arising out of a legal responsibility. *See also* **respondeat superior.**

waiver. An intentional release of a known legal right.

warranty. Guarantee by a manufacturer, wholesaler, or retailer to a purchaser that a product will perform according to identified standards. An express warranty is in writing. An implied warranty is an unwritten understanding that the product will do what it claims to do.

writ. A written court order or a judicial process.

writ of certiorari. An order of the U.S. Supreme Court that directs a lower court to send up a case for review.

List of Cases

Index

About the Authors

Annie Clement, PhD, JD

Annie Clement is currently a member of the graduate faculty at the University of New Mexico. She has taught at The Ohio State University, Bowling Green State University, and Cleveland State University. She also held appointments at the University of Iowa and Florida State University. Her bachelor's degree is from the University of Minnesota, Duluth. She also has a master's degree from the University of Minnesota, Minneapolis, a doctorate from the University of Iowa, and a law degree from Cleveland State University. Dr. Clement is the author of three books, twenty-two book chapters, and over fifty articles and one hundred presentations. Her areas of research are intellectual property, gender equity, aquatics, and risk management.

Dr. Clement, a Fellow of the American Bar Foundation (ABA), is also a past president of the National Association for Sport and Physical Education (NASPE). Among her national awards are an Honor Award from the American Alliance for Health, Physical Education, Recreation, and Dance (AAHPERD); an Aquatic Council Merit Award; a Joy of Effort award from the NASPE; an ABA Section of Business Nonprofit Lawyers Award; and a Distinguished Scholar award from the Safety and Risk Management Council.

JOHN GRADY, JD, PhD

John Grady is currently an associate professor in the Department of Sport and Entertainment Management at the University of South Carolina. He teaches graduate courses in Sport Law and Risk and Security Management, and undergraduate courses in Sport and Entertainment Programming and Risk Management in Sport. Dr. Grady's research interests focus primarily on the legal aspects of the business of sport, including implementation of the Americans with Disabilities Act by the sport industry as well as intellectual property protection in sport, specifically right of publicity and ambush marketing.

Dr. Grady received his bachelor's degree in Management with Honors in Finance from Penn State University. He received his JD and PhD from Florida State University.

His research has been published in outlets including the *Journal of Legal Aspects of Sport,* the *Journal of Sport Management, Sport Marketing Quarterly,* and the *Marquette Sports Law Review.* He is co-editor of the "Sport Marketing and the Law" column in *Sport Marketing Quarterly.* He also serves on the editorial review board for the *Journal of Legal Aspects of Sport* and is associate editor of the *Journal of Venue and Event Management.* He was the recipient of the Sport and Recreation Law Association Young Professional Award and has also received awards for excellence in teaching, research, and undergraduate advising at the University of South Carolina.